THE PHANTOM
IN FOCUS

THE PHANTOM IN FOCUS

A NAVIGATOR'S EYE ON BRITAIN'S COLD WAR WARRIOR

DAVID GLEDHILL

FONTHILL

Fonthill Media Limited
Fonthill Media LLC
www.fonthillmedia.com
office@fonthillmedia.com

First published 2012
Reprinted 2014

British Library Cataloguing in Publication Data:
A catalogue record for this book is available from the British Library

ISBN 978-1-78155-048-9 (hardback)
ISBN 978-1-78155-421-0 (paperback)
ISBN 978-1-78155-204-9 (e-book)

Typeset in 10.5pt on 13pt Sabon.
Printed and bound in England

Connect with us

 facebook.com/fonthillmedia   twitter.com/fonthillmedia

Contents

XV470 in a Box 4 formation over the North German Plain.

Foreword

By Air Commodore Rick Peacock Edwards, CBE, AFC, FRAeS, FCIM

It gives me great pleasure to write the foreword to this book about the F4 Phantom in RAF service. This versatile aircraft, used in the RAF in the ground attack, air defence, and reconnaissance roles, is one of the best known military aircraft ever produced and is still in service in a number of countries and in various roles. That in itself is testament to its all-round capabilities. The F4M was procured for ground attack and air defence roles with the RAF; the F4K was initially used for carrier operations with the Royal Navy, and later, with the demise of HMS *Ark Royal*, these aircraft were transferred to the RAF in the air defence role; and the F4J was later procured for the air defence role with No. 74 Squadron. I flew both the M and K versions whilst on No. 111 Squadron at RAF Leuchars – a memorable tour for many different reasons.

This book will be a welcome trip down memory lane for all those involved with the Phantom in RAF service, but for those who weren't it should be a fascinating insight into a brilliant aircraft with an impressive all-round fighting capability. Before flying the Phantom I had done two tours flying the single-seat Lightning, itself an iconic and impressive aircraft to fly but without the same war capability of the Phantom, a real war machine. That is how I will always remember it as an operational platform, from the significantly improved radar capability, the inertial navigation system, the number of weapons that could be carried, and their capability and, of course, the amazing firepower of the Gatling gun. The Phantom was an operational aircraft that meant business.

I am so pleased to see that Dave Gledhill has so intuitively covered the major milestones and areas of specific operational interest in this book. Just to read the table of contents brings back so many memories. However, the chapters on the Phantom in Germany, Quick Reaction Alert, and the Falkland Islands will, in my view, be of special historical interest. As a member of the Ten Bear Club – i.e.

I had intercepted ten or more Russian aircraft – I have particular memories of those multinational missions way north of the UK mainland where we would intercept Russian aircraft on a range of different missions. Every mission would carry a different story. I also remember how we planned to use some very short runways on remote Shetland islands if we had a problem, itself a mouth watering thought, but we were prepared for all eventualities. Flypasts at the radar station at Saxa Vord on the return trip to Scotland were always a morale booster to those ensconced in such faraway military establishments.

The Phantom achieved so much in its foreshortened life in RAF service, and for those who flew it the experience carries so many diverse and wonderful memories; the stories abound. The affection in which the aircraft was and is still held can be clearly seen at the annual Phantom reunion that takes place in a pub in central London on the same Friday each November; the camaraderie and banter remain and the stories never stop flowing. The Phantom era was a special chapter in RAF history.

But what about the author himself? I commend Dave Gledhill for putting this book together, and I can think of no one more likely to take the initiative or to produce such an exceptional result. Dave is himself one of those inspirational aircrew who it is not only a delight to know but even more of a delight to work with; he was always in my 'First Team', and if I ever had to go to war then he would be very close to me in both the ground and airborne environments. He was an exceptional fightergator, a round peg in a round hole. This book reflects his memories, his own achievements, and his own affection for a magnificent aircraft.

I really hope that you enjoy reading this wonderful book, and I have no hesitation in commending both the work of the author and the book.

Author's Note

There have been many books published about the Phantom. It is one of those iconic aircraft that attracts the enthusiast. I can't come close to matching such learned volumes, nor was it my intent. What I can add is a visual record through the countless photographs I took over my years in the back cockpit. As a young and enthusiastic aviator I found the Phantom a delight to photograph. Cameras that were affordable to the public were more basic, and using wet film I was more selective than I am with digital pictures today. The pictures may not be professionally staged, but they show daily life on a Phantom squadron exactly as it happened and from the vantage point of the cockpit and the flight line.

Apart from a few passing references, I have concentrated on the FGR2 version. I began flying the Phantom in 1975 and moved on in 1985, so the pictorial history focuses on that period. Having never served at Leuchars, I flew the FG1 on only one occasion, and I had already moved on to the Tornado F3 when the F4J arrived on the scene. During its service life, pictures inside the cockpit were difficult to take as photographs of some of the equipment were sensitive. This left a gap in my collection, which I was able to fill due to the help of Mike Davey who owns XV490's cockpit.

Female pilots and navigators never flew the Phantom as it was retired before they were cleared to fly combat aircraft. For that reason, the use of the masculine pronoun is not done with any chauvinistic intent.

Most of the material is from my personal recollections and I captured most of the photgraphs, but I spent time leafing through some outstanding books that had been published previously. Gordon Moulds' outstanding summary of the Operational Conversion Unit *The Phantom O.C.U. 1968-1991* is a trip down memory lane and captured many of the key events from the words of past Squadron Commanders. I have included a few images from my collection which I did not take simply because they are too good to ignore. If you recognize your work please let me know and I'll ensure my charities receive a bonus. Inevitably, I refer to a number of accidents and incidents, most of which are burned indelibly in my memory. I did, however, check the facts in the Military Aircraft Accident Summaries that are posted on the MOD website. That way, I can be sure that my memories haven't faded over the years. The aircrew who were lost were friends and colleagues serving their country to the best of their abilities. I would not wish to sully their reputations.

Modern combat aircraft enjoy an enviable safety record. The Tornado F3 had been in service a number of years before the first aircraft was lost, and the Typhoon has had an equally impressive introduction. My perception of the Phantom during my time in the cockpit was that it was a safe aeroplane when compared to the Lightning, which was its closest peer in the United Kingdom. Even so, losing an aircraft a month was not uncommon. Some squadrons seemed lucky whereas others seemed to lose aircraft on a regular basis with no apparent underlying reason. It was certainly not the case that some squadrons were less able or cavalier about flight safety, just the 'finger of fate'.

All told, I was lucky not to have to attend too many service funerals during my flying career. Inevitably, though, I lost good friends, and this book is dedicated to the memory of those who have passed away: Flt Lts Dick Mott and Ian Johnson, who died in a Phantom in Germany during the filming of the *Man Alive* programme for the BBC; Flt Lts John Gostick and Jeff Bell, who died after crashing into a hillside in the Falkland Islands; and Flt Lt John Ravenhall, who died of natural causes in the mid-90s, having retired from the Air Force some years earlier. John was my pilot for the trip home from the Falkland Islands. A more capable pilot and instructor I've yet to meet. Group Captain Hylton Price, the pilot of the Phantom that engaged the approach end barrier at Wildenrath in 1980, was killed when his Grob trainer collided in mid-air with another Grob over Wales and was unable to parachute to safety. Hylton was a fine fighter pilot and a genuinely nice man who was respected by all who crossed his path. He died trying to pass on his love of aviation to a future generation of flyers.

I am safe in the knowledge that they gave their lives doing something they had always dreamed of achieving and loved doing. They also hold the ultimate accolade in that they died in the service of their country, and there is no finer cause. They will never be forgotten.

My thanks also go to a number of friends:

Rick Peacock Edwards for penning the foreword.

Andy Lister-Tomlinson and David Lewis for providing pictures and maps to fill in the gaps in my collection.

Andy Lister-Tomlinson, Ian Cameron, Dave Middleton, and Kevin Melling for reviewing some of my drafts and for making so many helpful suggestions.

Mike Davey for allowing me to photograph the cockpit of XV490. Mike is typical of the many aviation enthusiasts who keep the memory of the British version of the Phantom alive through tireless dedication to preserving the aircraft at great personal expense.

Steve Clarke of the Air Historical Branch for his advice.

Of course, I must also mention my family Jan, Gemma, Paul, and Tim who have suffered my endless ramblings as I prepared the book.

My motives for this enterprise have been charitable. I will donate to service-related charities, so I trust my peers will be equally charitable in debriefing my efforts. It proved remarkably difficult to donate to the high profile charities, so I looked for others that are often overlooked in these austere times. I have chosen The Battle of Britain Memorial Trust, which maintains the memorial to 'The Few' atop the White Cliffs of Dover. I was present at its inauguration, and it seemed fitting. My other choice is the RAF Museum, which preserves historic aircraft for the nation, celebrating our aviation heritage.

The final word should be reserved for all the aircrew who flew the Phantom over the years, and the engineers and groundcrew who kept this sometimes temperamental beast flying under the most arduous of conditions.

You could love the Phantom or hate the Phantom, but you could never ignore the Phantom.

MOD Caveats

The Phantom in Focus – A Navigator's Eye on Britain's Cold War Warrior

CHAPTER 1
The RAF Phantom

'The Phantom is the triumph of thrust over aerodynamics'

The Phantom was already a hugely successful aircraft before it arrived in the UK. A true multi-role combat aircraft, it was developed by McDonnell Douglas for the US Navy, which had a requirement for a fleet defence fighter that could be re-roled for the ground attack mission. During its early career it set many world records for performance, including time to height, maximum height, and maximum speed. In RAF service it was employed as a conventional bomber, a nuclear strike aircraft, a reconnaissance platform carrying a British reconnaissance pod, and as an air-to-air fighter. Such diverse roles showed its true flexibility. Reportedly, a total of 5,195 were built, making it the largest production run for an American supersonic military aircraft – a record unlikely ever to be matched in the future. The aircraft's emblem is a cartoon ghost called 'The Spook', which was created by McDonnell Douglas technical artist Anthony 'Tony' Wong and featured on all the celebratory shoulder patches that marked the milestones as crews passed each thousand hours of flight time. Whilst many new pilots would compare the Phantom unfavourably with other types they had flown, within a very short time the vast majority, and even the hardiest cynic, acknowledged its strength and flexibility as a combat fighter. Its handling might have lacked the finesse of some of its peers, but its effectiveness could not be disputed when flown well.

Its history has been well documented by other authors and it is not my intention to repeat their outstanding descriptions, but I will try to take you into the cockpit. A twin engine, two-seat fighter, it was its nine external hardpoints that allowed such a diverse load to be carried. Few of its peers could carry out a ground attack mission while still carrying a respectable self-defence missile load. The UK version was heavily modified from its US cousins, the closest of which was the F4J. Although the RAF eventually operated that version, it was markedly

XV409 with a full weapons load ready to be accepted for Quick Reaction Alert.

different to the British Phantom and I will leave discussion of its service record to others. Powered by Rolls-Royce Spey engines fitted with a reheat system that had been adapted from a civilian design, at sea level the aircraft was capable of 750 knots plus. Allegedly, the airframe could achieve up to Mach 2 at high level, although few pilots ever achieved that goal, particularly not in a Spey-powered aircraft. The wing tanks were essential to give the aircraft the range it boasted, yet limited the maximum speed to Mach 1.6 when they were carried. The maximum 'G' loading in RAF service was a healthy 7.5G, although this was typically limited to 6.5G, or less, to extend the airframe life.

Although the service ceiling was quoted as 61,000 feet, some pilots managed to zoom-climb to the mid to upper 60s before invariably one or both of the engines flamed out. Realistically, sustained operation at much above 45,000 feet was difficult. The Phantom could certainly reach 50,000+ feet but it grumbled throughout the process and made its discomfort evident. Inevitably, peacetime RAF rules superimposed additional restrictions, such as a maximum speed of 540 knots at low level overland. Over the sea, 600 knots was easily achievable under almost any conditions, which surprised many bomber crews who thought they had outrun the attacker. Fully loaded, the aircraft weighed an amazing 56,000 lb. In the air defence role, it carried the AIM-7E Sparrow semi-active missile, the Sidewinder AIM-9G, and later the AIM-9L infra-red guided missile, plus the SUU-23 gun on the centreline station.

A powerful pulse Doppler radar, the AN/AWG-11/12 built by Westinghouse, gave it a true look-down shoot-down capability against targets flying at extremely low levels. The capacity to engage targets at such heights was actually set by the ability of the missile to fuse on the target rather than by the performance of the Phantom or its radar. The radar also transmitted a continuous wave guidance signal that would guide the Sparrow semi-active missile. In its snap-up mode, targets flying up to 20,000 feet above the aircraft could be engaged. Although the radar had relatively sophisticated electronic protection modes for its era, the Phantom had only rudimentary electronic countermeasures with which to respond. Despite this, few other aircraft at the time could boast a better capability. A radar warning receiver indicated to the crew when they were being illuminated by either hostile or friendly radars, and it was the square cap on the fin that housed the antennas for this equipment which gave the British Phantom its distinctive profile. Later in its life, chaff and infra-red flare dispensers were fitted to the underwing missile pylons. If threatened, the crew could dispense these countermeasures to confuse an incoming missile. Other than a small training device, the Phantom Electronic Warfare Training pod or PEWT, the aircraft was never fitted with an active jamming pod, unlike its Allied counterparts.

The British Phantom needed about 7,500 feet of runway to operate comfortably. For training sorties, unstick during the take-off roll was at about 150 knots using about 4,000 feet of runway, unless heavily loaded when the take-off roll was longer. 'Go speed' was 140 knots and, in theory, after an abort up to that speed, the aircraft could still stop in the remaining runway length. Landing speeds were broadly similar. The basic approach speed was also 140 knots, which was increased depending on the fuel remaining. An allowance was also added if a single engine or a flapless approach was needed. The arrival on the runway was firm, although the rugged undercarriage inherited from the carrier days was more than up to the hammering it took every day. Indeed, it was often said that a Phantom landing was more like a controlled crash than the flared landing of comparable types. The brakes were never particularly effective so a drag chute was deployed on landing to slow the aircraft down. Normally deployed by the pilot once the wheels were firmly on the ground, it was jettisoned after the aircraft turned off the runway. Some of the ex-Royal Navy pilots were rather more confident in the drag chute's capabilities. With a maximum deployment speed of 200 knots and typical landing speeds of 165 knots, there was a small window where the chute could be deployed while still airborne. By popping the chute on very short finals, a much shorter landing roll was assured, which could be extremely useful on short runways. Given the trim changes that this must have produced, it was not a technique for the uninitiated. Suffice it to say that most pilots preferred the aircraft to be firmly on the ground before deploying the chute.

For emergency use, and when operating from a carrier or a shorter runway, it was equipped with an arrestor hook that could be used on a daily basis if required. The hook was used in anger in RAF service when it proved operationally necessary to operate the aircraft from the short 6,000-foot runway at RAF Stanley in the Falkland Islands.

The Phantom had a chequered introduction to service in the UK and was, in reality, a third choice option. Original defence plans called for a supersonic vertical take-off and landing aircraft in the shape of the P1154 for both Royal Navy and RAF use. The ill-fated TSR2 was to have complemented the P1154, but, with its cancellation, alternatives were sought. A package of American aircraft was offered to fill the gap, including the C-130K, the F111 and the Phantom. A 'sweetener', giving a large work share package to UK industry, proved irresistible to the politicians, and although the C-130K eventually gave sterling service, the F111 was also cancelled, leaving the Phantom as the only fast-jet option. In the event, the Phantom was acquired as a stopgap ground attack aircraft pending the delivery of the SEPECAT Jaguar that had been ordered for that role but would not appear until the early 1970s. However, the long-term plans saw the aircraft transferring to the air defence role to supplement, and eventually replace, the Lightning. The Jaguar proved to be an effective platform and gave sterling service during many operational campaigns but it never matched the Phantom for speed, endurance and load carrying capability.

With the first deliveries in 1968, there were a number of teething problems, but undoubtedly the major issue was with the engines. There had been many difficulties clearing the Rolls-Royce Spey, which was unique to the British Phantom, for service use. In theory, the Spey gave more thrust, shorter take-off runs and better fuel consumption. It was a popular choice with the politicians as it was a British product and guaranteed work for the aviation companies. In practice, the difficulties of bolting a reheat system onto a civilian engine became apparent. That a complete redesign of the centre fuselage was necessary to house the larger Spey should have rung alarm bells, but it was some time before the air staff realised the full impact of this political decision. The Royal Navy, which was the original UK operator, struggled with engine performance in the carrier role, and during testing, the US flight clearance authorities were critical of the overall performance. Both the RN and the RAF received the F4K/FG1 version of the Phantom, with the first RAF squadron being No. 43 (Fighter) Squadron.

F4K FG1 Phantoms of the Royal Navy aboard HMS *Ark Royal*.

An armed 43 (F) Squadron FG1 Phantom.

The RAF version was almost identical to the Navy version and lacked the inertial navigation system and the high frequency HF radio of the later F4M/FGR2 but the FG1 had some airframe modifications to adapt to carrier operations. The nosewheel extended to increase the angle of attack on take-off, although this feature was inhibited in RAF service. The ailerons drooped to improve handling on approach to a carrier, and the stabilator had a fixed slat, again for handling reasons. It also had some limitations in comparison with the FGR2. Most importantly, the FG1 had no battery, which made an internal start impossible, and it relied on an external power set. On a carrier this was no problem, but it was to prove frustrating when the land-based RAF aircraft deployed.

Despite best efforts, the aircraft delivered to the RAF did not perform to specification. There were deficiencies in maximum speed, combat ceiling, radius of action, and combat air patrol (CAP) loiter time. The most restrictive for the crews was the fact that the reheat could not be selected above 43,000 feet and would not stay lit above 51,000 feet. This meant that procedures had to be adapted to achieve a decent high level performance, particularly ensuring that the reheats were engaged at lower levels before climbing into the upper air. These figures were worse than expected and limited the effectiveness as a high level fighter.

During the early 1970s, engineering issues entered the equation with the reappearance of jet turbine rotor blade failures. This meant that all the engineering estimates of mean time between failures were completely wrong, leading to shortages of engines and spares at the front line. In 1972, engine availability became critical and the RAF was forced to adopt drastic measures. Some palliative measures were introduced as crews were asked to manage engine performance in the air, but it was obvious that even more drastic action was needed. The flying task was reduced by as much as 25 per cent to allow Rolls-Royce to rectify the supply problem and deliver enough engines to keep the fleet flying. Aircraft began to be grounded through lack of engines. The operational priority was to protect the RAF commitment to NATO, so the RAF Germany squadrons were protected and UK squadrons and the Operational Conversion Unit (OCU) had to bear the brunt of the restrictions. Squadron hours were cut and, at one stage, the OCU was training only essential personnel such as exchange officers and squadron executives. A number of courses were cancelled completely and aircrew were diverted to other aircraft types, principally the V Force, much to their dismay. The OCU returned to full capacity only in 1974/75.

The aircraft systems were not immune from problems. There were ongoing plans to update the radar, fit the inertial navigation system, fit the instrument landing system, and install a radar warning system. All of these modifications required the aircraft to be returned to the maintenance facility at RAF St Athan,

The Rolls Royce Spey Engine.

meaning they were unavailable to the squadrons for extended periods. This was not ideal for the squadrons, particularly at an early stage in the aircraft's service.

The airframe life had to be managed throughout the aircraft's time with the RAF. 'Fatigue Index', commonly known as FI, was an engineering calculation that determined how much stress was being placed on the airframe by particular operational profiles. A medium level practice interception sortie was relatively benign and attracted a low FI rating. Air combat or supersonic flight, particularly supersonic G, was penalised heavily. It was calculated by the engineers, and a monthly allocation, specific to each airframe, was managed and recorded by the squadrons. At times, stringent G limits were imposed to prevent an aircraft being grounded before it was delivered for major servicing. Quite often this could mean an aircraft could not pull more than 3G during a sortie, so it had to be allocated to gentle duties or, more likely, placed on Quick Reaction Alert (QRA) where it would not fly very often. Naturally, a Squadron Commander's ability to manage his aircraft fleet was a key feature of his performance report, so squadron flying was directly affected by this engineering limitation. If high FI events such as an air combat phase or air-to-air gunnery were planned, invariably the preceding months were fairly gentle in terms of 'G' allowance. A more diligent Squadron Commander had been known to send crews on long navigation exercises around the country in order to build hours without using precious FI. This was fiercely unpopular with the aircrew as there was little training value in such sorties. Ironically, when the aircraft was retired, routine fatigue management had successfully extended the life by many years. Some aircraft were chopped up in the RAF Wattisham 'graveyard' with more usable fatigue life than had been available for much of the aircraft's service. Certainly, the last crews enjoyed more freedom than their predecessors in enjoying the full performance capability of the airframe.

One of the enduring problems that frustrated crews and engineers alike was radar serviceability. The powerful AN/AWG-11/12 missile control system, as the radar was known, was innovative. The inclusion of the pulse Doppler mode meant that targets flying at low level could be broken out from ground clutter. To meet the specification, it had to be able to detect a low flying fighter-sized target at 40 miles plus. In order to do that, it had to transmit an enormous amount of power through the antenna mounted behind the radome in the nose, and to carry that power it was fitted with heavy waveguides and solid state electronics typical of 1960s technology. Unfortunately, modern digital processing was in its infancy and the electronics were not up to the task. Had the failures been minor, navigators could have worked through and found alternatives. Regrettably, the most common manifestation was the failure of the transmitter, which meant that it was impossible to detect any targets at all.

Despite the title, navigators in a Phantom did little navigating. Their role was to operate the radar and the systems and, if these failed, it led to many wasted flying hours, effectively 'sandbagging'. Flying with a failed radar was known as flying 'lead nosed'; in other words, the highly effective radar became a piece of metallic ballast. The performance was eventually improved in the early 1980s with the introduction of the radar serviceability programme. Statistics gathered on the squadrons had proved to the air staff that there was undoubtedly an issue, and a replacement lower powered transmitter was designed. With associated improvements in the electronic line replaceable units, despite the fact that the power output was reduced to a fraction of the original design, the detection performance was not markedly affected. More importantly, the modified aircraft became massively more serviceable. Arguably, despite the emergence of extremely capable air defence fighters, the Phantom was at its most effective during the mid-1980s when these modifications were implemented. It was with some trepidation that Phantom crews transferred to the new Tornado F2 with its much maligned Foxhunter radar, leaving behind a simple but effective AN/AWG-12.

Of the 118 F4Ms delivered to the RAF, two were YF4Ms that were used for testing. The F4M/FGR2s operated from RAF Wattisham, RAF Coningsby, RAF Wildenrath, and RAF Stanley, moving to RAF Mount Pleasant. The fifty-two F4K/FG1s delivered to the Navy and the RAF were eventually all transferred to the RAF and were operated by the squadrons at RAF Leuchars. At its height, there were six operational RAF squadrons and a large Operational Conversion Unit operating the Phantom. Even though it had a good reputation for safety, over its service life in the RN and the RAF many Phantoms were lost. Between July 1969 and January 1991, thirty-two FGR2s and seven FG1s crashed. The RN lost eight FG1s during their time operating the aircraft and the RAF lost a single F4J. In all, thirty-two pilots and navigators lost their lives.

It was against this background that I was introduced to the Phantom.

CHAPTER 2
Operating the Phantom

Sitting in the cockpit of a Phantom you immediately became part of the machine and there could be no doubt as to its heritage. It looked and felt like a 1960s fighter, with stark black consoles and conventional gauges and, by fighter standards, both cockpits were huge.

The front cockpit layout, shown in Plate 4, had a traditional centrally mounted control column on a raised pedestal. The control column sat lower than in British aircraft cockpits of the same era and was hinged high on the cockpit floor, which had the effect of leaving extra room around the pilot's lower legs; ideal considering the bulky documents pilots carried in their lower leg pockets. The handgrip was also angled so that the top was slightly to the left of the bottom, and the front was rotated 15 degrees anticlockwise. This meant that the handgrip sat naturally in the pilot's right hand with all the associated buttons easy to operate.

The two throttles, mounted on the left console, controlled each engine individually, although, invariably, they were operated together. The throttles used a series of gates to control the thrust of the engines. From the 'off' position, pushing the throttles forward through the first gate set idle power and latches prevented the engines from being shut off accidentally. Pushing them forward again to the next gate exercised the engines in the 'military power' range, giving variable 'dry' power. To select reheat, the throttles were rocked outboard into minimum reheat and then further forward to the 'firewall' for full reheat. It was rare to operate the individual engines at different thrust settings. Only if an engine failed, or if minimum reheat was used for air-to-air refuelling at the higher levels, would the throttles be mismatched. Even in the event of an engine failure, there was little asymmetric thrust given that the engines were set close together in the fuselage. This meant that there was none of the dramatic yaw associated with wing-mounted engines in aircraft such as the Canberra. This made asymmetric handling much more comfortable for the pilot. Most importantly, having two engines gave the reassurance of a 'spare' when problems did arise. The second engine meant that an engine failure required only a reasonably routine diversion to the nearest suitable airfield rather than an ejection if flying an aircraft such as the Hawk.

The switches and levers were designed to be understood by US Marines, so they were shaped to represent the function they provided. The undercarriage was selected up and down using a huge illuminated wheel-shaped lever to the left of the instrument panel. The flap lever looked like a small flap, the canopy jettison was painted yellow and black and looked like a small canopy, and the illuminated hook lever, which lowered the arrestor hook, looked like a hook. To assist with fault diagnosis, the wheel handle flashed when the gear was in an unsafe position, for example if the undercarriage failed to lock in the up or down position. The hook light illuminated when the hook was unlocked but not fully down.

This seemingly bizarre policy was the result of hard-won experience from just after the Second World War. The USAF lost a large number of B24 Liberator bombers, many of which crashed during final approach when the flaps were accidentally raised, causing the aircraft to stall. After comprehensive investigations it was discovered that the switches to lower the gear and to raise the flaps were not only identical but operated in the opposite sense to each other. Pilots aiming to lower the undercarriage were accidentally operating the wrong switch, thus raising the flaps and crashing in the process. The shaping of levers and switches in the B24 immediately cured this phenomenon and the practice was carried across to the latest generation of US aircraft undergoing development.

The front consoles were littered with systems controls and avionics, with the more important items towards the front, making them more easily accessible to the pilot. Unlike modern aircraft, the F4 did not benefit from comprehensive multiple warning systems. Captions on the warning panel would illuminate to warn of a problem or a change of system status, with serious problems accompanied by a 'Master Caution' light. This red warning light flashed to attract the pilot's attention, and a repeater in the rear seat alerted the navigator. The navigator, ironically, was better served, as the repeater was positioned directly in front of his eyes immediately under the flight instruments. It was often the navigator who warned that the 'Master Caution' had illuminated. In the front cockpit, hidden under the cockpit coaming, the critical warning was badly positioned. It was hard to see from the normal seated position and almost invisible in strong sunlight. It was much later in the aircraft's life before this problem was fixed by moving the warning light. To make matters worse, there was no audio warning. Simulator instructors remarked that in a busy cockpit, or when the navigator was peering down into the radar display, it was not unusual for crews to fly for several minutes with the 'Master Caution' flashing away.

The flight instrument panel was also traditional with standard-looking instruments typical of many American fighters of the period. A traditional 'T' made up of the basic flight instruments was flanked on the right by the engine instruments and on the left by the weapons panel. The gunsight or lead computing optical sighting system (LCOSS) was immediately in front of the pilot and projected very limited weapons information through a sight glass in the windscreen, somewhat reminiscent of a Second World War fighter gunsight. Below this, a radar repeater allowed the pilot to monitor the navigator's display. The LCOSS was flanked on the left by an angle of attack gauge giving a slightly cluttered appearance to the windscreen. Another critical gauge, the 'G' meter, was relegated to a position lower on the console by the weapons control panel. Between the pilot's legs, a centrally mounted console carried mostly bombing controls, although it also carried a few key systems gauges.

The pilot selected and fired the weapons. The main controls were on a small panel at the lower left side of the main instrument panel. By modern standards, where fighter pilots enjoy 'hands-on throttle and stick' controls, this arrangement was not ideal. The pilot had to lean forward to reach the rotary switch to select the Sparrow, Sidewinder or gun, and under 'G' this could be difficult. Other essential controls such as the continuous wave radar for the Sparrow and the seeker head coolant for the Sidewinder were also tucked away on this panel. For safety reasons, all weapons were routed through a 'Master Arm' switch. With the switch off, nothing could be fired; however, with the switch on, all weapons were live. The status of the weapons was also displayed on the missile status panel with small illuminated displays. If in order to selectively lighten the load in the event of an emergency the pilot had to jettison weapons from the aircraft, this was also done on the missile panel. There was a huge difference between the Phantom and the present-day touch screen displays, and the aircraft was firmly rooted in the analogue era.

The view from the front cockpit was reasonably good, apart from the ironwork around the front canopy arch. The side view was unimpeded but few pilots could see further aft than the aircraft's wingtips. Although mirrors were fitted, they were convex in shape and gave a distorted wide-angle view that was next to useless in visual combat. The view from the back seat was somewhat better and in any hostile situation the navigator was responsible for, and spent much of his time, 'checking the six'. Even so, the view from the cockpit never matched that of the later bubble-canopied aircraft such as the F15 and Su-27 Flanker or indeed older aircraft such as the P51 Mustang. For that reason, every sortie was a physical workout if the crew were to remain unmolested by other attacking aircraft. It was routine to spend much of a sortie twisting and turning against the straps in the seat to gain a better view of the world outside.

The Spey engines that powered the aircraft were never really well liked and attracted much criticism from pilots transferring from other types. Despite this, some of the strengths of the engine were often overlooked. The bypass turbofan was reasonably frugal and worked extremely well at low level. It was well suited to low level operations in RAF Germany. At higher levels, however, the engine response was sluggish in comparison to a true jet such as the original J79. The reheat system, which was essential yet a bolt-on afterthought, was slow to light and could be hesitant. The Spey was less smoky than the J79 but, even so, minimum reheat was essential to reduce the smoke plume in a combat engagement. Acceleration was reasonably good through the middle range speeds of 350 to 500 knots, but to coax the aircraft into supersonic flight, where it was happiest, took effort.

A standard acceleration profile was developed, which began with a level dash before climbing to the tropopause, normally about 36,000 feet. At that point, a firm push over, or 'bunt', would persuade the jet to break Mach 1. The gentle accelerating descent pushed the speed into the low supersonic range before a zoom-climb would give the best speed for that day. Normally Mach 1.3 to Mach 1.5 was easily achievable, but Mach 2 was invariably elusive, and impossible carrying external fuel tanks. Sadly, unlike the clips from films such as *The Right Stuff*, breaking the sound barrier in a Phantom was completely underwhelming. If you watched closely, you might just see a slight twitching of the instruments through the Mach but, that aside, there was little to signify the transition to supersonic flight. Unlike Concorde, there was no illuminated sign to record the event. I was able to compare the fuel efficiency between the two types of engine during a squadron exchange with the German Luftwaffe F4Fs that used the J79 engine. Operating in the low flying areas in Wales we took a mixed 'four ship' at high level through the UK airways and dropped into low level over Cardigan Bay. After about 30 minutes in the area chasing Jaguars, the F4Fs were out of fuel and aiming home, consistently leaving their Spey engine cousins to play for some time longer before recovering to RAF Coningsby. That said, over-enthusiastic use of the reheat by our German cousins could have easily invalidated that assessment.

Early on, pilots learned to respect the aircraft. In normal flight, a stability augmentation system used servos to damp down the tendency of the aircraft to oscillate. This gave a much smoother feel for the pilot and, when disengaged, the aircraft became markedly unstable. Often, new navigators flying in the squadron twin-stick aircraft would ask to fly the Phantom for a little 'stick time'. It was a well-known trick for pilots to flip off the 'stab augs', leaving the young navigator vastly impressed at the prowess of his pilot in being able to control the unwilling beast. Handing control back, remarkably the jet returned to its normal docile self as, unknown to the hapless navigator, the 'stab augs' were switched back on! A feel bellows system fed artificial loads into the controls at high speed and 'G', making it harder to over-control or over-stress the aircraft. That, of course was not to say that pilots never over-stressed. Minor excursions over the limit were routine, but a serious underestimation of the height left one airframe on the hangar floor for many months after the pilot pulled 10G recovering from a dive. With large areas of stressed skin panels, a good deal of rehabilitation was needed before that aircraft flew again. Nevertheless, the airframe was rugged and there were few failures that could not be handled by a competent and well-trained crew.

Only a few in-flight emergencies needed immediate actions, so caution was generally the norm. Although the pilot was well drilled in completing 'bold face drills' for each emergency, there was normally time to think things through, and careful use of the flight reference cards was the order of the day. With a few exceptions, crews were trained to follow the drills carefully and discuss the implications of the failures before leaping in. Of course, endless practice emergency drills in the flight simulator helped enormously. Flight reference cards evolved over the life of the Phantom and reflected hard-won experience distilled by analysing successes and mistakes from many in-flight emergencies. Furthermore, the drills were drafted in the quiet of an office and not the heat of a cockpit. Used properly, responses to the emergency relied less on memory and more on careful consideration of the guidance in the cards, which, in turn, led to a safe recovery to terra firma.

The old adage for the Phantom pilot was, 'If it buffets, use your boots.' He flew the aircraft to its limits using angle of attack. AOA is the angle between a reference line drawn through the wing and a line representing the relative motion of the aircraft through the airflow. Most importantly, AOA was used as a measure of turning performance and, for the Phantom, 19.2 'units' angle of attack gave the optimum turn.

The advice in the Aircrew Manual for taking the aircraft into a stall read like a horror story:

> Normal 1G stalls are preceded by a wide band of buffet margin. The stall sequence is as follows: Onset buffet starts at 15 units AOA. Slight wing rock may occur at 22 units AOA and the pedal shaker is activated at 22.3 units AOA. Wing rocking increases at 24-25 units (about 10 kts prior to the stall). If recovery is not taken at this point, the AOA rapidly reaches 27-28 units AOA and the aircraft is then fully stalled. The aircraft then pitches nose up and/or yaws in either direction. Recovery from this stall is by setting 5-10 units AOA while maintaining neutral rudder and increasing power as required.

It was with this advice in mind that the Phantom pilot began to explore the handling of his new mount. To be effective in combat he had to be able to fly at these limits, and sometimes beyond. To help the pilot when glancing at the AOA gauge, optimum performance was indicated by a white area on the AOA gauge with a marker at 19.2 units. Pull to less than that figure and the aircraft was not being operated to its limit. Pull more than that value and the aircraft was operating beyond its maximum aerodynamic efficiency and turn rate suffered. The normal operating AOA limit was 21 units but, with care, the aircraft could be operated beyond this. As the aircraft passed 19 units the pilot would 'lock' the stick with both hands, restricting it to fore and aft movement. From that point, roll was initiated and controlled by large rudder inputs. By doing this the aircraft could be flown and fought beyond its published limits. The indexers, shown in Plate 6, were installed on the right-hand side of the LCOSS and easily visible from the normal seated position in the cockpit. They were indicative of the naval genealogy of the UK Phantoms and were intended to provide the pilot with an indication of AOA for landing on a carrier. Simple in concept, a 'doughnut', which was a small round symbol looking like its namesake, illuminated when the pilot pulled the control column to 19 units. Upper and lower chevrons prompted the pilot to ease off or pull harder on the control column to keep the aircraft at its most efficient. The indexers were vital to carrier operations where it was essential to land at an accurate AOA, but they were also extremely helpful when trying to extract the best performance in air combat. Unlike its land-based counterpart, the Navy FG1 Phantoms had an additional audio tone that could be heard when the landing gear was down. This tone consisted of slow beeps at low AOA, associated with a bottom chevron indication, and the frequency increased until it became a constant tone at 19 units. Beyond 19 units the tone remained constant as operations required the Navy Phantom pilot to land at a minimum of 19 units.

The aircraft had a rather disturbing handling vice – adverse yaw – and the stalling advice alerted the pilot to the risks. At very slow speed and at a high angle of attack, if a pilot took the aircraft beyond the normal limits it could 'depart' unless handled carefully. In layman's terms, that meant that it would stop flying in a straight line and do something completely unpredictable. Pilots could often be drawn into this flight regime, particularly if reacting to a threat, as the speed could wash off quite quickly. Even so, the Phantom gave fair warning. At just beyond the normal AOA setting of 19 units, the aircraft would start to buffet quite noticeably and at this stage the pilot would 'use the boots'. Take it even further and it entered 'wing rock'. At this stage the aircraft would rotate around its longitudinal axis, giving the effect of the wings moving up and down in sequence, hence the term 'wing rock'. Push it even further or try to use the ailerons and the aircraft entered the last and most dramatic phase, 'nose slice'. At this point, the nose literally sliced in the opposite direction to the demanded turn and the aircraft could enter a spin. Spin recovery was briefed on every combat sortie and it was quite possible, using an appropriate control input and by popping the drag chute, to break the spin. More than one pilot returned without a drag chute after an aggressive combat engagement, leading to questions and an inevitable dual check with the squadron Qualified Flying Instructor. Unfortunately, if the spin ever developed into a flat spin there was no known recovery other than by using the ejection seats. A video showing the fate of the test crew who established that fact was shown at many air combat phase briefings as a warning to the unwary. Despite these known characteristics and the danger of entering a spin, many pilots used high AOA for short periods in order to gain turning advantage during air combat manoeuvring. This was a short-term gain as the speed and energy washed off very rapidly, but the extra performance could be just enough to achieve a firing solution for the Sidewinder or the gun.

One of my old pilots explained lucidly how the aircraft could bite when pressed too hard:

> I regularly used 24 to 26 units and knew I could get away with 28! I tried more in Decimomannu once and as the AOA went through 29 units the whole world let go; I pushed the stick forward so hard I thought I'd smash the HSI ... the jet did two full 360 degree rolls, very rapidly, and recovered in exactly the right plane to get a Sidewinder shot on the opposing aircraft ... throughout the whole event my navigator didn't say a word, not 'unload', not 'recover', nothing. However, as I took the shot he quietly mumbled an expletive about luck ... or maybe something less subtle.

The aircraft was most efficient, fuel-wise, at about 350 knots or slower, but that was not a good fighting speed. Best cornering was at around 420 knots, but the preferred tactical speed was supersonic if at all possible; however, higher speeds used more fuel. For that reason, tactical transits were at the slower speeds, but on the first signs of an engagement the speed was immediately pushed up. Because of peacetime regulations it was difficult for Phantom crews to train at higher speeds, which could lead to bad habits. In UK airspace, supersonic flight was allowed only over the sea and, even then, the aircraft had to be at least 30 miles from the coast and pointing away from land. Residents on the coast could become nervous at the loud bang of a supersonic boom and such incidents made headlines. For that reason, many engagements were flown at a slower than ideal speed, which could place the Phantom at a disadvantage.

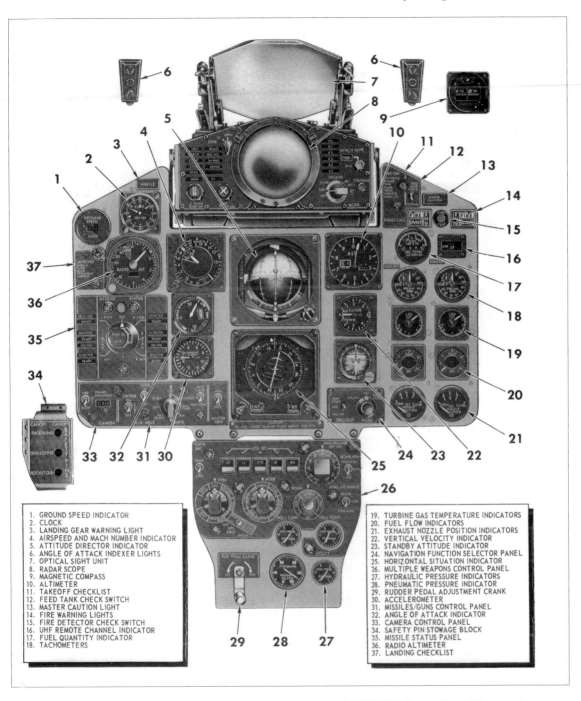

1. GROUND SPEED INDICATOR
2. CLOCK
3. LANDING GEAR WARNING LIGHT
4. AIRSPEED AND MACH NUMBER INDICATOR
5. ATTITUDE DIRECTOR INDICATOR
6. ANGLE OF ATTACK INDEXER LIGHTS
7. OPTICAL SIGHT UNIT
8. RADAR SCOPE
9. MAGNETIC COMPASS
10. ALTIMETER
11. TAKEOFF CHECKLIST
12. FEED TANK CHECK SWITCH
13. MASTER CAUTION LIGHT
14. FIRE WARNING LIGHTS
15. FIRE DETECTOR CHECK SWITCH
16. UHF REMOTE CHANNEL INDICATOR
17. FUEL QUANTITY INDICATOR
18. TACHOMETERS

19. TURBINE GAS TEMPERATURE INDICATORS
20. FUEL FLOW INDICATORS
21. EXHAUST NOZZLE POSITION INDICATORS
22. VERTICAL VELOCITY INDICATOR
23. STANDBY ATTITUDE INDICATOR
24. NAVIGATION FUNCTION SELECTOR PANEL
25. HORIZONTAL SITUATION INDICATOR
26. MULTIPLE WEAPONS CONTROL PANEL
27. HYDRAULIC PRESSURE INDICATORS
28. PNEUMATIC PRESSURE INDICATOR
29. RUDDER PEDAL ADJUSTMENT CRANK
30. ACCELEROMETER
31. MISSILES/GUNS CONTROL PANEL
32. ANGLE OF ATTACK INDICATOR
33. CAMERA CONTROL PANEL
34. SAFETY PIN STOWAGE BLOCK
35. MISSILE STATUS PANEL
36. RADIO ALTIMETER
37. LANDING CHECKLIST

The Phantom front cockpit as shown in the Aircrew Manual. UK MOD Crown Copyright (1975).

Above: The throttles on the pilot's left console.

Left: The canopy jettison (yellow and black) with the undercarriage lever (red) below.

Opposite above left: The hook lever on the right hand side of the instrument panel with the telelight panel behind.

Opposite right: The control column.

Opposite below left: The control column functions.

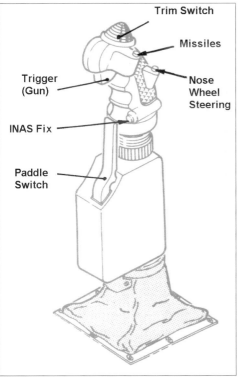

Trim Switch

Missiles

Trigger
(Gun)

Nose
Wheel
Steering

INAS Fix

Paddle
Switch

The pilot's instrument panel.

The missile status panel.

The weapons control panel.

A pilot's eye view through the gunsight of XV490.

The rear cockpit, shown in Plate 5, was uncharitably described as an 'ergonomic slum'. The first thing you noticed when closing the canopy was that the glass area was actually larger than it appeared from photographs. The rear ejection seat sat well down in the cockpit, leaving only the navigator's head visible above the canopy rails. Despite that, the view was surprisingly good, although the large intakes limited the view to the side and below. Air combat required constant movement in the cockpit to check for other aircraft around your own. Hauling against the bulk of the seat straps and twisting the upper body to be able to see into the tail area was a sport in itself and developed unusual muscles, particularly in the neck. The other thing that was instantly noticeable when the canopy closed was that it sloped downwards from back to front. When airborne, this created a false horizon, giving a feeling that the aircraft was not flying level. This could be extremely disorientating until you acclimatised.

Strapping in was a relatively frustrating process. In the early days, the seat was fitted with an American-designed torso harness that was attached to the lifejacket and was strapped on before walking out to the aircraft. A webbing harness fitted tightly around the upper body and the groin, and was pulled tight with straps on the lifejacket. Once in the seat, a personal equipment connector slotted into a receptacle linking you to the services such as oxygen, the radio, and the 'G' suit. Lap straps pushed into a lower box and were pulled tight and connectors known as Koch fasteners were then clipped onto the shoulder straps by the groundcrew. Small retaining pins were inserted to ensure that the fasteners did not disconnect inadvertently after an ejection. A bulky manual parachute release handle protruded from the left shoulder strap. The flying helmet completed the ensemble, with a flexible oxygen hose from the mask clipping onto a chest-mounted oxygen regulator. Once strapped in, movement was extremely limited and crews felt restricted. 'Trussed up like a Christmas turkey' was a phrase used by one squadron joker. The lap straps held the lower body firm in the seat, the only movement being in the upper body once a 'go forward lever' was released after take-off. Later, the torso harness was replaced by a combined harness, literally combining the parachute harness and the seat straps into one unit, which was fitted to the seat and remained in the aircraft. This meant that the lifejacket donned by crews before walking out to the aircraft was much less bulky, and it made the whole process of strapping in much easier.

The majority of the life support and radio systems were on the left console. The HF radio, V/UHF radio, and TACAN tactical radio navigation aid were joined by the controls for the radar camera. The right console housed the inertial navigation system and, behind that, a test box for the radar.

The key equipment was the radar; the controls were to the front and almost seemed to be an afterthought despite their importance. The radar display unit was housed in a huge metal cradle on the floor. The display tube was only a few inches square, and by struggling with a stiff handle on the right it could be eased out from its stowed position to sit just a few inches away from the navigator's face. Although that made it much easier to see the small display, the proximity of such a huge piece of metalwork was daunting, particularly at low level. The box was explosively stowed in the event of an ejection; literally, explosive bolts sheared the retaining mechanism. It always seemed a leap of faith to assume it would clear the navigator's legs before the seat moved up the rails and, given time, most navigators would stow the radar unit manually. The radar control panel was located by the navigator's left knee and was also pulled out when in use. The final piece was the navigator's hand controller, mounted on another plinth that pulled out from a stowage on the right-hand side. With everything in its operating position the vast space in the back cockpit was suddenly filled and it became extremely claustrophobic, particularly at night.

Visibility forwards was poor. Iron bars that had originally housed the controls for the reconnaissance pod sat between the cockpits, and the view was even further limited by the pilot's ejection seat. Peering around those bars to gain sight of an opponent in an air combat engagement was a fact of life for the Phantom navigator. The saving grace was that they were extremely effective grab handles to pull the upper body around in the seat against the pull of the seat harness allowing the navigator to 'check 6' in a combat engagement. This was a luxury the pilot did not have, so the navigator could see deeper into the '6 o'clock' than the pilot. The visibility was reduced even further when the defensive aids controls were fitted to these bars later in the aircraft's life. For the Phantom reconnaissance navigators, a forward view was an impossible luxury given the size of the recce control panel.

Operating the radar was an ergonomic challenge, particularly as 'the office' often turned upside down. Even with the radar scope fully extended, sun reflecting from the display was a constant problem, and many navigators used a locally produced scope visor to shield the display from the sun. Without one, the navigator was forced to lean over the display using a hand as a makeshift visor, so when the 'G' forces came on, it placed enormous strain on the back and neck due to the weight of the flying helmet. The control panel was on the left but the hand controller that controlled the radar scanner was on the right. Knowing precisely which particular button controlled which function became a vital skill to ensure that in the heat of an intercept, the correct mode was selected at the right time. In a similar way to the key levers and switches in the front cockpit, some of the key radar controls were shaped subtly differently. The gain controls for clear, clutter, and pulse were shaped like a cross, a serrated circle, and a hexagon, respectively. While this should have been helpful, in practice it was very hard to tell the controls apart by feel alone, through the thickness of a flying glove. The fact that this was the only sop to ergonomic design says much about how little thought went into designing the rear cockpit.

One of the unavoidable risks was that many navigators had the opportunity to 'listen to the radar' if the pilot unexpectedly snapped into a high 'G' manoeuvre. Unexpected 'G' forced the head forward and, once trapped with his head against the radar scope, it was an unwise navigator who tried to recover to a normal upright seated position as injury to the back or neck was extremely likely. It was much better to accept the ignominy and wait for the pilot to relax the 'G'. I learned the lesson very early in my career but, unfortunately, despite my experience, was still caught out many years later by an experienced pilot during an air combat engagement. Such lessons were known as crew co-ordination, and enthusiastic pilots could help inexperienced navigators with a call of 'G coming on' as an appropriate warning.

With experience, most navigators would anticipate a manoeuvre as their situation awareness developed. At the merge during an air combat engagement, the pilot would generate a minimum separation pass, in other words fly past the 'bogey' on an opposite heading as close as possible, leaving the opposing pilot no turning room. As the threat aircraft flashed past, the navigator could safely assume that a turn would follow imminently and brace accordingly, even though he would be straining to look over his shoulder to keep sight of the 'bogey'. At that point, with the aircraft entering a dynamic manoeuvre, the world literally turned upside down and normal rules by which the body lived were shelved temporarily. Another example of poor crew co-ordination would be that unannounced expletives from the front cockpit were received equally unenthusiastically in the back cockpit.

Whilst apparently minor, such lessons could be critical. One experienced Phantom pilot re-roled onto the Tornado GR1 bomber. His aircraft passed close to another fast jet in the low flying area and he made an evasive manoeuvre to avoid a collision. Being a true-blue fighter pilot he then reacted as would any air defence pilot, but the sudden manoeuvre surprised his navigator who was head down in the cockpit working the radar. As the aircraft entered a nose low manoeuvre, the navigator, thinking that the pilot had lost control, ejected them both from the aircraft. An air defence navigator would have been accustomed to such gyrations but the breakdown in communications between the crew may have contributed to the loss of an expensive airframe.

The radar was controlled from a panel next to the navigator's left knee. There were three principal modes: pulse Doppler, pulse, and mapping. The first two modes were used for airborne interceptions whereas the latter was used for navigation purposes. In the ground attack days, the radar was used for precise radar navigation and for radar bombing. For an air defence fighter that no longer dropped bombs, it was not needed for that purpose but could still be useful. As an example, crews operating well out into the North Sea would point at the coastline and get a radar 'fix' to update the navigation equipment from a known landmark such as Flamborough Head. Although the navigation kit could be updated from radio aids such as TACAN, the mapping mode gave some redundancy. For today's aircrew, such modes seem archaic in the GPS era.

Other switches allowed the radar to be used in the best mode for the particular type of attack. Although the radar could detect targets out to its maximum range, the range control determined how much was displayed to the crew. Typically, the radar could see large airliners or Soviet bombers out to about 70 miles, which was very respectable for its generation. A fighter-size target would be detected at 50 miles at medium level, but maybe only 35 to 40 miles at low level when on a medium level combat air patrol. On a low level CAP overland, typically flown at 1,500 feet, the detection could be as little as 20 miles but was largely driven by the radar horizon which is much closer at low level.

The scanner sat in the nose of the aircraft and directed the radar energy out towards the target aircraft. The navigator used two main controls. A radar hand controller on the right-hand side in the back cockpit was fitted with a small thumbwheel that moved the scanner up and down, allowing the radar to be pointed precisely towards the target. Another control on the radar control panel allowed the scan pattern to be narrowed in azimuth, increasing the data rate once the navigator had detected his nominated target. By refining the search, the radar was less likely to lose the target, although it increased the navigator's workload as he had to highlight the target more precisely using these controls. It was also possible to select multi-bar scans that would search a greater volume of airspace automatically. Most navigators preferred to leave the radar set in single-bar scan as the data rate was low in multi-bar scan. If the radar was mishandled, evasion by the target might lead to a lost contact leaving an embarrassed navigator asking for help from the ground controller.

To find a target, the navigator either needed to know its height or he had to set up a methodical search using the thumbwheel to point the scanner. If the Phantom was at 15,000 feet and he was searching for a low level target, a mental calculation would give a scanner angle of minus 3 degrees for typical detection ranges. By rolling the thumbwheel forward, the navigator could point the scanner where he expected the target to appear and begin to search. As the target flew closer, the volume to be searched increased. Navigators became adept at mental arithmetic to work out the sums for different ranges and heights.

The displays were unique and took some time to understand. pulse Doppler would give a display of azimuth against speed but would not display range until the navigator locked on to the target. The advantage of PD mode, however, was that it could see targets at longer range and those flying in ground clutter unlike the earlier pulse radars fitted to aircraft such as the Lightning. Lock-on was achieved by moving a cursor on the display over the target and squeezing a small trigger on the hand controller. The radar would then enter an acquisition mode and point directly at the point in space where the target was flying. Once it saw the target, it would then track automatically, allowing the crew to concentrate on other priorities such as the intercept geometry. A lock was also needed to provide the additional guidance data needed to launch a Sparrow or Skyflash missile.

Interpreting the displays took some time to learn. The standard display was known as a 'B Sweep'. Looking ahead, the centreline of the Phantom was at 0 degrees azimuth. To the left and right, the angle off the nose was measured in degrees out to 60 degrees each side of the nose. In both air-to-air modes, the baseline – or zero range – was expanded to allow the navigator to interpret close range information more easily. A horizon bar showed the angle of bank on the radar display. Small vertical acquisition markers allowed the navigator to designate a target. Elevation strobes on the right of the scope showed which position the navigator had demanded. A vertical line swept back and forth to show the instantaneous azimuth of the scanner. Once a target was detected, the navigator would move the acquisition markers over the target, squeeze the trigger on the hand controller and the radar would then track the target automatically.

Pulse mode was easiest to understand as it measured azimuth across the top and range down the side of the scope. The target shown below (Pulse Search Mode) is 15 degrees left of the nose at 37 miles range. In pulse Doppler mode, it was more complex. Although azimuth was still displayed across the top, speed was displayed vertically, with targets with a higher closing speed showing higher up the screen. There were two electronic notches known as the Doppler notch and the Fo (F nought) notch. A target that was crossing the Phantom's heading at 90 degrees had little closing velocity and could not be tracked easily. The radar 'notched out' these targets to prevent clutter. To be displayed, a target had to have a closing or opening velocity relative to the Phantom. The target shown in pulse Doppler mode is 20 degrees right and has a closing velocity of about 400 knots. The Fo notch served a similar purpose for targets flying at the same speed in a similar direction. Once locked up, both pulse and pulse Doppler displays were similar, although PD had an additional velocity display on the left. The target was tracked automatically and the inner elevation strobe tracked the target height. A steering circle in the centre of the scope showed the area within which a missile could be launched and grew larger as the Phantom closed to the optimum launch range for the Sparrow missile before collapsing

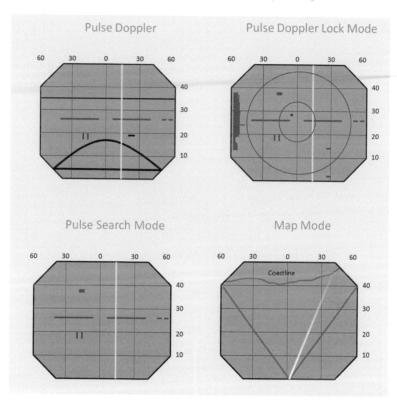

The radar air-to-air and mapping modes.

again towards minimum range. A steering dot showed the best heading for the optimum missile shot. By centring the dot, the pilot could fly a collision heading giving the missile the best chance of success. Small markers showed the missile engagement ranges. A larger ring around the outside of the scope was known as Vc (V Sub C). A gap in this ring rotated around the display and showed closing velocity. At 7 o' clock on the display the combined closing speed was 700 knots. By interpreting the movement of the steering dot and the Vc the navigator could determine if the target was evading. Unlike the air-to-air modes, mapping mode showed a traditional sector scan display with a single point at the baseline.

The radar could also be orientated to suit the scenario. In normal flight, the radar was ground referenced; in other words it was scanning parallel to the ground so that aircraft flying at a particular height could be easily detected. Unfortunately in air combat, once the aircraft began to manoeuvre aggressively, the ground was not a good reference as the aircraft might be upside down or manoeuvring aggressively in height. At that stage, the radar had to be re-referenced to the wing line; effectively scanning left and right, up and down relative to the crew and not the outside world. This was known as 'Gyros Out' mode, and as the aircraft looped and rolled behind its target attempting to take a missile or guns shot, the radar would remain pointing ahead, scanning parallel to the wing line despite the changing attitude. The crew could then exchange information on target position relative to their position in the cockpit, even when pointing vertically upwards.

The radar was also equipped with a number of self-protection modes that allowed the navigator to counter active jamming from an opponent. Electronic countermeasures could be employed against the radar, which could break the lock or show false targets. Navigators were taught to recognise these jamming techniques and could use manual tracking modes to keep the radar pointed at the target, even if the automatic functions were being 'spoofed'. There was also a mode that allowed the navigator to prime the Sparrow missile by setting a manual target velocity to prevent an enemy from jamming the Sparrow guidance. Once launched, the missile would have a better chance of tracking its target despite the countermeasures.

There were two types of Phantoms, known colloquially as single-stick or twin-stick aircraft. At the outset, the RAF recognised that pilot training was important and specified a version with dual controls. A control column was fitted into a housing in the centre of the floor of the rear cockpit and a set of throttles was fitted on the left console. This meant that many of the control panels occupied slightly different positions in a 'twin-sticker' in order to make room for the additional hardware. Rudder pedals were installed and could be adjusted away from the navigator's feet if not in use to give a modicum of comfort. A few additional instruments such as engine gauges were located on the front panel, and nice touches such as indexers to show the angle of attack were located above the main instrument panel. Some of these modifications were a bonus but some caused the navigator problems. The transmit switch on a single-stick aircraft was positioned on a floor-mounted foot rest. In a twin-sticker, the foot rest was replaced by the rudder pedal, so the transmit switch was moved to the inboard throttle similar to the front cockpit. Inadvertent use of the footswitch in a twin-sticker meant the navigator would introduce a healthy yaw on the controls, which upset the pilot considerably. The biggest drawback of the twin-sticker was that when the stick was in place, the radar could not be withdrawn from its stowed position as it would foul the controls. When stowed it was extremely difficult to see the display, and the navigator had to peer over a gyrating stick in order to see it. Even when not fitted, a small stub extended above floor level into which the rear stick was fitted. Navigators carried flight documents in a small canvas bag which many hung around the radar scope. If the strap was too long, the bag could foul the stub causing a control restriction. This was guaranteed to elicit a reaction from the front cockpit. Equally, jokers who asked to take control from the rear of a single-stick Phantom were debriefed comprehensively by the 'Pilot's Union'.

The Operational Conversion Unit had a much greater proportion of twin-stickers given the heavy pilot training workload. Generally, the engineers would remove the rear stick if an intercept sortie was planned. Occasionally, the stick was still in place. For an instructor navigator, a ride with a staff pilot when the aircraft was acting as a target was good news as it meant he could fly the aircraft for much of the sortie. Conversely, for a productive training sortie, it meant an hour jousting with a rapidly gyrating control column trying desperately to see the radar display beyond. On the OCU about 50 per cent of the aircraft were twin-stickers whereas on a squadron only one dual-control aircraft was normally on strength.

One of the unusual design flaws in the Phantom was that the cockpit heating and ventilation controls were fitted only in the front cockpit. A pilot could set a temperature that was comfortable in the front, yet the conditions in the back could be arctic or tropical. The normal rig for most of the year in the UK was an immersion suit worn over a knitted 'bunny suit' and under the lifejacket. While this thermal protection was a positive disadvantage in the cockpit, it was literally a life saver after an ejection into the North Sea. Unfortunately, dressing to survive in a dinghy meant that most aircrew overheated easily and airsickness was a common problem among navigators due to the motion and heat stress. Happily, as they were able to anticipate the manoeuvres, pilots were not similarly affected, as airsickness could be debilitating and would make the physical challenge of controlling an aircraft quite demanding.

The ease of navigating in a Phantom was much improved over previous aircraft that had relied on electronic navigation aids such as TACAN, which could be jammed. The Phantom inherited a Ferranti-designed inertial navigation system, or INAS, from the ill-fated TSR2 project. Although an early analogue design, the system was flexible and provided a huge leap in capability when flying at low level at high speeds. Six waypoints could be programmed, and the range and bearing to each was displayed on the flight instruments in both cockpits. An additional 'TO' or target of opportunity mode was available. If the aircraft flew over a point to which the crew wanted to return, a simple selection would give a range and bearing readout until cancelled by the navigator. The INAS was quite accurate considering the technology available.

There were a number of ways to align the system, although two main options were normally used. On a regular training sortie, the full or 'normal' alignment was carried out. This took 12 minutes once the platform oil had warmed up. The AN/AJB-7 heading reference fed a course heading to the inertial platform. After inserting the present position, the navigator selected 'align' and the 'ALN' light began to flash, rapidly at first, slowing as the platform aligned. Once the light showed steady, 'NAV' was selected and only at this point could the aircraft be moved. Any disturbance during the alignment would disrupt the process, taking much longer to align the system. Taxiing when still in 'align' mode could cause terminal damage to the gyros and it was important to co-ordinate with the pilot before the aircraft moved. Any mistakes meant another lengthy alignment and led to a frustrated wingman or leader. A rapid alignment allowed the INAS to be aligned in only 90 seconds and was generally used by QRA crews to allow a rapid scramble. Although swift, this alignment was much less accurate than a full alignment, so was used only when time was of the essence. The INAS was aligned in 'normal' mode and the heading noted before completing a Q shutdown. The lamp test button allowed the heading to be locked in when the system was reactivated, which reduced the alignment time markedly. The limiting factor was the temperature of the oil that protected the gyros. From cold this could take some minutes to warm up before the system could begin its alignment process. During this process the 'H' lamp illuminated, showing that the INAS was cold. For that reason, QRA aircraft were fitted with a 12-volt external power supply that kept the inertial platform oil constantly warm. A final option remained in the event of a failure, as the system could theoretically be aligned in the air. Unfortunately, this mode required the pilot to hold a steady heading for many minutes while the navigator aligned the platform. Suffice it to say that after the original trials sorties, this method was rarely, if ever, used in anger other than for novelty value and to give bragging rights in the crewroom.

The system could be updated or 'fixed' during the flight using the large red push button in the centre of the display unit. If the navigator could establish an accurate position from external fixpoints, the present position could be updated using the more accurate information. The system was normally accurate to within 2 miles during an average sortie. For air defence work that was generally acceptable, although ground attack crews would update the system much more regularly to give sufficient accuracy for bombing.

In air defence, the required navigational accuracy depended on the tactical scenario. Clearly, operating overland in tight airspace required better accuracy than operating on a remote combat air patrol many miles off the coast where 2 miles was acceptable. In reality, Phantom navigators did little pure navigation other than when deploying overseas, spending most of the time operating the weapon system or looking out of the cockpit for opponents. The term 'navigators' in the RAF was changed to 'weapon system operators' in 2003, supposedly to reflect the real duties in modern aircraft. This brought the RAF in line with terms used by the US Air Force and other NATO nations. Despite the change, most navigators were fiercely protective of their old brevet and few made the switch to the new flying badge where 'RAF' replaced the traditional 'N'. To the last, most back-seaters who trained as navigators resisted the change and would always call themselves navigators not WSOs.

The UK Phantom was modified extensively over the years. A simple but effective modification was the addition of an external rear-view mirror. This was literally bolted onto the rear canopy frame outside the cockpit but gave a much better view into the '6 o'clock'. Attacking aircraft that otherwise may have been unnoticed were suddenly more visible.

For many years the Phantom was not well equipped with defensive aids. In the mid-1970s, the aircraft was fitted with a British-designed radar warning receiver with the snappy title of the Marconi ARI 18228. Initially known as the passive warning receiver (PWR), the name was changed to the RWR (radar warning receiver) shortly after its introduction to service. The renaming was supposedly to deny an enemy the knowledge that the system worked passively, but anyone with even basic electronic warfare knowledge knew precisely how such things worked. The enormous rewriting of books and publications that the move caused seemed a huge waste of money at the time.

Three receive antennas were fitted in a cap on top of the tail, giving the British Phantom a distinctive square top to the fin. The antennas looked forward, backwards, and upwards to give as close to all-round coverage as possible. The capability of the RWR system was extremely limited. A small display tube showed a line at the bearing of an incoming signal. An attacking aircraft that locked up immediately ahead would appear in the 12 o'clock position. The actual frequency of the threat could be determined by the type of line; an I Band threat, which was typical of another fighter aircraft, showed as a solid line. Various other warning lights helped to identify the type of threat. Small warning lights showed if the aircraft was being illuminated by pulse (P) or track-while-scan (TWS) threats. Four green lights in each quadrant showed if a continuous wave equipped threat was present in that sector. CW threats were generally quite lethal, and urgent defensive reaction was required to negate such a threat. For example, a MiG-23 Flogger which used CW radar to support the AA-7 Apex missile would show up as a dashed line with an associated CW quadrant light. The rotary control on the lower panel allowed different strategies to be selected, and the six toggle switches enabled different parts of the electronic spectrum to be selectively monitored. Another toggle switch allowed the navigator to monitor the raw audio signals of the intercepted radar in his headset. From then on, with the audio turned on, the cockpit of a Phantom became flooded with squeaks, bleeps, and alarm tones but, without it, critical tactical information was lost. If life was hard before that time, it suddenly became much harder to concentrate on the job in hand. Ground training sessions taught crews how to identify the characteristics of threat radars from the bizarre warbles. One fellow navigator tried some 'one-upmanship' on the squadron boss when, during a ground training session, he substituted the warbling of a telephone for a Soviet attack radar. Despite losing the first skirmish, the boss's revenge ultimately proved much more effective.

In reality, the RWR was limited in its performance due to the presence of the Phantom's own radar. The receiver had been designed in isolation rather than as an integrated element of the Phantom weapon system. In a laboratory it worked well. The dense electronic environment, particularly over the North German Plain, saw potential enemy aircraft operating in the same electronic 'band' to that of the Phantom. The powerful emissions of the Phantom radar were detected by the RWR as a hostile aircraft, causing false signals to be displayed on the screen. It was not uncommon for both forward hemisphere CW warning lights to blink rhythmically in tune to the sweep of the Phantom radar coupled with a nuisance alarm tone in the headset. This meant the navigator had to deselect some important functions when the tactical situation was calm, reselecting them at critical phases of an intercept. Not ideal! As a consequence, the electronic interference from the Phantom meant that certain radar warnings from an incoming attacker came very late or not at all. In stark contrast, the same equipment fitted to the Buccaneer worked well. The Buccaneer lacked the powerful Air Intercept radar and was fitted only with a lower-powered navigation/bombing radar which the navigators used selectively. In this role the RWR was very effective and well liked by the bomber crews.

Later in the aircraft's life, and following the Falklands War, defensive systems began to be fitted to the Phantom in the form of chaff and flare dispensers. The AN/ALE-40 was a proven American countermeasures dispenser system. The dispensers were fitted to each side of the Sidewinder missile pylons under the wings. A base plate on each side of the pylon was fitted with an adaptor that rotated the chaff and flare dispensers through 45 degrees so that the expendable rounds would be fired below and behind the aircraft. As it was a new fit for the British Phantom, much work went into determining the best settings for how many flares and how much chaff would be used in each sequence and to work out optimum dispense patterns to protect against key threats. The navigator programmed the sequences using a control panel fitted in the rear cockpit. Numbers of expendables and the interval between each dispense were set on the upper control panel. The lower panel activated the system and showed the number of flares and the chaff bundles remaining in the dispenser. Dispense buttons in each cockpit allowed either crew member to dispense chaff or flares when needed. In broad terms, chaff was used against radar guided missiles whereas flares were used against infra-red guided weapons. A jettison function allowed the dispensers to be emptied in the event of an emergency. The precise details of countermeasures expendables and how they replicate the aircraft they are protecting is a complex chess match. Understanding the threat against which the Phantom might be pitched helped experts to produce flares that looked exactly like the heat signature of the Rolls-Royce Spey engines to an incoming missile. Precise sequences and associated tactics were developed by aircrew and scientists working for the Central Tactics and Trials Organisation (CTTO), now known as the Air Warfare Centre. Once developed, the tactics were issued to the squadron weapons instructors and taught to squadron crews who practised during regular training missions.

Chaff, or window as it was originally known when developed during the Second World War, consists of small pieces of metallised glass fibre. When ejected from a chaff dispenser, the small bundles bloom in the airflow appearing like another aircraft to a threat radar or a radar guided missile. Flares are pellets of combustible material which ignite when ejected and burn spontaneously to simulate the infra-red energy emitted by the host aircraft. The intention with any of these countermeasures is to seduce a threat missile away from the host aircraft, hopefully passing outside the lethal range.

One of the more innovative ideas to emerge was fitting the Telescoping Optical Sighting System or TESS. During a quiet day on the squadron, a trails officer from CTTO arrived with some rough sketches of a proposed trials fit. One of the problems of operating autonomously in Germany was the need to identify the target visually before shooting. It was generally thought that in the fog of war there was a risk of engaging friendly aircraft unless we could positively identify that the target was hostile. One of the safer ways to do this was to identify the threat with the 'Mark One Eyeball'. However, the most effective attack tactics for the F4 were to employ a frontal attack. Small-size head-on targets were notoriously difficult to identify accurately, especially in the poor visibility on an average day in West Germany. The concept was that if a telescope was fitted in the back cockpit, the target could be identified at a greater range, allowing the use of the Sparrow missile in the front sector. Rumour had it that the rudimentary piece of kit that was bolted into one of the squadron jets for the trial sorties was a modified sight from a Centurion main battle tank. I never knew whether that was fact or fiction. The optics were built into a quarter panel between the front and rear cockpits. A sight protruded into the airflow to the side of the canopy and was aligned with the weapon's boresight looking forward. The viewfinder protruded into the cockpit and was protected by a very large rubber boot into which the navigator was expected to peer.

With very little pre-briefing I was launched into the low flying area to evaluate the sight in the harsh environment of the Phantom cockpit during a low level intercept sortie. My pilot and I set up a combat air patrol in a low flying area and waited for 'trade', which was never long in coming. Immediately, I found a target on the radar and as we reached the point where we thought it would be possible to identify the target, I popped my eye to the 'shufty scope' expecting miracles. With the radar locked on, the pilot could place the Sidewinder steering dot in the centre of the radar scope, which would place the target directly in the weapon's boresight. As the TESS was fixed on the boresight, the target should have been in the centre of the optics, or so the theory went. Even under normal conditions, the cockpit environment of the Phantom was hot, sweaty, and in perpetual motion. The norm was nothing in comparison to the view of the world that greeted me through the rolling eyepiece. Through this new gadget, the movement of the background terrain was magnified and was gyrating violently. Even though I was reasonably good at identifying the other inhabitants of the low flying areas, a wobbly image of a jet would pass, briefly, through the field of view, leaving seconds to snatch the identification. Although uncomfortable, TESS was undoubtedly effective. With typical identification ranges in the hazy visibility typical of the North German Plain being about 3 to 5 miles, TESS almost doubled that. Suddenly, the option to engage with a Sparrow at low level, having already visually identified the target, became a reality. The challenge was how to prevent the squadron navigators from being decimated by airsickness. After the initial tests, procedures were developed to make best use of the sight and to use it only at the optimum moment during an intercept. Used in that way, it was extremely effective. The trials fit put the sight in the right-hand quarter panel window. I found it rather difficult leaning over the radar hand controller to peer through the sight, so the production fit moved the sight over to the other side of the cockpit, which seemed to help. Unfortunately, it proved impossible to bring the glass panel used in the test fit into production, so a steel panel was used in the final version. Although this reduced visibility from the back cockpit still further, TESS provided an innovative visual identification system at low cost and it was quickly introduced into service. Unlike some other vastly expensive failures, it was a credit to those involved in the procurement programme.

One of the constant discussion themes is how good was the Phantom against its peers? The Phantom is not, and never was, a 'dogfighter'. Basic combat manoeuvring, air combat manoeuvring, within visual range engagements – all terms for the 'knife fight in a phonebox' – were never the aircraft's ideal environment. It could cope, but it depended on good front-seaters and, equally, good back-seaters to get the best from the airframe and equipment and avoid the many pitfalls. Ultimately, the maturity of the weapon system at each stage of its development dictated how effective the Phantom would have been in combat for the RAF. The key to all tactics is having a bigger 'stick'. If your missile has

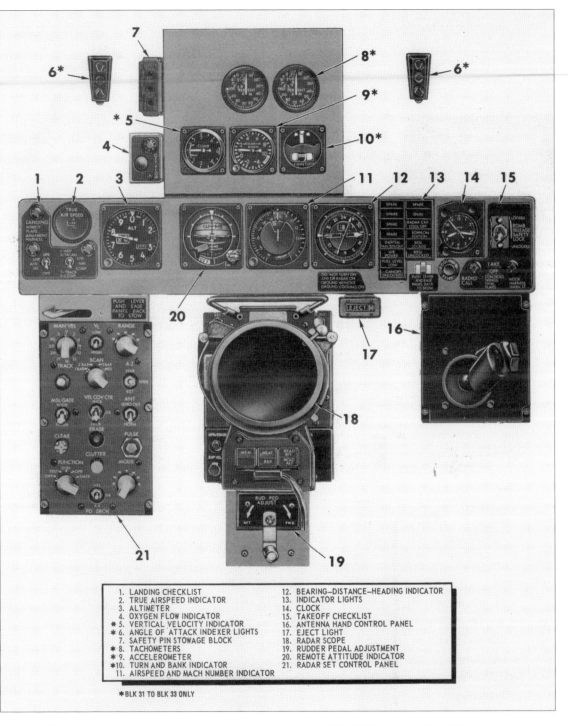

The Phantom rear cockpit as shown in the Aircrew Manual. UK MOD Crown Copyright (1975).

1. LANDING CHECKLIST
2. TRUE AIRSPEED INDICATOR
3. ALTIMETER
4. OXYGEN FLOW INDICATOR
* 5. VERTICAL VELOCITY INDICATOR
* 6. ANGLE OF ATTACK INDEXER LIGHTS
7. SAFETY PIN STOWAGE BLOCK
* 8. TACHOMETERS
* 9. ACCELEROMETER
*10. TURN AND BANK INDICATOR
11. AIRSPEED AND MACH NUMBER INDICATOR

12. BEARING–DISTANCE–HEADING INDICATOR
13. INDICATOR LIGHTS
14. CLOCK
15. TAKEOFF CHECKLIST
16. ANTENNA HAND CONTROL PANEL
17. EJECT LIGHT
18. RADAR SCOPE
19. RUDDER PEDAL ADJUSTMENT
20. REMOTE ATTITUDE INDICATOR
21. RADAR SET CONTROL PANEL

* BLK 31 TO BLK 33 ONLY

Above: The radar display with the hand controller to the right and the control panel to the left. The radar scope camera has been removed.

Left: The navigator's radar hand controller.

Opposite: The navigator's radar control panel.

The Inertial Navigation and Attack System.

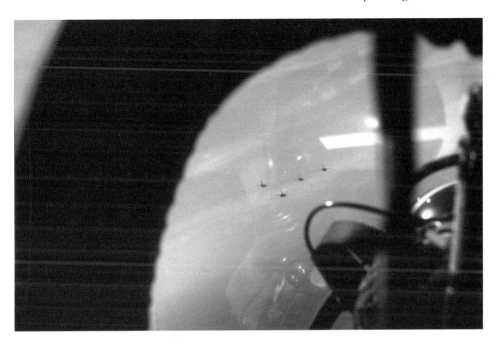

Visibility looking past the pilot's ejection seat was poor.

The mirrors showing the enhanced view through the external mirror. The ejection seats pins are stowed below meaning the seat is live.

Above: The Marconi radar warning receiver antennas on the fin.

Left: The radar warning receiver display.

The radar warning receiver controls.

The AN/ ALE40 Chaff and Flare Dispenser controls.

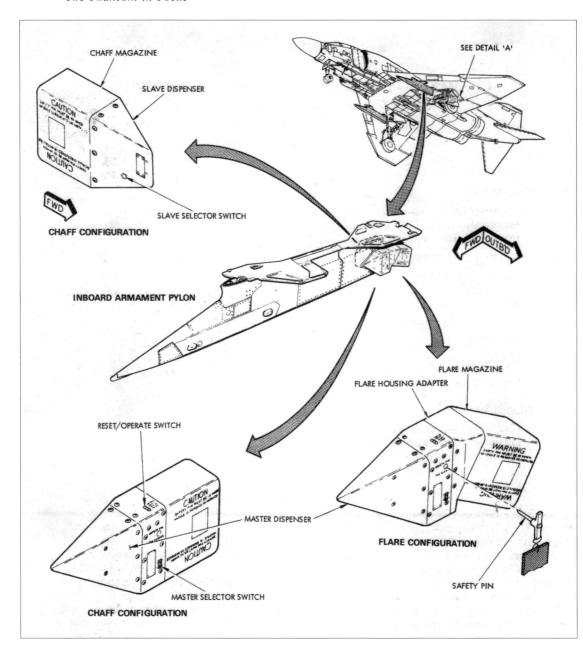

Above: The AN/ALE 40 countermeasures dispensers fitted to the missile pylons. UK MOD Crown Copyright (1981).

Opposite above: The telescopic sighting system mounting.

Opposite below: The telescopic sighting system eyepiece in the rear cockpit.

a longer range than your opponent, and your missile is fired inside parameters and is reliable, you win. End of story. Despite the impressive displays of turning prowess at an air show, no fighter pilot will enter a close turning engagement through choice, and that includes agile aircraft such as the F22, F15 and Su-27. The dynamics of a turning fight, even with the stealthiest aircraft, the best defensive aids, and the best situation awareness, are too unpredictable. Modern avionics can help because they are automated, but often automation is only as good as the system software, which can be flawed or badly programmed. A wily fighter pilot will stand off from the fight and target his opponent clinically at long range and destroy it without ever coming into visual range. In that situation his cockpit environment is calm and ordered, unlike the mayhem of close combat. Invariably, opponents conspire against this ideal but as missiles become more efficient with huge guaranteed kill zones, the ideal closes on the reality. Sadly, Phantom crews rarely had that luxury. In order to survive in combat, the weapon system has to be developed over the life of the aircraft. A Formula 1 racing team could not finish a season with the same car that began the season. In order to win, and there are no prizes for coming second in war, your aircraft must adapt and evolve with your opponent. In the mid- to late 70s the Phantom was a multi-role aircraft with an innovative pulse Doppler radar that gave true look-down shoot-down capability against opponents such as the MiG-21, MiG-23, and Soviet bombers. Phantom crews trained against US Air Force F4Es, F104s, and F5s, as even the USAF had not fielded a good pulse Doppler-equipped fighter. These pulse radar-equipped fighters faced a huge challenge locating targets in the ground clutter, yet the RAF Phantom was unconstrained by that limitation and so had an immense advantage and was considered to be king of the fighters by those who operated it at this time. Indeed, during its early years, the Phantom's beyond visual range Sparrow shot was discounted during training engagements. Perhaps bravado, but despite the fact that the Phantom may have already achieved a head-on 'kill', discounting that shot pulled the aircraft into a turning environment it didn't enjoy. Although opposing pilots gained training value from the engagements, such false scenarios set false learning patterns and were detrimental to true tactical employment of the Phantom. It took some years before other types fielded similar capabilities and every shot began to count. Even so, employing the aircraft effectively relied on knowing who the enemy was and ensuring that you could prosecute a kill at longer range. Even with modern techniques identification is never assured.

For Phantom crews, identification and rules of engagement were paramount, often placing the emphasis back on the ground controller to give clearance to engage. Although the Phantom had rudimentary identification equipment, it was never adequate to declare a target 'hostile' electronically without backing up the identification from another source or by 'putting eyeballs on target'. Even then, a visual identification was not irrefutable as, in later conflicts, the same aircraft type might be operated by NATO as well as opposing forces. The MiG-29, post Cold War is a good example. The most effective identification might be an intercept controller located near the forward edge of the battlefield who had watched the hostile track launch from an East German airfield. It could equally be an airborne early warning controller who had been advised by his NATO counterparts of the origin of the track. At the Phantom crew's level, if identification was not forthcoming, the head-on shot could not be employed, requiring the target to be visually identified, potentially pulling the Phantom crew in close. It was for that reason that the Vietnam era doctrine suggesting that air combat was consigned to the history books proved false. Honing air combat skills would be a constant feature in operating the British Phantom.

In the early 80s, the advent of the MiG-29 and Su-27 as opponents, and the F15 and F16 as training opponents, meant the Phantom was out-performed but, initially, not out-ranged. Indeed, the early F15A radar was hard to operate, a handful for a single pilot at low level, and could be unreliable. Often, the UK F4 was still the platform of choice to lead NATO Mixed Fighter Forces throughout the early 80s until the F15C entered service. Early F16A aircraft flown by the European nations had great turn performance but also suffered from radar problems and limited numbers of stern hemisphere only Sidewinder missiles, rendering them less effective than the elderly F4. Given decent rules of engagement, the Phantom still coped. Low level overland missions sometimes conducted autonomously by the Wildenrath Wing in poor weather were a good example of how tactics could compensate for equipment deficiencies. The Wildenrath Phantoms operated at 250 feet every day of the week in sometimes appalling weather conditions. It was expected that even the Soviet Tactical Air Armies would have penetrated at lower levels, so being able to work at low level where the flying was more demanding and required additional skills was essential. There were few equals to the Wildenrath crews, the tactic of operating at low level compensating for other tactical constraints. If the opponent approached at a slightly higher level, the Phantom crew was offered the easy look-up shot. If the opponent approached in the medium to upper air, the missiles employed in the NATO missile engagement zones would have exacted a heavy attrition rate. If, however, the Phantom was forced to climb to those levels the scales balanced. At medium level, airframe deficiencies began to outweigh pilot/navigator skills, and employing the Sparrow became almost essential. Ultimately, the famous 'catch all' tactic was to adopt a 'Mach 1.3, guns a blazin, whistle through the fight' option. Such high speeds were difficult to counter by even an agile opponent, although, in fairness, it rarely produced kills from the Phantom crew.

Eventually, the arrival of the Generation 3 and 4 air superiority fighters sounded the warning bells. As the missiles fitted to Soviet fighters became increasingly effective and their ranges increased, the Phantom lost its advantage. With new western fighters on the drawing board, upgrades became less affordable and rarer. In the mid-1980s, the aircraft began to suffer from under-investment as the Tornado F3 entered the inventory and the Typhoon began development. In the cut-throat arena of MOD spending rounds, funding for Phantom upgrades was rationed. Sparrow did not have sufficient range and was becoming less effective in the electronic battle. Skyflash had arrived and was an improvement, but the missile was still semi-active, meaning it had to be tracked by the radar to impact drawing the Phantom closer to the threat. An active version of Skyflash was not funded and even it was out-ranged by later Soviet missiles such as the AA-10 Alamo. With the aircraft becoming 'out gunned', the death knell sounded.

The German F4F was eventually upgraded with the AN/APG-65 radar and the active Advanced Medium Range Air-to-Air Missile (AMRAAM), offering a new lease of life and proving that the airframe could still be effective, but it was still basically a 1960s design with many analogue avionics. Integrating modern digital avionics into an analogue aeroplane was complex and costly. In UK service, the truth was that the Phantom's lifespan was being determined by politics. In a bid to reap the Cold War windfall, the Phantom would retire earlier than originally planned, used as a pawn in the Conventional Armed Forces in Europe Treaty.

CHAPTER 3
Operational Conversion

My first recollection of the Phantom was as a boy at the RAF Finningley annual air show but, I have to admit, it was not my immediate favourite. Like many young kids I was seduced by the noise of four Vulcan bombers with their Olympus engines at full throttle as they simulated a nuclear scramble from the operational readiness platform. The sight of those huge aircraft in a close stream with the last jet rotating into the vertical over the downwind threshold of the runway, but with all four aircraft still in camera shot, is an image that will last a lifetime. The wider, although still noisy, display of the 'newcomer on the block' didn't even seem to match that of the Lightning which never failed to please the crowds. Despite my early indifference, when it came to a posting from navigator training, the last thing I wanted was to sit in the dark confines of the rear crew compartment of a Vulcan pointing backwards. Fast-jet postings were highly prized, and only two of us on my course of ten trainees were lucky enough to be selected: me to the Phantom and the other to the Buccaneer. The Officers' Mess at RAF Coningsby sits adjacent to the northern taxiway. My first, still vivid, memory was gazing through the Ante Room window seeing the camouflaged bulk of a Phantom taxi past, knowing that very soon I would be in the cockpit. The boyhood dreams rapidly became reality.

No. 228 Operational Conversion Unit had been selected as the numberplate for the Phantom OCU. With a distinguished history, it was an appropriate choice, having been associated with training fighter crews for many years. Formed at Leeming in May 1947, the unit trained crews for Mosquito night fighter squadrons until 1951. Between 1952 and 1961, it re-equipped with Meteors which by then carried Air Intercept radars, but the greater demands of the new jets meant a move to RAF Coltishall. Following the relocation, Javelins and then Canberras were introduced before 228 OCU saw its first association with RAF Leuchars in Scotland, which was to feature again in its final days of operating the Phantom. It relocated to RAF Coningsby in 1968 with the introduction of

An early airborne shot of a Phantom of 228 OCU. The scarab beetle denotes the shadow numberplate 64 Squadron. © David Lewis.

XT895 of 228 OCU over Lincolnshire in early 1976.

the Phantom. During its time as the Phantom Conversion Unit, 228 OCU trained an amazing 1,320 aircrew between 1968 and 1991. The number is surprising as the average two-seater squadron comprised approximately thirty aircrew and an average tour of duty was three years. In the early days, the courses produced mainly ground attack crews, with courses running from late 1968 to 1975. The first three courses on the OCU were unusual in that the pilots and navigators were allocated to different courses. This feature didn't last and by Number 4 Course, pilots and navigators were brought together and received the same training. With the replacement of the Phantom in the ground attack role by the Jaguar in the early 1970s, the emphasis shifted to producing air defence (AD) crews, and by mid-1974, Phantom squadrons were forming in the AD role and dedicated AD courses were the norm. By the time I arrived at Coningsby in 1975, Number 25 Ground Attack Course, the last of the 'mud movers', had already finished.

I flew my first trip in a Phantom in XV472 on 26 March 1976 with one of life's gentlemen, the boss of the OCU, Wing Commander Mike Shaw who commanded the unit from 1974 to 1977. Before I made that giant leap I had been trained as a navigator. Navigator training in the early 1970s was still biased towards traditional plotting skills, producing aircrew for Transport Command and the V Force. The majority of the sorties were flown in the back of the Varsity and the Dominie, where plotting position lines on a paper chart and taking sun shots with a sextant were the recognised skills. The only relevant training for a prospective fast-jet navigator was 12 hours in a Jet Provost learning how to navigate with a map and stopwatch at low level. After the award of my coveted Navigator brevet I progressed to the Air Defence Lead-In, which had only just been introduced to give a limited insight into air defence tactics. This phase offered a further 12 hours but, with the JP's lack of avionics, the training was limited to pairs formation flying and visual intercept training known as 'Rat and Terrier' exercises. The two aircraft set up at planned navigation points 15 miles apart and aimed towards each other flying pre-planned tracks. The student navigator in the 'Terrier' would attempt to spot the 'Rat' and set up a visual intercept using suitable commands to his pilot. The student navigator in the 'Rat' would try to spot the incoming 'fighter'. Although it was simplistic, the training had some value in developing the ability to control an aircraft using verbal commands, which was to become a core skill in the Phantom. It was also crucial to be able to spot another aircraft in the air before your opponent – not as easy as it sounds – so both students began to hone their visual detection skills. Moving on, more plotting followed, but by now flying in the Dominie at higher speeds. Radar Lead-In training consisted of a few sorties of low level radar navigation in the back of the Dominie and four sorties in the darkened crew compartment of a

Hastings equipped with the Vulcan navigation bombing system. Using this huge 12-inch circular display we were to navigate around the UK using only the radar. None of this seemed of particular relevance to conducting air interceptions using the complex weapon system in the Phantom, so staying motivated as my OCU approached was a problem for a keen young aviator ready to get on with it. An invitation to return to Scampton to try some remedial exercises on the Hastings reminded me to take the training rather more seriously. So, at this stage, it was apparent even as a brand new prospective Phantom navigator that I was not particularly well prepared for my future career.

While the anticipation of climbing into the back seat of a Phantom was immense, the reality came as a shock when the day finally arrived. Despite the extensive groundschool, even the physical stress of being weighed down by the heavy survival gear came as a surprise. The first sortie passed in a blur as I stumbled through my hesitant procedures, trying to make the Phantom systems do my bidding. The early reality was cruel. A fighter aircraft never operates as a 'singleton', and standard RAF tactics are based on 'battle' formation where the wingman sits about a mile abeam his leader but separated in height. This formation gives visual cover around the formation, with each crew member allocated areas of the sky to search. The 'first spot' of an attacking fighter is a highly coveted prize on any mission. When the Phantom was introduced to RAF service, most fighters of the day were armed almost exclusively with air-to-air missiles that had to be launched within 60 degrees of the target's tail. This explains the old fighter pilot's adage of 'Check 6'. The '6 o'clock', or your own tail, is where the attack would most likely arrive. It is still the hardest area to cover visually, although with modern avionics giving a 'God's-eye view' and fed by datalinks, it is less likely that a Typhoon pilot would be surprised by an unexpected attack. The first member of the formation to spot a threat would call to the lead pilot, directing a defensive manoeuvre if the threat was imminent. This would take the form of a radio call: 'Bogey 6 o'clock, one mile, break left.' It was a brave pilot that ignored that call, but for a young navigator it took some courage to hit the transmit button for the first time. The first action when 'bounced' was to engage reheat to try to gain 'energy' or speed before quickly turning towards the threat to defeat the missile shot. Sadly, this made the hot metal around the engines of your aircraft an attractive target for a heat-seeking missile as the afterburners bit. One of the early lessons for pilots during air combat training was deciding what to do next, once the Phantom became a slow and unmanoeuvrable 'lump'. To my eternal shame, my training had been so rudimentary and had involved such little tactical formation flying that my first ever call on the radio was to give a punchy defensive reaction against the other aircraft in my own formation. That simple mistake cost me a good deal of credibility amongst my peers on the course, not to mention a few beers, for some days; well weeks. Training improved over the years, so my successors were better armed as they began their air defence careers, but for me it was not an auspicious start!

The students on the early AD courses came from a variety of backgrounds, but Strike Command Headquarters decided that about 50 per cent should be Phantom qualified transferring from the ground attack role, 25 per cent should be ex-Lightning pilots, who would understand air-to-air techniques but would need to adapt to the vastly different capabilities of the Phantom, and 25 per cent would be ab-initio, namely straight from training. Although not a problem on the course, this mix led to some tensions on the squadrons as different skills clashed. The first AD Squadron Commanders were almost exclusively ex-Phantom ground attackers, as were the majority of the supervisors. The 'muds' called the shots and many of the Lightning pilots were ignored in the early days, which gave a tendency for squadrons to adopt old ground attack tactics and procedures rather than those more suited to the new role. For this reason, it was some years before experience grew and the Phantom matured into a capable air defence platform. As a newly arrived ab-initio it was easy. We knew little, could add little, so we remained quiet, listened, and watched the occasional fireworks.

Originally, because of their varying backgrounds, students on the OCU received tailored courses. Ex-Phantom crews received a six-week conversion to the air defence role called a 'Squadron Course'. Lightning pilots received a twelve-week conversion to the Phantom known as a 'Lightning Course'. Newly trained aircrew underwent a full seventeen-week course known as a 'Long Course'. It proved impossible to sequence these courses to finish on the same date to form squadrons, so by early 1977, the options had been rationalised to deliver either a 'Short Course' or a 'Long Course' depending on background.

The OCU was set up in three distinct squadrons: No. 1 Squadron was the Groundschool Squadron that delivered the academic systems training and operated the flight simulators and the Air Intercept or AI Trainer; No. 2 Squadron was the flying element; the final, but by no means least important, section was No. 3 Squadron, which provided the engineering support to keep the Phantom flying.

The syllabus was broken up into five phases, completed in strict order:

The Groundschool/Simulator Phase
The Conversion Phase
The Basic Radar Phase
The Combat Phase
The Advanced Radar Phase

The Phantom Flight Simulator (Coningsby M1) preserved at Newark Air Museum.

On arrival at Coningsby, the new pilots and navigators were paired as crews. Student crews would fly the simulator sorties and AI Trainer sessions together, although instructors would fly most of the airborne events with a student in the other cockpit. The reason the Phantom worked so well was that experience in either cockpit was synergistic, so I found myself as a young inexperienced ab-initio paired with an ex-Lightning pilot who was about to command a squadron. A strong pilot could help a weaker navigator and vice versa and, in turn, I found myself helping young pilots throughout my later career. In the air, any new profile would be flown with a staff pilot or navigator before flying the exercise as a student crew, hopefully building confidence. Despite that, crew rides often seemed more like 'the blind leading the blind'. Although additional handling exercises were included in the flying syllabus for the pilots, all aircrew underwent the same training on the ground and an almost identical syllabus in the air. It was key that the navigators understood the aircraft systems as comprehensively as the pilots and, equally, the pilots had to be familiar with how the radar system worked. This fundamental principle was never compromised, even with the advent of the Tornado F3. As experience built, the sign of an effective crew was when each member became adept at sharing each other's workload without even realising it. Too much chat in the cockpit was often the sign of a crew who had yet to gel. Clearly this did not apply to the instructor, who prided himself on being able to talk longer and louder than the student at any time during the mission and well into the debrief.

The first event on the course was a comprehensive groundschool phase that lasted about four weeks. During this time, the complexities of the Phantom's systems were unveiled in excruciating detail. Understanding how the Rolls-Royce Spey jets provided not just thrust but less obvious functions such as bleed air to drive a myriad of secondary systems that would keep us alive was absolutely critical. Interspersed between lectures were simulator sorties where the operation of these systems was demonstrated and we began to understand how to get the Phantom into the air. More importantly, the simulator sortie would include demonstrations of how quickly life could become exciting when these systems failed.

Emergency drills were practised time after time until they became second nature. Despite endless drills, simulator training would give only an inkling of the complexities of real emergencies that were invariably more intricate. Imagine the havoc caused by a detached fan blade from a jet engine that slices through various pipes on its route through the outer skin of the jet. At that moment, the telelight panel which flags up system failures to the crew would be as brightly lit as a Christmas tree on 25 December. Understanding the nature of an emergency was important. Reacting properly and conducting the correct drill was essential. For that reason, an early task was to become intimately familiar with the flight reference cards that were carried on every sortie and ran to nearly fifty pages. This meant crews being able to recite parrot-fashion and execute immediately the 'bold face drills' that were needed in an emergency. The cards contained the follow-on actions that would configure the Phantom in the best way to counteract the failure. I recall one particularly stark drill. The hydraulically driven power controls or PC operated the flying surfaces of the Phantom. There were no bold face actions for a double PC failure. The cards read simply: 'Anticipate loss of pitch control. If flight conditions permit, attempt to control the aircraft in pitch by use of engine and lateral control. Manoeuvre the aircraft into an area suitable for ejection. If hydraulic pressure does not recover or control is completely lost – EJECT'. Life could be seriously simple operating the Phantom.

Very early on, the mind-blowing complexity of air interceptions was introduced. This was to become the cornerstone of virtually every sortie I would fly during my career. A grizzly old staff navigator from the flying squadron delivered a series of lectures, introducing topics such as turning circles, collision angles and relative tracks, the final turn, intercept profiles, visual identification procedures, and shadowing techniques. These terms may be unintelligible to the layman, but without this grounding it was impossible to position two aircraft flying at well in excess of 400 mph, and at different heights, to a point within missile or gun parameters. It was important to understand how the Phantom reacted to its environment. If you asked for a 5G turn at 45,00 feet, not only would it not be forthcoming but the aircraft stood every chance of departing from controlled flight and returning to Earth faster than it had reached 45,000 feet. Pilots were quick to point this out. Armed with the knowledge of what a 180 intercept looked like on a radar scope – a 180 is two aircraft pointing at each other on opposing headings – the student crew began practising the various profiles in the Air Intercept Trainer.

The AI Trainer was a training aid that allowed crews to run through the different types of intercept in the comfort of a classroom environment. The radar and weapons controls were replicated in two rudimentary cockpits. Targets could be programmed into the trainer by the staff navigator who would position the fighter and target at appropriate heights and ranges, with the 'air picture' being displayed by a large projector onto the wall. The technology would be alien to modern youngsters. 'Programming' meant turning analogue rotary wheels on a console that moved potentiometers behind the console to position the two aircraft in space. This sounds simple in comparison with modern digital graphics but was cutting edge technology in the early 70s. Typically, the starting positions were 40 miles apart, but, at the cruising speed of the Phantom, an intercept lasted a few seconds rather than many minutes. Not surprisingly, the projected map of the air picture was a feature which the staff navigator could turn off, and most often did. This meant that the radar scope was now the only means to work out the complex air situation as you sped towards your target at high speed. Once the basics had been mastered it was time to fly.

At this point, crews moved across the airfield to the flying squadron. The first task was to acquaint the new crews with the cockpit environment and the flying characteristics of the Phantom. During the Conversion Phase the flying was inevitably pilot-centric. The student pilot's first four sorties were flown with a Qualified Flying Instructor (QFI) before being let loose with a staff navigator on a 'First Solo'. The Phantom could not be flown by a single pilot as key systems were operated from the back seat, so even a transit sortie had to be flown with a full crew. To that end, this was as 'solo' as a pilot ever flew on the RAF Phantom. The first couple of sorties for the student navigator involved operating the inertial navigation system and the radar for real. In those early days, the avionics fit was relatively simple and it was only later that the complexities of a radar warning receiver, chaff and flare systems, an IFF interrogator and the telescoping sighting system were installed in the back cockpit. After just a few hours on type, the staff instructors retired to the crewroom and the student crew was launched alone and unafraid with an expensive fighter aeroplane in their charge. The first crew solo was a gentle affair, giving the opportunity to play with the equipment on a benign profile. The pilot practised a few scripted manoeuvres, and the navigator played with the radar hoping to find the odd opportunity target to track. Throughout the sortie the new crew prayed that the aircraft remained serviceable, as they had no desire to practise the newly learned emergency drills. However, there was no time wasted before the QFIs took over again and the intricacies of handling at various speeds, operation of more of the systems, formation flying, instrument flying, supersonic handling and night flying were explained to the new pilots. This period was the biggest difference in training between front- and back-seaters, with the pilot flying about sixteen sorties during 'Convex' whereas the navigator flew only four.

After only a couple of weeks, crews moved on to the Basic Radar Phase where the real task of learning how to use the Phantom as an operational weapon system began. This first phase reinforced the fundamentals of intercepting another aircraft which had been learned on the ground. With combined closing speeds of 800 mph, things happen quickly. More importantly, at those speeds, if the intercept was not flown precisely, things could go wrong very quickly and the fighter could end up way out in the North Sea with the target over Lincolnshire. The breakdown of responsibilities was easy in the Phantom. Although the pilot had a repeater display, the navigator handled the radar controls, controlled the intercept and passed commands to the pilot, giving headings, heights, and speeds to fly. Once visual with the target, the pilot took over, engaging the target with the weapons while the navigator 'checked six', looking for other threats that might engage the aircraft. In instrument conditions, when the pilot could not see the target, the navigator might have to control the intercept all the way to calling the missile shot, with the pilot flying the whole profile on instruments. Intercepts were controlled using a standard convention. Nautical 'banter' still ruled, so left and right was port and starboard. 'Go port' meant start a standard turn to the left using 45 degrees angle of bank. 'Harder' would increase the angle of bank by 15 degrees, and 'Ease' would reduce it by 15 degrees. 'Go up' would give a 1,000 feet rate of climb, and 'Go down' the same rate of descent. 'Set 400 knots' would give that speed. Using these simple commands the navigator would position the aircraft during the intercept. There were two basic tactics. An 'Attack-Reattack' would position the Phantom on a collision course, 2,000 feet below the target at a point in space in front of the target where the Sparrow missile could be launched. Once the missile was on its way, a breakaway manoeuvre was initiated, putting the target towards the edge of the radar coverage before turning hard back towards the target and turning in behind. Once inside Sidewinder missile parameters, a second shot could be taken in case the first Sparrow shot had failed. This profile could be achieved very simply. On his radar display, the pilot had a steering dot which would set up a collision. By manoeuvring the aircraft to put the dot in the centre of a steering circle, the Phantom would arrive at a point in space where a missile shot could be taken. Being British, we of course had to make it far more complicated and came up with a number of esoteric profiles controlled by the navigator, which, in truth, achieved a similar aim. That said, once 'Combat Ready', a crew who had formed a working bond could share the workload. If there was an easy way to complete the intercept, the one with the best tools would 'do the business' and the other crew member would be scanning the skies for potential aggressors. The other type of attack, a 'Stern Attack', threw away the prospect of a head-on Sparrow shot and the aircraft was flown into the target's stern hemisphere. The disadvantage was that the target invariably saw the fighter approach and could react to the attack, making life harder for the incoming fighter. Nevertheless, by going round the back the Phantom crew could identify the target, so the risk of engaging a friendly target was reduced.

One of the main roles of the Phantom was to provide the UK Quick Reaction Alert. Once scrambled, the Phantom would be vectored to intercept unidentified tracks entering UK airspace. The stern attack was the preferred profile for coming alongside an intruding Soviet Bear or for intercepting a wayward civilian aircraft. The most efficient way to arrive in close formation was to complete a stern attack followed by a visual identification procedure. It was the OCU instructor's role to ensure that the mechanics of this attack became ingrained. This type of intercept was set up using 'keys'. A key was a range and bearing of the target from the fighter. By a complex series of mental calculations using basic geometry, a displaced attack could be set up. From opposing headings, a final turn initiated at a 'key' of 40 degrees right at 12 miles would achieve a two-mile roll out behind the target aircraft. Errors could be taken out by controlling the rate of turn as the fighter manoeuvred in behind. Simple really, especially when strapped to tons of metal, about 4 miles above the Earth, travelling at 400 mph, on a collision course with a target that may not want to be intercepted! These intercepts were practised over and over again by the student crews until they were imprinted in the brain. Once firmly imprinted, the staff briefed the target to make an evading turn which completely changed the intercept profile, meaning it had to be recalculated during the run.

At the end of every sortie, each aspect of the mission was debriefed carefully to ensure that all the learning points were drawn out. The final event was the film debrief, which lasted up to 30 minutes and was run by the staff navigator. The Phantom carried a camera that filmed the radar display in the back cockpit. The technology was rudimentary by modern standards, producing wet film that had to be processed by the station photographic section as soon as the aircraft landed. This old-style cine film was delivered back to the squadron and the staff navigator then dissected each intercept with the student crew. I well remember the rattle of the cine projector in the background and the often not so gentle explanation of why being 5 miles behind my target instead of 'in the saddle' at 2 miles was not a good thing. At that time smoking was the norm, and the wisp of cigarette smoke through the light beam of the projector filling the atmosphere of the tiny cine room seemed perfectly normal.

While the Conversion Phase focused on the pilots and the Basic Radar Phase switched the pressure to the student navigators, the next phase challenged each student irrespective of which cockpit he occupied. The pilots, who were now more comfortable with flying the Phantom, were challenged to fight the aircraft to its limits during the Air Combat Phase. Equally, navigators, who had begun to grasp the concept of a three-dimensional fight, now had to learn to control the aircraft in a 3D world. The goal of keeping tabs on your opponent was absolutely crucial, and if your pilot could not see the threat, navigators were given the tools to control the manoeuvres by verbal commands. 'Roll left', 'Roll right', 'Pull', 'Push', 'Buster', and 'Gate' became the means to position an opponent where the pilot could regain visual contact. Obviously, the staff pilots and navigators would allow the students to control the fight in order to demonstrate the learning points. This was enormously advantageous, particularly if the staff instructors 'intentionally' lost visual contact.

With the advent of missiles, it had been thought that the dogfights of the Second World War were over and that missiles could be launched 'beyond visual range', making air combat more clinical. The Vietnam War proved that this logic was flawed and that the basics of air combat were still needed. The Phantom was not a good turning aircraft, but, flown well, using its superior weapon system, it was a match for any fighter operationally deployed at the time. Only the advent of the F15 in the early 80s and later the Soviet MiG-29 Fulcrum and Su-27 Flanker left it outclassed. In its heyday it was a match for any opponent. However, in the 'close fight', things were different. The pilots were taken through the basics of air combat manoeuvring by a pilot Air Combat Leader sitting in the back cockpit. They then flew their first sortie against another aircraft, and bizarre terms such as a 'High Yo-Yo', 'Low Yo-Yo' and 'Lag Pursuit Roll' were explained and demonstrated. These were the basic fighter manoeuvres, or BFMs, which were the building blocks of learning to fight the Phantom to its limits. It is easy to sit on the ground and think of aerial manoeuvres in two dimensions. In reality, air combat is a three-dimensional game, and learning how to interpret the world in 3D when 'the office' is upside down is a skill hard won and takes years to develop. The basic sorties showed how to prosecute an attack when you were on the offensive, in other words safely in missile parameters behind your target. Once established 'in the saddle', the defender would counter the attack employing BFMs to evade the missile and the attacker. The manoeuvring would become highly dynamic, rapidly entering the vertical, and would conclude with either a kill or a stalemate. One of the more worrying manoeuvres was known as a 'scissors' where the two aircraft would pull hard towards each other, pass close aboard before reversing the turn and repeating the lunge. This would continue to a stalemate or until one pilot managed to spit the other out in front where a shot could then be taken. The whole sequence was flown in full reheat, so lessons had to be mastered quickly as fuel was short. Once mastered, the profile was repeated but now on the defensive. Against another Phantom it was possible to use BFMs to hold off an attacker. Against an agile opponent, such as the F5 Freedom Fighter or the Hawk, it was an entirely different and more humbling experience, as the tighter turning ability meant a kill often followed quickly. The secret was to learn how to avoid being placed in that position. The 1 versus 1 exercises were followed quickly by 2 versus 1 sorties, so the learning curve was steep. In these sorties, the pair of Phantoms was pitted against a single target flown by a staff crew. This taught the principles of fighting as a pair, which was how the Phantom would be flown on the squadron. Again, communicating and co-ordinating two fast-moving aircraft to engage an aggressive enemy was a challenge. The target would attempt to engage one of the pair unseen but, when spotted, would switch his attention between the attackers trying to launch a missile and force an error. A well-flown pair should always have defeated a single attacker, but lessons were often hard won. The concepts of a 'free' and an 'engaged' fighter were introduced. As the singleton attacked one of the pair, the aim was to hold him off, making him predictable so that the other Phantom could position for a missile shot. That was the principle, but the 'bogey' often upset the carefully crafted plan. As an aside, the great comedian John Inman has no idea how often his catchphrase was mimicked during air combat engagements: 'Are you free?'

The final phase of the OCU course was the Advanced Radar Phase. This was more operationally focused and taught the variations that were needed to intercept targets operating at low level, flying at supersonic speeds or at very high level, and flying in tactical formations. Some of these intercepts were conducted as a single fighter but some were flown as a pair, adding complexity to the mission. The intensive training was brought together during the end-of-course 'War'. The student crews were launched from ground alert by Squadron Operations to a combat air patrol. Targets as diverse as Jaguars, Buccaneers, Vulcans, and Canberras provided by other units, in addition to OCU aircraft flown by staff crews, were tasked to fly through the defended area and were intercepted by the students. The proof of success was to return with a radar film capturing the missile shots which could be validated by the staff instructors. 'No film; no kill' was the tough rule that was never compromised and would be a feature of all future operational missions.

The OCU course had deficiencies. It was as late as 1990 before air-to-air refuelling was added to the syllabus, nor were the complexities of intercepting an aircraft that was jamming the AN/AWG-12 taught at that stage. The evasion that the targets were allowed to perform was very limited, and full 'day tactics' where the target had free rein was included only late in the Phantom's life. Although Phantom crews had been operating overland in Germany for many years, the more difficult techniques that the low level overland environment demanded were not introduced in training until 1990. Additionally, most raids against the UK were more likely to be conducted by large formations of aircraft, but tackling such formations was introduced only at squadron level. Air-to-air gunnery using the SUU-23 cannon and practice missile shots were impossible to incorporate in the short time at the OCU and were also extremely expensive. These skills would also be taught during the operational work up on the squadrons and beyond.

The OCU was also a fully operational squadron declared to NATO. When the 'hooter' sounded, the OCU staff crews became 64 (Reserve) Squadron and generated aircraft like any other squadron. As yet unqualified to be let loose with a Phantom, the students were farmed out to fill roles around the station, but 64 (Reserve) Squadron 'went to war' like any other squadron. Despite the complexity of the Phantom, these exercises in the 1970s were reminiscent of films such as *Battle of Britain*. The jets sat in neat rows on the aircraft servicing platform. Crews operated from the peacetime buildings and, when scrambled, drove to their jets in buses or Land Rovers or ran across the concrete if the jet was close by. Life was gentlemanly. It was only the advent of hardened buildings in the mid-1970s in Germany and the early 1980s in the UK that brought the reality of modern and, potentially, chemical warfare into sharp focus. Even so, I recall one squadron sage offering advice that I recalled on many occasions through later life. After a typical exercise 'faff', he said, 'The more you bleed in peacetime, the more anaemic you'll be in war.' Wise words indeed.

The first aircraft to be delivered for RAF service was XT891, which arrived at RAF Coningsby on 23 August 1968. It now sits as a gate guardian at Coningsby, hopefully preserved as a lasting reminder of the Phantom's connections with the station. After refurbishment, it was returned to the colour scheme it wore on delivery before the markings of 228 OCU were applied. It was then placed on a plinth inside the main gate of the station. The colours lasted for quite a few years before being replaced by those of 6 Squadron during the brief time when the Jaguars operated from RAF Coningsby in 2009.

I spent a gruelling four months at Coningsby completing the OCU course, but the station was to feature large in my life again when I was posted back to

XT891 the gate guardian at RAF Coningsby restored to its delivery livery.

become a radar tactics instructor in 1982. My last days at Coningsby, first time around, were spent in the formalities of the ceremony to receive the squadron standard for my new squadron, the newly re-equipped 56 (Fighter) Squadron. As the squadron moved to RAF Wattisham I finished the last few sorties of my OCU course before heading south to join my first squadron.

CHAPTER 4
Squadron Combat Ready Training

Conversion course over, arriving on the squadron was just the first step in becoming operational. The 'chop rate' through training and failure to meet combat ready standards was high. Only a small percentage of pilots and navigators actually made operational status on a fast-jet squadron compared with those who started training a number of years before. Even at this late stage, failure was a strong possibility and there was no relaxing until the coveted 'Op patch' was firmly fixed to your flying suit. It was with some trepidation that I walked past the No. 56 Squadron Lightning gate guardian at RAF Wattisham on that first day. Wattisham in the 1970s was a cosy station in the old-school style. Much smaller than many RAF stations, the NATO hardening programme had not yet begun, so the squadrons lived in two of the four large Second World War vintage hangars that fronted the flight line. In the other two hangers occupied by Engineering Wing, the Phantoms received their second line servicing. Both squadrons operated their aircraft from the huge concrete aircraft servicing platform and, in true 70s style, the line hut, where crews signed the jet in and out for a flight, looked like something from a wartime movie.

At 7,500 feet long, the runway was a little short for the Phantom, with braking distance being the critical figure. For a Phantom carrying three external tanks and a full missile load, 8,000 feet of concrete gave a comfortable margin for error when landing using the brake parachute. Although the squadrons lived in the hangars, Quick Reaction Alert, or QRA, was at the eastern end of the airfield some distance away. A fast access track joined the main runway to the Q shed about 1,000 feet in from the runway threshold. This gave only about 6,500 feet for take-off during a QRA scramble, so if the afterburner failed on take-off it could be an exciting roll down the runway in a heavily loaded Q jet. With cold engines, the burners could be slow to light. It was possible to launch with only a single afterburner but not advisable unless it was essential. However, it was always a difficult decision for the pilots on QRA; had the burner failed or was

The Wattisham Wing with 23(F) Phantoms in the foreground.

it just being temperamental? An aborted take-off would invariably mean taking the overrun cable and thereby blocking the runway. In that situation, the second QRA aircraft could only get airborne by taking off over the jet in the cable, so guaranteeing meeting the QRA scramble commitment was a real concern.

The Cold War was at its height so, as the air defence Phantom squadrons formed, pressure was on the squadron bosses to declare their squadron operational on the planned dates. In 56 (F) Squadron's case that target date was mid-1976. There was no shortage of aircraft as the Germany ground attack squadrons had already begun drawing down, so Phantoms were being freed up at a steady rate. The Lightnings had already been withdrawn from Wattisham and the remaining airframes were being consolidated at RAF Binbrook in Lincolnshire. The Air Officer Commanding No. 11 Group was keen to see his new air defence Phantoms fill the void but he went about it in a strange way. On the first Officers' Mess dining-in night after RAF Wattisham had been declared operational, the AOC was invited to give an after-dinner speech to rally the new Phantom crews. Either his aide had given him the wrong speech or he was a dyed-in-the-wool Lightning fan, because he spent 15 minutes singing the praises of the Lightning as an air defence fighter; to the stunned silence of the new and highly motivated Phantom crews. The ex-Lightning pilots in the dining room allowed themselves the odd smirk despite their new loyalties. Despite the AOC's 'help', the highly experienced team of aircrew and engineers achieved the operational declaration on time, although moving from 'declared' to truly capable took more time.

The squadron operational work-up was slightly frustrating as it repeated much of the content of the Coningsby operational conversion course. There were variations in how individual squadrons operated, and tactics could be significantly different even between squadrons on the same base. The academic intercept profiles were repeated to check understanding and to prove that the ab-initio crews could adapt to the squadron environment which was much more self-policing. The ability to intercept a low flying bomber, a 'high flyer' or a supersonic target had to become second nature before the squadron would shift new crews to more operational profiles.

One of the earliest tasks was to understand the language of flying. Just understanding the conversation on a squadron was a challenge for the newcomer. Aircrew love acronyms and abbreviations. Crews needed to know that the ILS was the instrument landing system, the MCS was the missile control system, and the TAF was the terminal approach forecast (weather) and so on. New aircrew were slowly initiated as they passed through the training system, becoming almost unintelligible to the layman by the time they were declared operational. To add to the melting pot, unsecure radios meant that simple codes were needed to give a modicum of security. One of the routine calls was to give a ten minute warning prior to landing. This allowed the engineering staff to allocate groundcrew, position them for the see-in and to allocate tradesmen to debrief any faults. A simple code using a prefix letter, a number, and a suffix letter indicated the serviceability state of the aircraft. For example, 'X Ray' meant the aircraft was serviceable whereas 'Zulu 10 Bravo' meant the radar was unserviceable and identified the pulse Doppler mode. We all assumed such a cunning code was uncrackable. The RAF fielded communications security monitors to listen to the radio calls when a base was being evaluated. This kept radio users alert to the risks of poor radio discipline. 'Loose lips sink ships' was the wartime slogan that highlighted the problems. Speaking to the experts later in my career, it became obvious how ineffective these simple homespun codes really were. Like the aircraft spotters who sit at the airfield perimeter fence listening to the air traffic control frequencies, a comprehensive picture of how the exercise was progressing was easily formed. In practice, some of the information that was freely passed over an open frequency was truly staggering.

Once the basic flying language was mastered, the next issue was brevity codes. NATO published a codeword list to allow simple actions and objects to be identified. A 'bogey' was a hostile target, 'judy' meant I have control of the intercept, and a 'hooter' was an electronic jammer. It is surprising how many of

Preparing for a training sortie. UK MOD Crown Copyright (1978).

these codes have made their way into regular use. 'Heads up' actually means 'I have missed the intercept and a hostile target is coming your way'! Search on the internet and it now takes only moments to find a full decode of the NATO brevity codes. So much for operational security in the digital age.

The ultimate spoof known as the Falcon Code was a good example of aircrew humour. Born during the Vietnam conflict, it was another way to pass on cryptic information by using a numbered code. In this case, however, the content was much more tongue in cheek. As an example, Falcon 269 meant 'Apparently you have me confused with someone who gives a (expletive)'. Falcon 222 meant 'Now you have (expletive) it up I suggest you find a way of un(expletive) it', and Falcon 102 meant 'Get off my (expletive) back!' Written in the original Anglo-Saxon, the code could be modified for local use. It was, in theory, used only between aircrew on a tactical frequency. In practice, it was adopted universally and, surprisingly, many ATC officers raised a chuckle in the cockpit despite the risk of retribution from the ATC standards evaluators.

A 360 Squadron Canberra T17 intercepted during a QRA training mission. UK MOD Crown Copyright (1978).

One of the skills that the OCU could not develop was the ability to intercept an aircraft that was electronically jamming the Phantom's AN/AWG-12 radar. For the air defence units, this training was provided by a specialist squadron, No. 360 Squadron under the nickname of Exercise 'Profit'. Although the squadron operated Canberra T17s from RAF Wyton, quite often the crews would deploy to the fighter base to carry out face-to-face briefings and debriefings. The Canberra had been adapted from the original bomber and carried radar jammers in ugly bulges that had sprouted all over the airframe.

With knowledge of the characteristics of the Phantom radar frequencies, the Canberra Electronic Warfare Officer (EWO) could send out an electronic jamming signal that masked the radar signal of the Canberra from the Phantom navigator. This jamming signal was known as 'noise' and had changed little from the early days of electronic warfare during the Second World War. On the radar scope, the small blip which was how a normal aircraft appeared on the display was masked by a narrow band of interference that made it impossible to determine the target's range. This meant that the navigator had to adopt different intercept techniques to work out how far away the target was from the Phantom. The EWO could also generate more complex deception signals that looked like another target on the Phantom radar. With skill, the EWO could make his own aircraft's response look like a formation of aircraft. Phantom navigators had to learn how to use the electronic protection measures built into the radar to counter these jamming techniques. By using an auxiliary radar function, the navigator could recognise the real target from the false targets. Making various switch selections, he could track the 'jamming strobe' and launch a Sparrow missile against the jammer despite the electronic deception. This electronic chess match was completely invisible outside the confines of the two cockpits. These techniques were practised regularly, but the ultimate test was when the exercise was scheduled at night. An old adage was 'A peek is worth a thousand sweeps'; in other words, one reassuring sight of the target through the cockpit canopy was better than all the clever information displayed by the Phantom's radar. There was no chance of a 'sneaky peek' out of the window during a night jamming exercise as there was little ambient light over the North Sea and the jamming was difficult to counter. The 'pucker factor', knowing that you were pointing at a fast-moving aircraft using fallback procedures, was enormous. Height separation between you and the jammer became a precious commodity and was carefully maintained. It didn't help, however, in knowing that the opening gambit was to climb or descend to co-altitude with the target in order to work out its height. The concern was magnified by the fact that during most Exercise 'Profit' sorties, the Canberra EWO was also jamming the ground radars so your fighter controller might be equally 'blind'.

The Canberra crew could also dispense chaff. The use of these small pieces of aluminium foil, developed during the Second World War to confuse German radars, is still widespread. Surprisingly, it is effective even against some modern processed radars. Dispensers fitted in the rear fuselage of the Canberra dropped small packets of chaff that were whipped into a large cloud in the airflow behind the aircraft. Signals from the Phantom radar were reflected back from the chaff cloud, looking extremely similar to the real aircraft. Modern radars that use Doppler techniques are not affected, as the chaff immediately slows down once dispensed. The pulse Doppler mode available to the Phantom navigator was immune to chaff, as this mode used speed to differentiate targets. The radar processed the chaff response, showing it was stationary, so it would not show as a target. Despite this, chaff dropped at a critical point in the intercept if the navigator was using pulse mode fooled many a less wary Phantom navigator.

The Canberra also carried communications jammers that could jam the radio frequencies used by the Phantom crews. Normally only employed on exercise, the Canberra crews would try to employ 'spoofing' to divert the crews from their task. Some crews were persuaded to leave their combat air patrol for a non-existent tanker or ordered to shift their CAP position just before the 'mass raid', missing the incoming attackers. The Canberra crews also injected humour into an otherwise serious exercise. On one occasion, during a very quiet Joint Maritime exercise off the north coast of Scotland, the following exchange occurred:

Canberra operator: 'I'm upset' (or a very similar Anglo-Saxon expression).
GCI controller: 'Station calling Buchan, say again your callsign'.
Canberra operator: 'I'm not that upset.'

After revisiting the academic intercept profiles, the first major check ride on the road to operational status was the Phase 3 visual identification (VID) check; successful completion resulted in the award of a 'Limited Operational' category and clearance to sit on QRA. For this, the crew's ability to intercept and identify a target that was flying at night without navigation lights was tested. Two Phantoms would launch and operate under the control of a Ground Controlled Intercept (GCI) site well out into the North Sea. The aircraft would be positioned 50 miles apart by the controller and begin an intercept. The target, simulating an intruder, would extinguish all its external navigation lights and begin its run in. Against an invisible target, the pilot had to fly accurate headings, heights, and speeds to within a few feet or a few knots. The navigator had to control both the intercept and the identification, carefully controlling the radar and the scanner, giving precise commands to the pilot to meet the intercept profile. A two-mile roll out behind the target was the goal and from that initial position, with a target flying at speeds between 300 and 450 knots, the fighter would close in to identify the intruder.

Once the medium level profile had been demonstrated against a target flying at about 20,000 feet, the profile was repeated against a target flying at low level at 1,500 feet. The North Sea could be a dark and unforgiving place at night at low level. The fighter closed carefully into minimum range. The fuzzy blip on the radar was carefully positioned at a point 45 degrees off the nose, slightly below the Phantom, at 300 yards, at which time the fighter stabilised by matching speed and heading. The crew had to keep it there for some time until the pilot could make out the darkened bulk of the other aircraft and determine its identity. To ask for tiny adjustments of as little as one degree in the aircraft's heading in order to maintain position required skill and trust of the highest order in both cockpits. Quite often it was only possible to make out a vague silhouette against any background lighting. At medium level, this might be starlight. At low level, the target might be highlighted against a flare from an oil rig or the lights of a trawler. Surprisingly, accidents were rare, although frights were common. There was a very well-rehearsed breakout manoeuvre which, if the position became unstable, allowed the interceptor to reposition behind the target and repeat the profile. It was regularly practised and often used. Later, with the advent of night vision goggles, this whole identification procedure became massively simpler as the goggles turned night into day. From that time onwards, unless the target was flying in cloud, crews could see the target much earlier and identification became simpler. However, using the goggles was not without risk, as aircraft flying many miles away were easily visible. Once close, the lack of depth perception when looking at another aircraft through goggles meant that manoeuvring in close formation at night could be dangerous without skill and care. Surprisingly, the cockpit lighting had to be modified to make it compatible with the night vision equipment, otherwise stray light flooded the goggles. Although the dull eerie glare of low light devices is commonplace nowadays, and was the foundation of news reports during the Gulf War, the technology was stunning to the aircrew when it was first introduced, revolutionising night operations.

Once declared 'Lim Op', aircrew were cleared to hold QRA but not to take part in exercises. More tactical training followed before the new pilot or navigator would be finally accepted into the fold. The final check ride was called the 'Op check' when the new crew would be launched from ground alert using full scramble procedures to mount a combat air patrol with another Phantom in the exercise area. In the UK, the pair was the fighting element; however, on RAF Germany squadrons, this was often increased to a 'four ship', so the aircrew member being checked out was expected to be able to lead this larger formation. In both theatres the scenarios were similar. A series of targets would run through the CAP area and the fighters would be instructed to identify, shadow, or engage each intruder using the most appropriate profile from their by now extensive repertoire. In the UK, the targets ranged from Vulcans operating at 50,000 feet plus, through jamming Canberras, to low level formations of Jaguars and Buccaneers. Occasionally, a more challenging target would be included and, paradoxically, the most difficult targets to intercept were the least likely candidates. Intercepting a Shackleton flying at only 200 knots at low level tested the most experienced crew. With a typical speed of 350 knots plus for the Phantom, such a slow target gave challenges during both the intercept and the final identification. The Phantom could not stabilise at 200 knots unless the undercarriage was lowered. This was ill-advised in a tactical situation as it made the lumbering Phantom extremely vulnerable and unmanoeuvrable, so the pass was made at 250 knots, which was the slowest realistic speed. With 50 knots overtake, the final pass was quite dramatic and, for the navigator, taking the required photograph was a challenge as the target whistled past. At this stage of training, no longer were the targets subservient. Evasion limits of up to two 360-degree turns were allowed. These could be flown during the intercept to disrupt the approach geometry and once the players came into visual contact, making it extremely demanding to manoeuvre the Phantom into missile parameters. It was perfectly acceptable to use the full capabilities of the opposing aircraft, and the opposing crews enjoyed the challenge.

The final seal of approval was given once the radar film had been assessed back on the squadron when the kills had been confirmed. Being declared operational was a truly significant milestone for a 'first tour' pilot or navigator but even for more experienced crews, being declared operational on a new squadron was still an accolade. With it came the right to wear the 'Op patch' worn proudly on the right arm of the flying suit on a fighter squadron. The other rite of passage was the downing of the 'Op pot'. Each squadron had some type of drinking vessel to support the ceremony. This would generally be a tankard donated by a previous squadron member, often dating back many years. Normally large enough to hold a couple of pints of foaming beer, the pot was downed at the next 'happy hour' in the Mess bar to the sound of a squadron song or two. Any liquid was acceptable, and one teetotaller drank his Op pot in milk, to the amazement of the assembled aircrew.

Once operational, aircrew could take part in station and national exercises. In the 1970s and 1980s, the major annual exercise was known as Exercise 'Elder Forest' and was arranged by HQ 11 Fighter Group. In autumn every year, waves of aircraft operating from both the UK and the Continent would launch against targets in the UK. These targets could be fighter bases, GCI sites, radar installations, or other militarily significant sites. Formations would attack from the east, day and night, running though combat air patrols mounted by Phantoms, Lightnings, and Hawks. Quite often, UK forces would be joined by US fighters from East Anglian bases, which in the late 1970s was in the shape of Phantoms, but later F15s. The interest of 'Elder Forest' was the diversity of targets. Most NATO nations were involved, and targets varying from Mirages through F5s to F16s were common. This meant that crews would experience a differing range of tactics that provided new experiences. It was not unknown for a B52 to join the fray operating from the continental US. The B52 crews occasionally deployed to Fairford or Greenham Common, but it was not unknown for them to operate from their home base in America. These crews would fly across the Atlantic to hit targets in the UK before turning around and heading back to the USA – an amazing feat of endurance. Inevitably, there were fewer raids planned at night during exercises, and it was always depressing to be allocated the night shift. I remember sorties in the early hours of the morning with the radar scope depressingly clear, knowing that my pilot, I, and the fighter controller were the

QUALIFICATIONS & RENEWALS

(Instructor category, Command category, Servicing responsibility, etc.)

Date	Aircraft Type	Aircrew Duty	Qualification	Renewal Date	Signature	Unit
THIS IS TO CERTIFY THAT PILOT OFFICER D J GLEDHILL HAS COMPLETED						
A COURSE OF NAVIGATION INSTRUCTION AND HAS QUALIFIED						
AS AN AIR NAVIGATOR WITH EFFECT FROM 6 JUNE 1975						
					SQN LDR	
					OC 2 ANS	
6 JUNE 1975					No 6 FLYING TRAINING SCHOOL	
3 FEB 77	PHANTOM FGR2	NAVIGATOR	LIMITED OPERATIONAL AIR DEFENCE (IAW 11 GP ASO AS)	N/A	OC 56(F) SQN WG CDR	56 SQN
24 FEB 77	PHANTOM FGR2	NAVIGATOR	OPERATIONAL AIR DEFENCE (IAW 11 GP ASO AS)	N/A	OC 56(F) SQN WG CDR.	56 SQN

After nearly 4 years training, a simple entry in the aircrew logbook records the milestone of being declared operational.

only people who were still awake. There were few distractions on the 'graveyard shift', although navigators quickly learned the frequency for the BBC World Service on the HF radio, which gave a limited entertainment while scanning the empty skies.

One of the most popular exercises had the nicknames 'Hammer Blow' or 'Mallet Blow'. The main targets for the ground attack aircraft were located on the Electronic Warfare Training Range at RAF Spadeadam in north-west England. Before arriving at Spadeadam, the bomber crews would penetrate fighter CAPs located along the east coast of the UK before routeing overland into Northumberland and Cumbria. As Phantom crews developed overland skills the CAPs were extended into the low flying areas, improving the training value immensely. Surface-to-air threat systems, such as the Soviet SA-6, SA-8 and ZSU-23-4 gun systems, were positioned around the range and would engage the bombers as they were attacking their simulated targets. No one asked where these systems had come from. Indeed, a whole simulated airfield was cut into a Cumbrian hillside and old aircraft hulks were spread around in simulated dispersals to provide additional targets. With the popularity of the exercise, squadrons fought for slots and normally made sure that they launched large formations. Equally, fighter squadrons made sure all the available CAPs were manned, giving the attackers the maximum training benefit and the minimum respite from air attack.

Despite operational status, combat ready training did not end with the award of the 'Op patch'. Air combat training was one of those essential skills that had to be constantly practised. In the 1960s, the Americans had decided that with the advent of air-to-air missiles future air combat would not require basic fighter manoeuvres. The Vietnam War put paid to that thinking when US Phantoms were engaged in air combat by highly agile MiG-15s, MiG-17s, MiG-19s, and MiG-21s. After punitive losses, a programme to reinstate air combat training was hastily introduced.

Recently declassified, the 'Constant Peg' programme in the Nevada Desert allowed US crews to train against Soviet MiGs that had been acquired from various sources. The programme is described in fascinating detail by Steve Davies in his book *Red Eagles*. A whole squadron of MiGs, based at the desert airfield at Tonopah Test Range, was flown by US test pilots. Soviet tactics were studied and the aircraft flown to replicate the type of threat NATO crews would face in a future war. This allowed friendly tactics and capabilities to be refined, and crews could be shown how and how not to engage Soviet fighters. Although UK crews were not able to take advantage of 'Constant Peg', pilots and navigators were invited to a training facility where Soviet fighters were displayed on the ground, giving the chance to inspect the aircraft closely. This was a huge advantage given that most training on the squadron used grainy photographs. Experts offered details on strengths and weaknesses of the design to allow aircrew to form their own judgements. I recall my own experience. On being allowed into the enormous hangar, a feeling of being like a 'kid in a sweetshop' comes to mind. Inspecting the hardware, I remember being surprised at how agricultural the engineering seemed by western standards. The Soviets would happily run a pipe through a duct strapped onto the side of an aircraft, fixing it with rivets. The concept seemed to be 'if it works, why bother to over-engineer the solution?' Staring into the MiG cockpit for the first time, my senses were attacked by the duck egg blue colour. Apparently, this had been determined by Soviet scientists to be a restful colour that calmed pilots' nerves. My reaction was more akin to airsickness than calm. Such threat training displays are commonplace nowadays and most aircrew who have flown on Exercise 'Red Flag' at Nellis AFB in Nevada will have seen those threats at close hand in the facility nicknamed the 'Petting Zoo'. One of the effects of the end of the Cold War is that the facility at Nellis is now completely unclassified.

Part of the US air combat initiative was to form squadrons of Aggressors both in the US and in Europe. The European-based squadron was the 527th Aggressor

An F5E in the natural aluminium scheme replicating a Mig 21.

Squadron at RAF Alconbury, equipped with the Northrop F5E which closely matched the Soviet MiG-21 in performance and size. As with the sister 'Constant Peg' programme, the aggressor pilots were carefully briefed and trained to replicate Soviet skills and tactics.

After a comprehensive briefing, a typical sortie against the Aggressors would start with a ranging exercise. Most crews were used to flying against the much larger Phantom. Eyeballs had to be recalibrated to be able to recognise the missile parameters for an F5. An F5 flying at the correct release range for a Sidewinder seemed much farther away than a Phantom due to it being much smaller. Without recognising this, Phantom crews could be under threat from a small fighter such as a MiG-21 without even realising, and might therefore initiate the incorrect defensive tactic. A badly timed defensive break would merely allow the F5 to arc the circle and close the range, which it might otherwise not have been able to do. Conversely, a late break would allow an F5 to slot into an easy guns tracking solution. Early sorties would hone pilot handling skills against the more agile F5. The F5 pilot would position in loose formation at about 500 yards swept back from a position known as 'the perch'. As the F5 closed in range, the Phantom crew would begin a defensive manoeuvre to negate the attack, normally by breaking hard towards the F5 to defeat a missile shot and increase the angle off the tail. These exercises would be terminated quite early as the Phantom realistically had little chance of survival under those circumstances unless the missile failed. Once

The red numbers on the nose were typical of those worn by Soviet Migs.

this basic skill had been practised, training would move on to combat splits. The two fighters would turn away from each other and diverge to the limit of visual range. The aggressor pilot would call the turn back and the fighters would turn hard towards each other. The aim for the Phantom pilot was to point his aircraft at the opponent and generate a minimum separation pass. Give the F5 turning room and he would take advantage, arc the turn and become offensive. A close aboard pass, which for training purposes was 500 feet apart, followed by an extension, would allow the Phantom crew to extend and re-engage with enough space to lock and shoot a Sparrow missile head-on. What to do, and most importantly what not to do, against the agile F5 was demonstrated and practised repeatedly. Eventually, the training was completed by operating against pairs of aggressors employing Soviet tactics. NATO tactics were more flexible than the scripted Soviet tactics, which could be countered if crews were aware of how the MiGs would operate. The aggressors were extremely good. While the air combat manoeuvres were supposed to reflect the skills of likely Soviet opponents, fighter pilots are fighter pilots and there was always the risk that the 'horns would come out' when the chance of a kill presented itself to an aggressor pilot. They were trained to 'soak up the shot' to demonstrate the training objective but freely admitted that it was hard to resist the temptation to fight back. It was easy to destroy the confidence of a Phantom crew if the training was not delivered in a way that showed how best to employ the aircraft. Overall though, the aggressor

56 Sqn Phantoms alongside USAF RF4Es before a combat sortie.

pilots were extremely professional and provided the opportunity to hone combat skills against a highly representative opponent.

One of the more bizarre Phantom accidents occurred during an Aggressor deployment in June 1980. A Phantom FG1, based at RAF Leuchars but temporarily operating from RAF Alconbury, had completed its sortie and was returning to land. After breaking into the circuit, the downwind checks were completed normally, but as the aircraft turned finals the radome latch, which held the radome closed, failed. As the aircraft slowed for landing, the airflow flipped the radome back. Instead of presenting a smooth aerodynamic shape to the airflow, the radome acted as a massive speed break. The aircraft became rapidly uncontrollable and the pilot lost control. The crew ejected immediately, albeit at very low level, and the aircraft crashed just short of the runway. The accident was captured by aircraft enthusiasts around the airfield perimeter. The image of the doomed Phantom in a terminal dive with its nose cone folded back is a rare shot of an aircraft in its final moments. Happily, the crew survived and were able to return to flying duties after normal medical checks.

Another aspect of a detachment to Alconbury was to be able to share ramp space with other Phantom operators in the shape of the resident RF4E

92 Sqn Phantoms on the ramp at IAF Decimommannu.

reconnaissance squadron. The other thing that a detachment to a USAF base showed was the vast difference in the way a US squadron and an RAF squadron operated. US Phantoms were centrally maintained. The operators on the squadron issued a weekly schedule detailing the flying effort. The maintenance staff were completely committed to meeting that schedule and were hit with a 'maintenance non delivery' should they fail to do so. The down side was that the targets set seemed deliberately easy to achieve and aircraft utilisation was poor. On this occasion, the squadron deployed five aircraft to Alconbury to meet the week-long air combat phase against the Aggressors. Four of the five aircraft flew up to three waves per day. In comparison, the majority of the RF4Es barely moved a wheel during the whole week. The US pilots were extremely jealous of the RAF approach in which aircraft were owned and operated at squadron level, extracting the absolute maximum from the airframes.

One of the technological innovations of the 1980s that revolutionised air combat training was the introduction of the Air Combat Manoeuvring Installation or ACMI. The first range in Europe was set up at the Italian Air Force base at Decimomannu in Sardinia by the American company Cubic Corporation. Some years later, a similar range was set up in the North Sea and operated by BAE Systems. Debriefing facilities were set up at Coningsby and Waddington in Lincolnshire to allow RAF crews to fly air combat missions from their home bases. Paradoxically, as the UK was committed to Decimomannu, other NATO nations used the UK range far more than the RAF due to the inevitable lack of defence cash to fund both ranges. RAF crews were left to

An airborne instrumentation pod on the Sidewinder pylon.

'piggy back' on training sessions arranged by other nations while the range was under-utilised.

The ACMI was an instrumentation system that tracked the position of any aircraft on the range carrying the ACMI pod. A tracking and instrumentation subsystem, the TIS, was equipped with distance measuring equipment that measured the range of the aircraft to interrogator substations. The TIS comprised a master station and up to seven interrogator stations mounted on buoys anchored to the sea bed. Data transmitted from pods on the aircraft was sent via each station back to a control system at Decimomannu and recorded for debriefing purposes. Up to twenty aircraft could be tracked simultaneously, allowing quite complex air combat scenarios to be practised. The pod that collected the data was a modified Sidewinder missile body and was carried on one of the missile pylons. The pod transmitted position data, flight parameters,

The RTO analyses tactics used during an air combat training sortie.

and weapon system information to a control system on the ground which was displayed in real time in the control room, showing the position of all the participating aircraft in three dimensions. Cockpit views could be displayed on screens to analyse tactics, missile shots, or gun shots. As missiles were launched, the system recorded the parameters and computed whether the shot was valid. If validated, a small coffin would appear around the victim and the Range Training Officer (RTO) in the cabin would call a 'kill removal', taking that aircraft out of the fight. At any time, the RTO could see the position of each participating aircraft and could act as a safety co-ordinator or as an air combat instructor.

The big advantage of ACMI was that, for the first time, real time information was displayed. Up to that point, the more experienced aircrew, who generally had better recall of what occurred in a fast-moving air combat engagement, would rule the roost. Uncharitably, it was said that he who talked loudest won the debrief. Although not quite accurate, it had more than a ring of truth. ACMI changed all that and suddenly debriefs became more circumspect, and many aircrew with 'legendary recall' were put to the test. Squadron weapons instructors insisted that a hot debrief was conducted without the help of the instrumentation. This ensured that the ability to reconstruct an engagement was maintained for times when ACMI was not available. Notwithstanding, it resulted in much more honest and concise debriefings prior to seeing the reality in the ACMI cabin. One of the biggest challenges was to ensure that RTOs did not become 'super GCI controllers'. With the sudden improvement in situation awareness that ACMI offered, it was tempting to help colleagues in the air in an unrealistic way. For real, the 'bad guys' would not carry ACMI pods, nor could GCI controllers, staring at the slowly revolving air defence radar, provide the type of control that ACMI allowed. The system had to be treated as a debriefing aid, not a combat enhancement. RTOs were quickly taught to bite their tongues even if it meant their colleagues in the air taking a missile shot from an opponent.

ACMI detachments varied in size from five aircraft to the whole squadron. The more complex missions required four aircraft on range, so five aircraft was the practical minimum. At that time, many other nations deployed to Decimomannu to conduct air-to-ground training on the NATO bombing ranges. Initially, dissimilar air combat training was conducted against other fighter squadrons such as US F15s, Italian F104s and German F4 squadrons. Later, the British ground attack squadrons were also cleared to use the ACMI range, giving greater variety. Squadrons prepared before the detachment by completing a period of 'like' 1 versus 1 air combat and 2 versus 2 against other Phantoms. That meant that when the wheels were on the ground at Decimomannu, it was straight into dissimilar 2 versus 2, leading up to the more realistic but complex 4 versus 4 engagements. The range was located just to the west of the island so, after a short transit, aircraft were within the range and ready to fight. Range slots were scheduled in thirty-minute blocks, but, for the Phantom, use of the reheat was essential to extract the maximum performance from the aircraft and engagements were inevitably fuel, not time, limited. Two or three combat merges was the norm, and the aircraft could operate to the limits of its performance. Supersonic flight was not only approved but positively recommended by the weapons instructors. But to avoid dropping a sonic boom on the Sardinian town of Cagliari, there was a termination line about 30 miles off the coast. At that range, all players had to be subsonic and began preparing for recovery to Decimomannu. Tactics developed quickly; the days of slow speed turning and burning were quickly replaced by long range Sparrow engagements followed by high speed runs through the combat area. With regular use of afterburner, sortie durations of only 30 minutes were common, with much of that taken up in flying to and from the range. Invariably crews would arrive back at base 'on fumes'.

Another feature of the squadron combat ready work-up was the armament practice camp where air-to-air gunnery techniques were rehearsed. Additionally, missile practice camps where air-to-air missiles were evaluated were conducted annually and both are worth exploring in more detail.

My first years on the squadron were reasonably stable. The normal postings cycle for an aircrew officer was a three-year tour before moving on to the next challenge. As most aircrew had joined 56 (F) Squadron as it formed in 1976, movements for the first couple of years were few and a great camaraderie developed. There was a tradition on the squadron that the junior pilot and junior navigator were the general dogsbodies. Normally, this exalted position was held only for a few months before the latest student arrived from the OCU. Being last in and seeing few new faces following, and even fewer old faces moving on, the accolade fell to me for some considerable time.

CHAPTER 5
Air Defence of the UK During the Cold War

At the height of the Cold War, the Phantom was a vital part of the air defence of the UK. The Lightning, which the Phantom initially supplemented and eventually replaced, was a short range interceptor. It lacked fuel and endurance and was lightly armed with only two missiles. Moreover, it had a simple pulse radar with limited capability at low level, so it was heavily reliant on the ground based fighter controllers. As a consequence, it was often operated from ground alert and scrambled to meet an incoming attack. The old joke was that a Lightning was short of fuel on take-off, so the interception had to be efficient and, ideally, close to the coast. Lighting pilots became adept at saving fuel and on occasion resorted to measures as extreme as closing down one engine. Other than operating a combat air patrol with the pilot spotting his target visually, it had little capability overland. Despite all the limitations, it was revered by its pilots. The arrival of the Phantom meant that a much more flexible strategy could be adopted. With its external fuel tanks and eight air-to-air missiles, the Phantom could operate well out into the North Sea and north into the Iceland-Faroes gap. Rather than sit on ground alert, it could be positioned well forward and begin to attack an enemy force well before it even entered UK airspace. This became increasingly relevant as the Soviet Air Forces were equipped with increasingly longer range stand-off weapons that could be launched hundreds of miles from the target. To counter the vast numbers of aircraft which the Soviets could muster, a layered structure had to be adopted to harry the potential attackers all the way to their target.

The result, now almost defunct, was known as the United Kingdom Air Defence Ground Environment or UKADGE. It was made up of a mix of fighters and missiles directed by battle managers and fighter controllers who would direct and fight the air battle from the ground. The first element was the Sector Operations Centres (SOCs) at Buchan in Scotland, Boulmer in Northumberland, and Neatishead in Norfolk. Each SOC was allocated a section of UK airspace, with the dividing lines lying roughly east/west. Northern airspace, which extended out towards Iceland, was controlled from RAF Buchan near Aberdeen; northern England and the Midlands from RAF Boulmer; and southern England from RAF Neatishead. Huge air defence radars were located at each of these sites and, when combined with the radar pictures from air defence picket ships and airborne early warning (AEW) aircraft, produced what was known as the recognised air picture or RAP. It was this information displayed to the battle managers that allowed them to employ the air assets available in as effective a way as possible. In reality it was a chess match, and controllers had to ensure the limited numbers of fighters had fuel and weapons and were positioned where they were needed. To support the fighters, tankers and AEW aircraft had to be positioned in the combat area well before the 'invading hordes' crossed the boundary into the UK Air Defence Region. The successful controller had assets in the right place at the right time and had refuelled his fighters before the raid appeared. Subordinate to the SOCs were a number of Control and Reporting Centres and Control and Reporting Points. These were located as far away as Saxa Vord on the island of Unst in Shetland. Some, such as Staxton Wold in Yorkshire and Neatishead in Norfolk, enjoyed the luxury of being located in the heart of rural England, so were significantly more popular postings for the controllers. Another unit, known as 1 Air Control Centre, was based at RAF Wattisham in Suffolk, but was mobile and able to deploy its radars and controllers wherever they were needed in times of crisis. In broad terms, the SOCs fought the battle and the CRCs directed the fighters and missiles into individual engagements. The structure is shown in Plate 3. With an improving air picture from the new early warning radars and the arrival of the Phantom with its better endurance, it became easier to cover the vast sea area surrounding the British coastline. A triple layer of combat air patrols was established, known logically as inner, middle, and outer CAPs. The inner CAPs were always close to the coast and were manned principally by Lightnings. The middle and outer CAPs could be hundreds of miles distant. The decision by controllers on whether to man these CAPs was threat dependent. In the eastern waters of the North Sea, the more likely threat was from shorter range tactical assets such as Fencer and Flogger fighter-bombers that would have moved closer to the Channel coast during the early stages of a war. In the northern waters and closer to the UK coast, the more likely intruders were strategic bombers. The CAP orientation was chosen such that the fighters' radars pointed towards the area from where the threat was expected to emerge. In the North Sea this meant that they were orientated easterly and north-easterly. In the Iceland-Faroes gap this was much more likely to be a northerly direction. A CAP was a holding pattern, normally flown in a left-hand direction with the CAP datum closest to the coast. At medium level, the outbound leg would be 4 minutes long. Once the navigator found a target, the Phantom would leave CAP to intercept the incoming 'bogey'. This pushed the actual intercept point even further from the UK shores, as the Phantom would travel some distance towards the threat before intercepting. The CAP heights could be nominated by the crews or the controller depending on weather and tactical conditions, but the Phantom was most comfortable operating at 15,000 feet as that was a good height from which to descend to intercept low level targets. The aircraft would use less fuel, however, if it patrolled at a higher level where its jets were more efficient. Equally, if the threat was expected to come through in the upper air, it made sense to fly at a higher altitude. Unlike in Germany, there were no hard boundaries between adjacent CAP areas, so fighter controllers had to make crews aware of where the adjacent fighters were operating and deconflict with their fellow controllers. The introduction of the Joint Tactical Information Distribution System (JTIDS) many years later gave instant situation awareness to fighter crews as the recognised air picture was fed straight onto the cockpit displays. This gave Tornado F3 crews a 'God's-eye' view of the airspace in which they were operating, allowing them to employ their formation much more effectively. Phantom crews never had that luxury, with the tactical picture being passed via radio calls from the ground. Interpreting the verbal air picture was an art rather than a science for the Phantom crew. It was important to understand that picture, as there were no prizes for shooting down your own tanker. Although fratricide has not been a major issue for air-to-air fighters during recent campaigns, public awareness of the problem in the air-to-ground arena has increased and 'blue on blue' has become a household term when bomber pilots misidentified their own ground troops.

The next defensive layer was provided by missiles. Despite the false hopes of the 1950s, missiles had not proved to be a total solution for air defence. In combination with fighters, however, missiles were very effective, and potential attackers would have had a torrid journey to the target penetrating both fighter engagement zones and missile engagement zones. In its heyday in the mid-1970s, No. 85 Squadron operated the Bloodhound missile and had operational sites at the RAF stations at North Coates and Bawdsey, with its headquarters at West Raynham in Norfolk. In 1983, No. 25 Squadron returned from Germany and its Bloodhounds were relocated to RAF Wattisham, RAF Barkston Heath, and RAF Wyton. Working together, these squadrons established a missile engagement zone, or MEZ, which blanketed the UK landmass in the south. From the aircrew perspective, identification became an even bigger concern to Phantom crews when the Bloodhounds were operating. The missile operators relied on the air picture being provided by the Sector Controllers to identify incoming hostile aircraft. Friendly aircraft were identified by an electronic system known as Identification Friend or Foe (IFF) that sent coded electronic signals to the

A Bloodhound Surface to Air Missile.

Practice missile firings by a Rapier fire unit near Port Stanley.

UKADGE. Unfortunately, IFF was never perfect, identification was never 100 per cent guaranteed, and mistakes could occur. Lock-ups by Bloodhounds were common and the radar warning receiver would quite often burst into life as we recovered to base. I am not the only returning fighter who was mistakenly engaged by a Bloodhound after completing many hours on CAP as I returned for my afternoon tea and medals! To avoid fratricide, procedures were introduced to make recovering aircraft appear as friendly as possible to the person with the finger on the trigger in his darkened control room. Unfortunately, speed was often the easiest discriminator to impose. An airborne track approaching at 250 knots looked far less hostile than one travelling at 500 knots, but it was hugely uncomfortable to recover at such a slow speed in a Phantom. If 'bounced', there was little hope of negating the attack, as the jet became almost uncontrollable if manoeuvred hard at such slow speed and very quickly became a 'sitting duck'. Unfortunately, being reliant on an intercept controller to warn of hostile aircraft in the vicinity, when he might be busy controlling an engagement at the limits of his cover, was asking a lot. Most crews preferred to return at a higher speed along a minimum risk route, hoping that the Bloodhound controller was alert.

The final layer of defence was provided by Rapier missiles operated by the RAF Regiment. The unit headquarters was at RAF Honington in Suffolk, but elements of the squadrons would be deployed to main operating bases to provide Base Defence Zones. The Rapier was a hugely capable weapon system but, in the 1980s, largely visually aimed and therefore short range. At the height of the Cold War, four squadrons including the Joint Rapier Training Unit were based in the UK with a further squadron in Germany. The UK squadrons were headquartered at RAF Honington, with the equivalent HQ in Germany at RAF Wildenrath. Additionally, following the Falklands War, a unit of Rapiers was permanently detached to RAF Stanley moving on to RAF Mount Pleasant when it opened to provide base defence of the airfield.

The final vital pieces of the jigsaw were the tanker towlines and the airborne early warning barriers. These were provided by Victor and VC10 tankers, although for a brief period after the Falklands War, a few Vulcans were hastily modified to fill the tanker role. Shackleton AEW aircraft soldiered on for much of the Cold War, awaiting the arrival of the Boeing E3D Sentry after the cancellation of the disastrous Nimrod AEW Mk 3 project. The AEW barriers were positioned sufficiently far forward to extend the radar cover without placing the AEW aircraft in hostile airspace. There were robust procedures to withdraw them in the event of attacking aircraft showing undue interest. Having completed many practice missions attacking 'high value assets', I know all too well that a regressing tanker crew that does not want to be intercepted can call on many friends to help. Physics dictates that a radar transmitter positioned at

1. XV437 over a snowy Norfolk landscape.

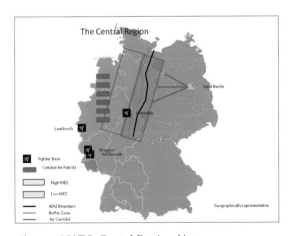

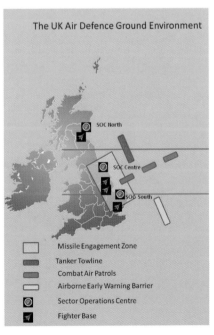

Above: 2. NATO Central Region Airspace.
Right: 3. The UK Air Defence Ground Environment.

4. The Phantom Front Cockpit.

5. The Phantom Rear Cockpit.

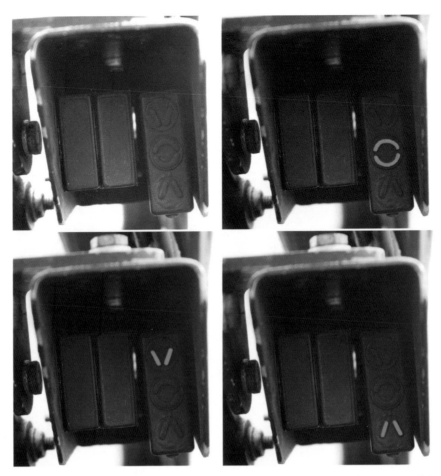

6. The Indexers display with top right, a maximum performance turn (18.7-19.7 units), bottom left a 'push' command (20.3-30 units) and bottom right a 'pull' command (0-18.1 units).

7. XV437 set against a snowy landscape.

8. XV468 of 56 Squadron, shortly before retirement.

9. In the cockpit of XV464.

10. XV500 taxies past the RAF Wattisham QRA sheds.

11. The RAF Wattisham Quick Reaction Alert Facility or 'Q Shed'.

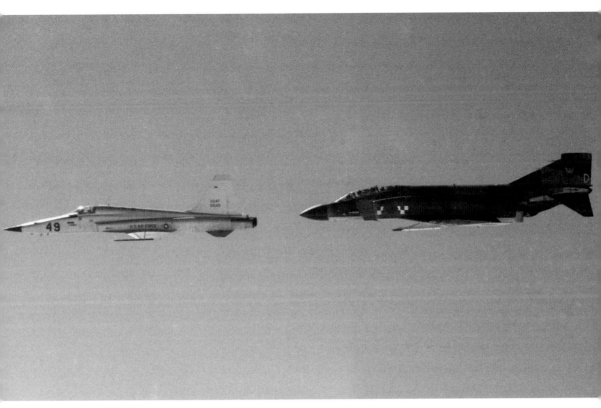

12. A 527th Aggressor Squadron F5E finished in a natural colour scheme to represent a Mig-21.

13. 56 Squadron crews including the author after a sortie against the US Aggressors. Note the old style torso harnesses.

14. XV434 at the Danish Air Force Base at Skrydstrup during a squadron exchange. The aircraft crashed in Yorkshire some years later.

15. 56 Squadron Phantoms at RAF Akrotiri configured for air to air gunnery.

16. XV490 outside the RAF Wattisham Quick Reaction Alert Hangar.

17. XV495 on Readiness 10 at RAF Wattisham.

18. A Soviet Air Force Bear 'Juliette'.

19. A Soviet IL38 "May" intercepted south of RAF Akrotiri in the Eastern Mediterranean.

20. XV495 on Readiness 10 at RAF Wattisham.

21. A Border marker post but small plinths marked the actual border.

22. A Border Watch Tower.

Halt!
Hier
Grenze
Bundesgrenzschutz

23. West German Border Police Warning Board – 'Halt! Border'.

24. A Border Watch Tower.

25. XT899 of 92 Squadron taxies past his wingman on the Delta Dispersal Loop.

26. XT899 of 92 Squadron taxies around the Delta Dispersal Loop.

27. A 92 Squadron Phantom leaves the HAS.

28. XV460 of 92 Squadron leaves HAS 54 on Delta Dispersal.

29. XV422 which shot down an RAF Jaguar with a Sidewinder on 25 May 1982.

30. A 56 Squadron Phantom lights the afterburners as dusk falls.

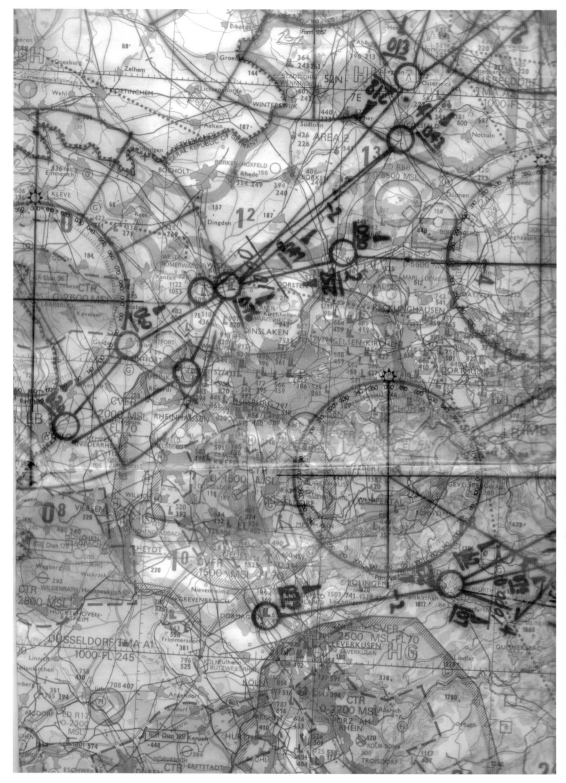

31. An actual Cold War low flying map showing the departures from RAF Wildenrath. The maps are creased from folding to make them easy to use in the confines of the cockpit. (*Courtesy Andrew Lister Tomlinson*)

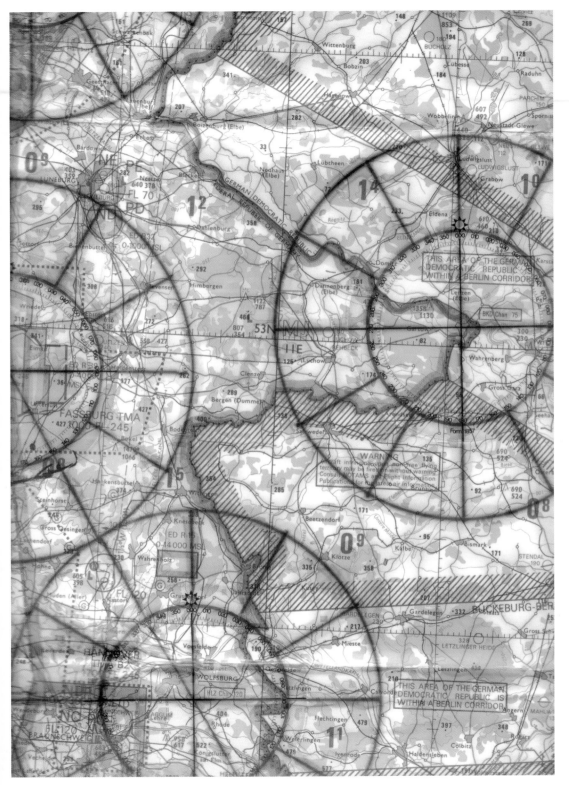

32. An actual Battle Flight map of the entrances to the northern and central Berlin corridors. Range and bearing rings have been drawn around the TACAN beacons to aid navigation. Fassburg TACAN sits to the left centre of the map. (*Courtesy Andrew Lister Tomlinson*)

Overleaf: 33. XV426 in the vertical.

ground level will have an area around the radar head where airborne targets cannot be seen. This gap in coverage is known in the fighter community as the 'dark area' and led to many politically incorrect jokes over the years. By feeding the picture from an airborne early warning aircraft into the recognised air picture these gaps could be filled. The other obvious advantage of AEW was that the radar coverage of the UKADGE could be extended by pushing the barriers forward, giving longer range warning of incoming raids, albeit at the expense of making the AEW aircraft more vulnerable to attack.

The improved capability of the Phantom allowed a little more flexibility in tactical employment, and tactics began to develop. There were a number of standard tactics that were common in the Phantom Force. UK-based Phantoms normally operated in pairs, with only two aircraft manning each combat air patrol. To ensure that at least one radar was always looking in the direction of the expected threat, the aircraft would position themselves at opposite ends of the racetrack. As one turned outbound, the other would turn back towards the coast. In the early years of Phantom operations, the GCI controllers' tactics were simplistic; single fighters would be committed against raids maintaining a presence on CAP. Later, this seemed amazingly naïve, and committing a pair of fighters was the norm.

Once a target was detected, the lead navigator would call it to the intercept controller who would give instructions, for example 'Engage' or 'Identify'. The navigator would select a tactic depending on the number of attacking aircraft and whether the threat had been declared 'hostile'. The wingman would join in battle formation to provide mutual support during the intercept and to bring as many weapons as possible into the engagement. If the ground controller had positively identified the track as hostile, the preferred attack was a bracket. Each Phantom would widen the battle formation to position outside the closest aircraft to each Phantom at the front of the enemy formation, hence the name bracket. Both Phantoms would launch head-on Sparrow shots as the leading target came within range. If there were more targets in the formation, once the Sparrow missile had destroyed the leading target the navigator would lock to the trailing aircraft on their own side of the enemy formation and carry on 'down the line', taking further head-on Sparrow shots. This made best use of the Phantom's weapon system and avoided the risk of turning into the middle of a formation which would probably result in close combat manoeuvring, particularly if the missile shots failed. If the targets could not be confirmed as enemy aircraft, an offensive visual identification could be flown. For this profile, the Phantom that gained first contact would accelerate ahead, opening about 3 to 4 miles of separation ahead of his wingman. As the lead aircraft sighted the target, the lead crew would identify it visually and call either 'friendly' or 'hostile'. If 'hostile', the second Phantom crew would lock up and engage with a head-on Sparrow missile. If 'friendly', the formation would be allowed to proceed unharmed. Although this tactic separated the Phantoms by some miles, mutual support was retained by use of the radio. If attacked, either aircraft could assist its wingman due to their relatively close proximity.

Another option if the target was unidentified was the 'Hook' attack. Both Phantoms remained in battle formation, line abreast about a mile apart, and set up an interception to one side of the incoming target formation. At about 5 miles, the Phantoms would pull hard towards the lead target and attempt to identify the type of threat. If 'hostile', a minimum range Sparrow shot might still be on the cards, particularly if the enemy aircraft saw the approaching Phantom and turned towards it. More often, the Phantom would be forced to convert the attack into a stern hemisphere approach. With the advent of the all-aspect AIM-9L, the tactic became much more flexible. Instead of being forced to manoeuvre into the traditional '6 o'clock' position, the AIM-9L allowed a shot to be taken on the target's beam. This allowed the Phantom to turn back down the threat axis and again avoided being drawn into a turning fight. With an AIM-9G, which could only be fired in the target's stern sector, there was but one option: to turn in behind and 'run down' the attackers. Whichever way the attack developed, turning behind an enemy formation was always risky unless you were absolutely certain that the targets being attacked were the back markers. Many a bomber pilot armed with air-to-air missiles watched with glee as an unwary Phantom crew dropped into his gunsight in the middle of the bomber formation after a poor intercept.

Bomber crews always had to meet a time on target, so were reluctant to 'turn and burn' before dropping their weapons. Equally, weapon loads are heavy, which made the bombers unmanoeuvrable before the target. Invariably, when approaching a target, attacking crews would try to avoid detection or evade an interception. Tactics were employed to make it harder for the fighter to detect the attacker, either using radar or visually. The preferred tactic was to descend closer to the ground, which made the aircraft harder to see. By splitting the formation it was impossible for a fighter to target all the intruders. As the fighter prosecuted the attack on one hapless bomber, it would drag the fighter away from the rest of the formation, making a follow-on attack more difficult, particularly in marginal weather. Surprisingly, a camouflaged fast jet is extremely hard to see from the confines of a Phantom cockpit at 500 feet, even against a fast-moving landscape. While searching, the Phantom crew would be forced into a predictable straight line chase, probably with the navigator's head buried in the cockpit, manipulating the radar which was tactically unsound. The 'Red Baron' had chided his circus members if they spent more than 20 seconds straight and level in the combat area, and his advice is still valid all these years later. Once the bombers had dropped their weapons and were returning from their target it was a different matter. It was often during the run home that the fiercest engagements occurred as bomber crews took the chance to practise their evasion tactics or air combat skills.

It was on one such tactical mission that a Phantom was lost in Yorkshire. The crew was practising overland interceptions against another pair of Phantoms that were flying in trail formation. Having found the rear aircraft of the formation, the crew of XV434, shown in Plate 14, turned in behind and took a simulated Sidewinder shot. Happy that the missile had achieved a simulated kill, they pulled around the aircraft they had just engaged and accelerated, searching for the next target some miles ahead. As the speed increased, the pilot felt a marked pitch down and tried to lift the nose. The aircraft responded, but more aggressively than he expected, and he found himself entering a series of pitch ups and pitch downs that were difficult to control. The 'G' increased and the oscillations became so violent that the pilot's head was forced down towards his knees, at which point he ejected, closely followed by his navigator.

The inquiry concluded that the most likely cause of the crash was that a blockage, probably an insect, had occurred in the feel bellows system. This pressure compensation system applied artificial feel to the controls when the aircraft was operating at high speed to prevent over-stressing the aircraft. In this case, the blockage affected the stick forces on the pilot's control column, causing unexpected demands on the control surfaces. Ultimately, the aircraft became uncontrollable as the pilot fed in compensating demands in his efforts to maintain control. This phenomenon is known as pilot-induced oscillations, although in this case it was through no fault of the pilot. The symptoms he experienced were more dramatic and, ultimately, more dangerous due to the proximity to the ground. Ironically, it is highly likely that something as small as a bumble bee had become lodged in the bellows tube, leading to the loss of a multi-million-pound combat aeroplane.

The pilot's ejection was remarkably uneventful given the immense forces acting on the stricken aircraft and he separated from his seat normally. The navigator fared much worse. The rear ejection seat in the Phantom was sequenced with the front seat to ensure that the navigator was not hit by the front canopy in the event of simultaneous ejections. For that reason, a Phantom navigator would always leave the aircraft about 2 seconds after the pilot if the handles were pulled at the same time. Unfortunately, as the Phantom was at very low level travelling at about 500 knots at the time of ejection, when the aircraft pitched down violently, the delay before his seat left the aircraft meant that the navigator was ejected towards the ground. The aircraft crashed in open moorland close to a gulley, but the navigator separated from his seat very close to the ground and his parachute drifted through the fireball. He was affected by both the traumatic nature of the ejection sequence and the intense heat from the burning wreckage that seared his parachute. Miraculously he survived, but it was some time before he was located by the search and rescue helicopter. The pilot was already moving around and was located quickly, but the navigator was hurt and it took a good deal of skill on the part of the rescue crew to find him. Eventually both crew members were taken to hospital. To our immense relief, the navigator, who is a true gentleman, went back to flying after a long and slow recuperation, although he lost his 'bang seat category' and was posted to the E3D Sentry. In subsequent years he was able to put his fighter experience to good use in the AEW community. I spoke to the crew in the months that followed and was touched not only by their accounts of the horror of the accident but by their courage and fortitude in coming to terms with their experiences. As with many accidents, the unique circumstances of the ejection provoked a healthy debate in the crewroom. The helicopter had taken quite some time to locate the navigator due to the fact that he was severely hurt and had been unable to operate his personal locator beacon. Modifications were made that led to the introduction of automatic inflation of dinghies and automatic initiation of personal locator beacons to cope with situations where the ejectee was incapacitated. These modifications improved the chances of survival for many crews in later years. As with so many accidents, good came from suffering.

There was one final secondary role given to Phantom crews. Many years before I began flying the aircraft, an Australian aircraft had accidentally fired at a fast patrol boat (FPB) and the Sparrow missile had punched a hole through the vessel, causing it to sink. A profile had been worked out where the Phantoms flew a split pincer approach onto a suspected FPB. The first Phantom would accelerate ahead and fly low and fast overhead the suspect vessel to identify it. The second Phantom on hearing the call of 'hostile' would pop up, lock onto the boat using the pulse radar, and fire a Sparrow missile. With hindsight, the thought of attacking a Soviet FPB armed with self-protection SAN-4 missiles without any self-defence jamming equipment or chaff and flare dispensers seems worryingly naïve even if the profile was loads of fun.

Another concept that emerged in the early 1980s was the Mixed Fighter Force. The Hawk training aircraft stationed at the Tactical Weapons Units did not have a war role. At a relatively small cost, the Hawk's missile pylons were modified to take two AIM-9 Sidewinders and the aircraft were declared to the Air Defence Commander as air defence assets. During exercises, the Hawks would deploy to the east coast fighter bases and join the order of battle. Concentration of force was accepted air power doctrine. Rather than buy more expensive fighters, the concept of a more capable pulse Doppler-equipped fighter leading a simpler but perhaps more agile fighter into the merge had been evaluated in RAF Germany in the late 1970s. The Mixed Fighter Force was intended to combine the strengths of the Phantom radar and weapons with the agility of the Hawk and to deliver the maximum force into the close engagement. In good weather and against the right type of formations it could be an extremely effective tactic. In poor weather or against tight formations it could be a liability. A Phantom ideally entered a fight at 500 knots or faster whereas the Hawk was struggling at speeds above 480 knots. The Phantom could easily leave the slower Hawk in its wake, preventing the essential concentration of force. Once the Hawk was mixed in with the attackers it could be difficult to co-ordinate, given the differing performance of the two types. Careful co-ordination was needed over sometimes poor radios to avoid the risk of 'blue on blue' engagements as the Phantom re-engaged. Additionally, with only two missiles and a gun, the Hawk quickly ran out of weapons and often could remain for only a single engagement if realistic weapons expenditure was being practised. Many exercise scenarios allowed the Hawk pilot to 'reload' in the air. Although this allowed the Hawk to remain on station and increased the training value, it could set bad habits among aircrew and intercept controllers alike who assumed the Hawk could achieve more than the two weapons allowed. The concept was well practised and could have been available to the Commander, but despite its excellent turning ability and the skill of its pilots, the Hawk was often better suited to manning the inner CAPs, similar to the Lightning. Without doubt, it was a welcome addition to the numbers of fighters available to defend the UK during the Cold War.

Despite the defence in depth strategy, the key improvement the Phantom brought to the UK air defence controllers was the ability to be pushed forward onto the outer combat air patrols. It was assumed that if the Soviet Union ever attacked NATO, nuclear war would follow very quickly. How far the Soviets pushed into West Germany would have dictated how far forward they were able to base their nuclear capable tactical air assets. Assuming that they reached the Channel ports in the few days that were forecast, it would have been only a short time before tactical air assets would have threatened the UK in a Third World War scenario. In the early stages of a war, it was far more likely that the principal threat to the UK would have been from the Soviet Strategic Aviation forces in the form of Bear, Badger, Bison, and Blinder bombers. The bomber variants of these aircraft, although able to drop conventional bombs, were more likely to have used nuclear stand-off missiles for the early attacks. These missiles, such as the Kelt and Kennel classes, in reality the size of a small aeroplane, were launched hundreds of miles from the target. Although inaccurate due to the unsophisticated technology, the Soviets compensated by fitting large nuclear warheads; in other words 'brute force over sophistication'. In order to counter this threat it was far more effective if the bomber could be intercepted before it launched its weapon rather than try to intercept the high subsonic or supersonic missiles once they had been launched. To do that, fighters had to be deployed forward and well distant from the UK coastline.

Although the Lightning was a great aeroplane, it was a point defence fighter with extremely short range and only two missiles. It was poorly equipped to operate hundreds of miles out to sea without a tanker and with only two missiles, giving realistically only one or two engagements. The Phantom, however, could complete two-hour missions and carry out up to eight intercepts at long range. Coupled with its much better radar, this meant that it could potentially negate, or at least significantly reduce, the manned bomber threat if it could be fielded in sufficient numbers in the right area. A 'Doomsday scenario' was rehearsed on every air defence exercise and was known as a survival scramble. The assumption was that the air defence base was under nuclear attack, probably from Soviet nuclear missile forces. On receipt of a 'Ringo warning', all serviceable fighters would have launched and made their way to pre-assigned CAPs, searching for incoming raids. It was expected that the first missiles would have been followed after 90 minutes by a wave of Soviet bombers, and it was these that the Phantoms would seek to destroy before they could add to the destruction. Any Phantoms not allocated to a tanker would have recovered to their bases, hopefully to be rearmed and launched again to return to the CAPs. How long this process could have been maintained, given that the bases would have been damaged and contaminated by nuclear fallout, is debatable. Nevertheless, the Phantom gave much more flexibility to have extracted some revenge which had hitherto been difficult.

The ability to intercept a high flying supersonic target was one of the core skills for a UK air defender and led to one of the more unusual exercises. When Concorde completed its testing phase and entered service with British Airways, the pressure on the prototype aircraft eased. In early 1977, British Aerospace offered a number of sorties by one of the prototypes, G-AXDN, in which it would act as a target for Phantoms and Lightnings to intercept. For the Lightning pilots this was exactly what the aircraft had been designed to do. A scramble from ground alert to meet a high level, high speed intruder could have been an extract from the original specification for the aircraft. For the Phantom, which was less comfortable flying in the upper air, it was more of a challenge. The realistic service ceiling for pulling alongside an aircraft was about 50,000 feet, and even then the Phantom had to keep both reheats burning and would probably pass the intercepted aircraft still flying at speeds greater than Mach 1. However, the advantage the Phantom enjoyed over the Lightning was that it carried the Sparrow missile which could 'snap up' and destroy an aircraft flying at a much higher altitude. This meant that Concorde flying at Mach 2 at 65,000 feet was certainly inside the envelope and could realistically be engaged.

On the day in question, a series of CAPs about 200 miles apart were established in the North Sea, and at the nominated time Concorde began its run from a point well north of Scotland. Phantoms from Leuchars, Coningsby, and Wattisham were given the opportunity to carry out a single intercept as it headed south. Although the exercise was repeated the following day, this was an almost unique opportunity, only a few crews having the chance to practise the profile. The range at which the Sparrow was launched in the head-on sector depended on the speed of the fighter, the speed of the target, and the target's altitude. The higher the value for each, the longer the range at which the Sparrow would be launched. Added to that, the Sparrow could take out only about 20,000 feet of altitude, so the Phantom had to climb to within that altitude of the incoming target. Against Concorde, that meant a launch height of about 45,000 feet. The weapons instructors pored over the manuals and devised an intercept profile to tackle a target flying at such extreme heights and speeds – far higher and faster than anything the Soviet Union could field at the time. It was decided that by accelerating to about Mach 1.5 and pulling up at about 26 miles, the Sparrow dot would be in the allowable steering error circle by the time the target came within Sparrow range. The profile was practised repeatedly in the simulator to prove that it worked. Armed with this knowledge, the lucky crews were dispatched onto CAP to await the arrival of Concorde. Miraculously, as Concorde blasted down the North Sea a series of inelegant lunges proved the theories, and simulated Sparrow missiles sped inexorably towards the pride of British aviation! The opportunity was never repeated as G-AXDN retired shortly afterwards and now resides in the Imperial War Museum at Duxford. Few visitors who gaze at its elegant lines will ever be aware that it was once offered as a target to allow an intercept profile to be validated.

The numbers game was always an issue, and most British taxpayers would have little idea how many fighters are needed to defend UK airspace. The reality is that to mount a single CAP constantly for 24 hours requires the resources of a whole Wing of twenty-four aircraft. With only three Phantom fighter bases, a permanent airborne presence could be mounted on only three CAPs. There are hundreds of potential CAPs around the UK, but it was never realistic to cover all these locations. Battle managers were forced to deploy forces thinly where they felt the greatest threat would materialise. For that reason, fighters were held on ground alert unless raids were expected. Once committed to a patrol area, provided they did not expend their missile load they would be kept on CAP to avoid wasteful transits to and from the home airfields, which could take

Above: The 16 Ship Phantom formation which marked the 60th Anniversary of the RAF. UK MOD Crown Copyright (1978).

Left: The 16 Ship Phantom formation overflies RAF Wattisham. UK MOD Crown Copyright (1978).

The crews formed up after the sortie in a Diamond 16 formation pose. UK MOD Crown Copyright (1978).

as long as 20 minutes or more. So, despite the flexibility the Phantom offered, it was often negated by lack of resources. A media campaign in the mid-1970s highlighted that the UK could call on a mere seventy-seven fighters to defend the home airspace. This deficiency had been identified by the planning staffs, and the Tornado F2/F3 was selected to reinforce the defences and finally replace the Lightning. A very respectable 165 Tornado F3s were ordered, which, added to the remaining Phantoms and Hawks, increased the fighter force to a decent size. Despite the lack of Phantom numbers. it didn't stop the senior leadership from launching large formations at any whiff of a celebration. It was a red-letter day when I was included in a sixteen-ship formation on 31 March 1978, flying in XV500, to celebrate the Diamond Jubilee of the Royal Air Force. The formation was led by the Station Commander and the squadron boss who was a navigator. The joint formation mounted by both 23 (Fighter) Squadron and 56 (F) Squadron put sixteen Phantoms and an airborne whip into the skies over Suffolk. The formation passed over key bases such as Neatishead and Coltishall before making a number of flypasts over RAF Wattisham. It was a fitting tribute, evoking memories of the large formations flown by the squadrons during the Hunter and Lightning eras. Above all, for a newly operational navigator it was an evocative experience to see such immense firepower in a single formation, even if I had a very small role in the proceedings, being a lowly number fourteen of sixteen. Afterwards, the station photographic section captured the event, with the crews forming up on the aircraft servicing platform in a diamond sixteen formation pose.

As the years went by, slowly the numbers were whittled away. With the demise of the Phantom in the early 1990s, once again a standing force of fewer than 100 Tornados defended the UK, albeit by then against a much weaker Russia. Nowadays, the planners cite a lack of threat or the greater efficiency of new aircraft types to justify the lack of fighters. Apart from that brief period in the late 1980s, Britain has never had sufficient fighters to counter a concerted attack on the country. The UKADGE has been a victim of changes in perception of the level of threat to the UK and to the inevitable and incessant defence cuts. The SOCs have been reduced to a single unit at RAF Boulmer, the missiles are gone, and only a single fighter type, the Typhoon, remains. With the end of the Cold War, perhaps the threat to the UK Home Base is a thing of the past. Let us hope that the collective wisdom is sound and that the UK will never again be attacked as it was in the dark days of the Second World War. If it should be, it is doubtful that today's 'Few' would have enough aircraft to stem more than a small tide.

CHAPTER 6
Quick Reaction Alert

The role of Quick Reaction Alert, or QRA, is to protect UK airspace, be it from intruding Soviet bombers, wayward light aircraft, or suspicious airliners. After seeing the devastating effect of an airliner being used to destroy buildings on 9/11, governments once again realised the value of having air defence aircraft on constant alert. During the Cold War, incursions by Soviet Bears were widely reported, but it was not unknown for Eastern Bloc airliners to stray from their planned track, passing close to sensitive installations in order to gather intelligence. Most tracks that appear daily on UK radars are aircraft that have filed flight plans and, by doing so, are cleared through UK airspace by the air traffic control agencies. Hundreds of such flights pass over the UK every day. An 'unknown' is exactly as the name suggests: a track for which no flight plan has been received and which appears to be on a heading that would penetrate the UK Air Defence Region. A track that is designated as a potentially hostile intruder is aptly named a 'Zombie'.

The UK ADR during the Cold War was a vast expanse of airspace stretching from the English Channel up the North Sea and into the waters around Iceland. It was monitored day and night by the Air Defence Commander from the Operations Room at Headquarters Strike Command, RAF High Wycombe. The watch officer was known as the UK Master Controller and was duty bound to investigate any track that could not be identified. To do this, the QRA aircraft were at his disposal. The UK held four aircraft on 'Readiness 10', which meant that the aircraft had to be airborne inside 10 minutes after a scramble message. RAF Leuchars in Scotland mounted Northern QRA with two aircraft and was closest to the action so normally would be scrambled first. Aircraft from Leuchars could be in the operational area in the Iceland-Faroes gap within 20 minutes but, if needed, would be replaced by southern-based aircraft that mounted Southern QRA from RAF Coningsby in Lincolnshire or RAF Wattisham in Suffolk on a rotational basis. By the time Southern Q were heading north, a tanker from

RAF Marham or RAF Brize Norton would have also been scrambled in support, allowing these aircraft to extend their time on task.

At the height of the Cold War, the Soviets tested the UK reactions on a weekly basis. Often the Master Controller would be alerted by his Norwegian counterparts as a track emanating from Russia passed a trigger line over the North Cape. If the controller was clever, he would call the QRA Commander at the duty air defence base and warn of likely activity. This would give crews time to put on their protective equipment and fire up the aircraft systems, particularly the navigation equipment, in slower time. Although the crews were prepared for a no-notice launch, a planned departure was invariably more efficient than a scramble.

There were a vast number of different Soviet types intercepted over the years. UK airspace was well distant from Mother Russia, so the types that had the range to operate in UK airspace belonged to the Soviet Long Range Air Force. The 'Milk Run' was flown by the Bear 'Deltas' which passed south of Iceland on a weekly basis en route to Cuba. Less common were the Bear 'Foxtrot' maritime patrol aircraft. The 'Foxtrots' normally operated in support of Soviet fleets in the Atlantic, but they would monitor the activity of NATO task forces, particularly during NATO exercises. The Tu-16 Badger was also a regular visitor. This aircraft had been adapted to fulfil a number of roles from conventional bomber, through missile carrier, to electronic intelligence gatherer. The latter was by far the most common, and anything other than these regular visitors caused considerable interest. Much less common, but occasionally seen, was the Coot 'Alpha' intelligence gatherer and the Bison jet bomber. QRA crews trained to recognise each of these different types and studied the different marks in fine detail. Tips were offered on how to tell a Bear 'Delta' from a Bear 'Foxtrot'; often it was as obscure as whether the aircraft had a particular blister on the rear fuselage or not. Crews came up with mnemonics to help identify the individual marks. The electronic jammer variant of the Badger was the Badger 'Juliette'. The mnemonic was 'J for Canoe' as the aircraft had a long canoe-shaped radome that stretched along the length of the underbelly. Why this stuck in the minds of the pilots and navigators is anyone's guess, and probably says something about how the fickle aircrew mind works.

QRA missions in the Iceland-Faroes gap could be long, and a seven-hour flight was routine from RAF Wattisham. There was no such thing as a packed lunch, and the ability to take a 'pee break' while strapped to an ejection seat wearing a full immersion suit was limited although not impossible. For that reason, scrambles nearly always came before lunch or immediately after a coffee break.

Each RAF air defence base had a separate facility for QRA, well away from the routine humdrum of squadron life. The squadron tended to be busy, and roaming Flight Commanders were always ready to allocate small extra duties to the unwary. These were known as 'SLJs' (silly little jobs), but QRA was an SLJ-free zone. The QRA crews were on duty for 24 hours and lived, ate, and slept in the facility. Once on QRA it took absolute priority over any other duty, activity, or function, but in some ways it was a welcome break. Having once visited a USAF QRA facility in Iceland, the palatial surroundings with pool tables, coffee bars, and large-screen TVs was light years away from any RAF facility I ever worked from. The typical UK Q shack was small and dreary, boasting only a TV and video recorder to play movies to while away the hours. The QRA shed at RAF Wattisham was typical of the type of buildings in RAF use. It was updated in 1976 after the arrival of the Phantoms to give more space for the additional aircrew, but even so was painfully small. The two alert aircraft were housed in adjacent hangars containing all the engineering equipment needed to service and start up the aircraft. A huge 'Houchin', or external power set, provided electrics to operate the avionics and radios until the engines were started and the internal generators were on line.

Crews would take charge of their Q jet at about 09:00 and give it a daily check. The inertial navigation system was run up and realigned, and the radios and telebrief system checked. The cockpits were set up to individual preferences, and the final preparation was to position the aircrew's lifejackets at the base of the steps and the flying helmets on the cockpit rail to allow rapid donning. The ejection seat was checked and the safety pins were pulled, with the exception of the firing handle pins. Crews had to know exactly where to find their equipment, so once aircrew had set up their equipment the groundcrew were forbidden from entering the cockpit. These preparations meant that in the heat of the scramble all the essential items were easily to hand to speed up the check-in. Once the handover was complete, tedium set in. New crews would pore over the 'Noddy Guide' which contained all the QRA procedures. After a couple of sessions on Q, that became second nature, and magazines, books, and TV were the diet. Video recorders and movies ran for much of the day, and most QRA facilities had enviable video libraries with all the latest films. Dress was hardly comfortable for the aircrew. In the UK, crews had to dress for the Iceland-Faroes gap where, in the event of an ejection, the sea temperature was 5 degrees Celsius or less. Life expectancy without proper protection was counted in minutes, so warm clothing was essential. Even then, it would be a long time before a helicopter could reach a likely ejection area, so getting into the small rubber dinghy that was packed into the ejection seat was paramount for survival. Aircrew underwear was not pretty and consisted of a long-sleeved vest and long johns. A knitted pullover, replaced later by a full-length knitted 'bunny suit', came next, followed by an internal 'G' suit around the legs. The single-piece immersion suit, made from a heavy rubberised material with integral bootees and rubber seals at the neck and wrists, was next. Flying boots fitted over the bootees. The lifejacket, torso harness, and flying helmet completed the ensemble. Once kitted out, not only did each aircrew member weigh 30 lbs more but the heat stress in the cockpit was significant.

The aircraft were serviced daily, which took about 10 minutes. During that time, the Duty Controller was warned and would hopefully give more notice of an impending scramble to allow the groundcrew to wrap up the servicing as soon as possible. Next to the hangars was a small brick-built annexe that housed a kitchen, separate lounges for the aircrew and the groundcrew, and bedrooms. Although meals were sent in from the station catering facilities, many crews elected for dry rations that they could cook in the small kitchen. The QRA curry was legendary. Being a captive audience, in addition to the obligatory TV many took the opportunity to study or took up hobbies to while away the hours. Despite many taking the risk and removing immersion suits to sleep, the sacrosanct rule that the jet was to be airborne inside 10 minutes from the 'hooter' sounding was never relaxed. There were no excuses and no concessions. The most demanding alert state was held in RAF Germany where the aircraft had to be airborne inside 5 minutes. On one Tactical Evaluation both alert crews were scrambled in the wee small hours, and the time from being asleep to 'wheels in the well' was a mere 3½ minutes. This was little short of miraculous, given that the INAS took 90 seconds to align.

I spent years sitting patiently on QRA hoping to coincide with a mission by a Bear, to no avail. Others would sit Q for the first time and return with that elusive picture and a 'war story'. In my case, it just never happened. I finally broke my duck many years later when lurking around the Operations desk on detachment in Cyprus. The Duty Authoriser took a call from the Sector Controller warning that a 'May' maritime patrol aircraft was heading our way. After a hasty scramble, my pilot and I intercepted not one but two 'Mays' just east of the island. It was not quite a Bear, but the large red star on the fin left no doubt as to its origins. Luckily, the Soviet crew could not know that we were armed only with ball ammunition in our gun pod. There had been no time to load live missiles.

The irony was that my first sighting of a Bear was at the annual air show at Fairford. After the fall of 'The Wall', the Soviets began to send aircraft to UK air shows. Ambling past the aircraft we came across the crew, and, pointing to my badge, by then showing a Tornado F3, I persuaded them to allow us to sit in the aircraft shown in Plate 18. Seeing the vast cockpit and crew compartment, it was apparent that the Soviet crews enjoyed much greater level of comfort than we did during those long missions over the North Sea. Needless to say, there was no animosity and we left feeling a little more reassured that aircrew are the same the world over.

A Soviet IL38 'May' intercepted south of RAF Akrotiri in the Eastern Mediterranean. A picture of the other 'May' is shown at Plate 19.

Despite the technology, errors could occur. I recall a scramble in the early hours of the morning for a live QRA mission into the Iceland-Faroes gap. The SOC at Neatishead had warning from the Norwegians that a Bear was routeing into the UK Air Defence Region. Given this advanced notice, it was decided that Southern QRA would be used for the intercept and we were scrambled from Wattisham, along with a Victor tanker from RAF Marham in Norfolk. We made the long transit north and were advised as we passed abeam Leuchars that a Shackleton Airborne Early Warning aircraft was being launched in case the Bear dropped down to low level. This made us think that it might be a Bear 'Foxtrot', the maritime surveillance version of the Tu-95. Although the Control and Reporting Post at RAF Saxa Vord had limited cover, there were some large holes in the air picture at those northern latitudes. Dawn was just breaking as we reached the combat air patrol datum that we had been given in the scramble instructions, and we began searching the vast areas of the ocean for the intruder. Unfortunately, almost immediately we heard that the Shackleton had aborted and returned to RAF Lossiemouth with a problem. An hour passed with absolutely

A 43 Squadron FG1 intercepts a Bear Delta taking up the classic pose. UK MOD Crown Copyright (1978).

no sign of anything that even vaguely resembled an airborne target on the radar scope, so we were pulled off CAP to refuel. Tanking as quickly as possible we resumed the search, but, frustratingly, our controller admitted that his scope had been empty during our absence. Almost immediately, I found a blip on the radar, called it to Saxa, and we vectored towards the contact.

The weather was extremely poor and we already knew that the main cloudbase was between 500 feet and 1,000 feet, but it came as no surprise that the contact was at low level so we began our descent. With the target flying well below our height, I was using the pulse Doppler mode on the radar to break the target out from the ground clutter. One of the limitations of the early generation AN/AWG-12 equipment was that it did not give a target range until the radar was locked on to the target. All I would see until that point was a blip at the azimuth of the target and a rough indication of its speed. The Bear was equipped with sophisticated electronic surveillance equipment and would hear the tell-tale pulses of our radar as we scanned the airspace. I had to remain in search mode to give as little warning as possible of our approach, which added to the complexity of the intercept. I was working hard to keep the target in track, but my pilot was working just as hard since we were still in cloud and he was flying the intercept on instruments. As we rolled in behind, I began to lose contact in pulse Doppler but we were just starting to break out of the bottom of the cloud. The weather

A close in shot from above a Bear Delta. UK MOD Crown Copyright (1978).

below was appalling, the visibility extremely poor, and being many miles to the north of the Scottish coastline and at low level, we had lost radio contact with our controller. The feeling of isolation was enormous.

I regained contact with the target in pulse mode, breaking out the contact from the background sea clutter, and we pressed in for a visual identification. By now, even in search mode, the Bear's radar warning equipment would be lit up like a Christmas tree so I decided to lock up. That would also prompt the Bear's pilot to react if he had plans to do so. Better to find out at this range than when we were making our final approach into close formation. There was no reaction to the lock, so we pressed in following the standard profile that would bring us in from above the target. Provided the target stayed below us there was no way we could be dumped into the sea by a devious Bear pilot, but this one was 'on the deck'. Unlike the academic targets we practised against on the squadron, this one was not meekly compliant. As we closed, he threw in a large turn and the radar contact skated towards the side of the radar tube. As I barked out a couple of commands to re-establish the approach, my pilot was glancing occasionally through the windscreen, which was being peppered by a passing rainstorm. He had intercepted Bears on a previous tour at Leuchars and was well aware of the risks and the challenges. A few less than positive noises were beginning to come from the front cockpit. Those who have intercepted the enormous Tu-95 aircraft, which is equipped with four engines with eight contra-rotating propellers, say that you can hear the throb of the engines as you approach, even in the noisy environment of the Phantom cockpit. All we were hearing was the routine drone of our own jets. As we finally closed the range to 300 yards, which was our minimum range, it suddenly became apparent that we had intercepted one of our own Nimrods. The disappointment was strong as I realised that intercepting a Bear had eluded me yet again. When we finally climbed out and reported the identification to the controller he seemed equally mystified as to why the Nimrod was there. With hindsight, we might have recognised that a Bear would be unlikely to operate at extreme low level in such poor weather. No one else intercepted the Bear that day, so perhaps having seen the weather at low level the crew aborted the sortie and returned to Russia. In any event, my best chance of making that elusive intercept had just been missed. Others over the years were more successful and crews brought home pictures of Bears on a regular basis.

Back on QRA, the more mundane procedures had to be practised. It was important that new crews experienced a training scramble as soon as possible to ensure they understood the process and how to launch from the Q shed. Ground controllers also had to exercise the system, and base personnel such as the photographic section had to practise their own part in the process. Practice scrambles were routinely arranged against aircraft returning to their own bases. One of the most important aspects of the mission was to bring back pictures of the intercepted aircraft. In the 70s and 80s, the QRA navigators carried a Pentax single lens reflex camera in the back cockpit. Frustratingly, it was loaded with black and white film as this was the only film that could be processed by the base photographic section within the stipulated response times. For that reason, most QRA photographs that ever made the news headlines were black and white pictures unless the crew carried their own camera. Even so, analysts learned many things about Soviet bombers over the years by poring over QRA pictures and looking at every last detail of the intercepted target. Once alongside, the navigator was expected to take a series of shots, trying to capture images against different backgrounds and close-ups of areas of interest on the intercepted airframe. Even these detailed aspects of the mission had to be practised.

In the Central Region, QRA had the far more imposing title of Battle Flight. It also had the more stringent requirement to hold 'Readiness 05' or in other words to be airborne inside 5 minutes from the scramble order. As mentioned before, the Phantom inertial navigation system took 90 seconds to align, so it left precious little time for the other things that had to be done to get the aircraft airborne.

The two squadrons at RAF Wildenrath operated from separate dispersals, but each squadron's QRA shed was located within the dispersal at the eastern end of the airfield, with 19 (Fighter) Squadron playing host. Each squadron provided

A USAF F-111E. UK MOD Crown Copyright (1978).

A 100 Squadron Canberra both acting as targets for my practice QRA scrambles. UK MOD Crown Copyright (1978).

a crew and aircraft for the QRA commitment throughout the year. Unlike the UK with its dedicated facilities, at Wildenrath a regular hardened aircraft shelter housed the alert aircraft, although the facilities in the small annexe that sat alongside were reminiscent of the UK equivalent. Like the UK, the facility was connected 24 hours a day to the QRA controller at the local control and reporting centre, which in the case of Wildenrath was at Uedem in Germany. The 'hooter' could be triggered by the Battle Flight Controller, by the Wing Operations Officer at in the operations centre at Wildenrath, or by the aircrew on Battle Flight. Once set in motion and a scramble message was received, only a coded response from a controller would prevent Battle Flight from scrambling.

A live scramble was taken very seriously and civilian traffic would be cleared out of the path of the QRA aircraft. Wildenrath sits 30 miles or so west of Cologne and was a long transit to the Inner German Border or IGB. It was not unknown to be cleared at transonic speeds across the congested West German airspace in order to get to the border as quickly as possible. The inclusion of the codeword 'gate' in the message meant 'use reheat and make best speed'. This type of scramble added adrenaline to an already heady mix. There were stringent procedures for operating in the vicinity of the IGB. Immediately adjacent to the West German border was a zone whose shape mirrored the line of the border on the ground. This was known as the Air Defence Interception Zone or ADIZ. A further sterile area, known as the Buffer Zone, butted onto the ADIZ, providing an element of protection. Aircraft could operate in the Buffer Zone under carefully orchestrated procedures, but operation in the ADIZ, other than QRA aircraft, was prohibited. The structure is shown in Plate 2. This ensured that there were no inadvertent penetrations of East German airspace which would lead to the inevitable diplomatic incident, particularly if a military aircraft was involved. Anyone mistakenly straying into the ADIZ would hear a call of 'Brass Monkey' on the international distress frequency. This was one of those unique radio calls that instantly captured everyone's attention. Anyone who considered, even remotely, that they were close to the border would turn immediately onto a westerly heading to clear the area. Failure to heed a 'Brass Monkey' if you were the offender led to an interception by QRA and guaranteed unfortunate repercussions.

The routine mission for Battle Flight was to bring wayward light aircraft back into safer airspace. As the air defence controller spotted the pilot drifting towards the border, Battle Flight would be launched. Slow civilian light aircraft were challenging targets that required the Phantom crew to conduct a 'passing VID'. With light aircraft speeds of only 100 knots in the cruise and a minimum speed of 200 to 250 knots for the Phantom, depending on how brave the pilot was feeling, it was impossible to formate on the small aircraft. In fact, the pass could be flown with up to 150 knots overtake. Once intercepted, the QRA pilot would call on the guard frequency for the light aircraft pilot to accompany the QRA aircraft away from the ADIZ. It must have been a dramatic sight for the pilot of a light aircraft, who would already be unsure of his position, to see the bulk of a Phantom pass, at speed, alongside. Western aircraft penetrating the ADIZ caused many scrambles, but border penetrations by Soviet fighters were far more common than one would imagine. Unfortunately, as Wildenrath was about 20 minutes' flying time from the border, any minor incursion of our airspace could not be prevented by QRA. The offending aircraft would invariably return to East Germany before any QRA aircraft could come close to intercepting. RAF Gütersloh, which sat much further east in the North Rhine-Westphalia region, often acted as a forward base for QRA Phantoms during periods of tension or higher activity in East Germany. In the Lightning days, QRA had been held from RAF Gütersloh, giving a much quicker reaction. With the changes in how the Phantom was employed, operating to the rear behind the missile belts, RAF Wildenrath was chosen as the base for the air defence fighters. To make sure that the rapid response could still be employed, QRA aircraft would be deployed forward from Wildenrath under Operation Easy Jet and operate from the old Lightning QRA sheds at Gütersloh, giving a much shorter transit to the Inner German Border.

One of the most famous incursions of the East was the case of the young pilot Mathias Rust, who after an epic flight to Moscow on 28 May 1987, landed his Cessna 172 in Red Square. His visit resulted in an extended stay, enjoying the hospitality of his Soviet hosts, and led to the sacking of a number of high ranking commanders of the Soviet air defence forces. His route took him through Finland and Estonia, so Battle Flight would not have been scrambled as he was outside the area of responsibility.

Some of the more dramatic QRA activity involved military aircraft. There was a bizarre event in the 70s when a Harrier pilot ejected from his aircraft after a birdstrike caused an engine failure. A subsequent account by the pilot of the Harrier established the facts surrounding the event. The force of his ejection cleared the remains of the bird from the engine, which restarted, leaving the pilot watching helplessly as his Harrier climbed away as he descended in his parachute. The Harrier climbed smoothly, reaching 20,000 feet and still transmitting its emergency code on the IFF. The incident had occurred close to the border, so QRA was scrambled in case it proved necessary to shoot the aircraft down should it head eastwards towards East Germany. The Harrier was still innovative technology in those days and no one wished to assist the Soviet Union in developing its own Yak 36 Freehand which was a copy of the Harrier. In the event, a German F104 was sent to intercept and found the unmanned aircraft flying quite normally, albeit pilot-less. The Harrier GR3 version had very short endurance and, shortly afterwards, the aircraft ran out of fuel and crashed harmlessly in an open field in southern Denmark. The Harrier had stayed airborne for a remarkable 38 minutes after the ejection.

The Eastern Bloc went one better in July 1989 when a Soviet MiG-23 was involved in a similar incident. This was widely reported in the media at the time, as unfortunately the aircraft crashed into a house, killing one of the occupants. The pilot experienced engine problems on take-off from the Soviet airbase at Kolobrzeg in Poland. He ejected after losing power on take-off, thinking he had experienced an engine failure, but the engine recovered and the aircraft continued to climb away, heading west. The unmanned aircraft crossed East Germany and West Germany and was intercepted en route over The Netherlands by QRA F15s from the US base at Soesterberg. The F15s were not cleared to engage, so the MiG-23, still heading west, entered Belgian airspace with French QRA now alerted. It finally crashed into a house in Kortrijk, Belgium, having travelled 560 miles. This proved to be one of the last incidents of the Cold War, as the Berlin Wall fell in November 1989 and all the Soviet fighters withdrew to Russia shortly afterwards.

The starkest reminder of the Cold War to most Germans was the Inner German Border that divided the two halves of Germany. Whether it was orientation or indoctrination, all QRA crews were taken to see the border in the area of Helmstedt. No one could have failed to notice the doctrinal divide between the two power blocs laid bare by the slash of the fence through the German countryside. Seeing the fence with the watch towers set less than 1 km apart, the cleared earth strips, claymore mines, and dog runs, left no doubt as to the lengths to which the Soviets would go to keep East and West Germany apart. Nothing could have persuaded a 'Cold War warrior' more convincingly than 'The Wall'. Repairs were obviously needed, and we chanced across a working party repairing a section that had been dismantled. Our guide pointed out that the personnel allocated to the duty were the Pioneer Korps, otherwise known as the '150 percenters'. The repair team worked in pairs and were armed. One would be a single soldier, while the other would be married, which guarded against unexpected bids for freedom. As a final guarantee, another armed soldier of unblemished reputation held guard on the western side of the fence and was also armed. There was little chance of any of this repair detail emigrating to West Germany.

Soviet Command bunkers dotted the landscape, controlling the individual watch towers. Imposing marker posts painted in the red, black, and gold of East Germany were positioned some way to the west of the wall. Surprisingly, these were not the actual border, which was marked by small unassuming concrete

The Inner German Border cuts through the trees behind a West German town.

plinths some way east. To add to the air of menace, the West German Border Force had positioned additional border signs warning of the border to the unwary tourist. Plates 21 to 24 capture the austerity of the border fortifications. The clearest sign of division, however, were the roads to nowhere. Small byways that had formerly linked local villages were suddenly barred by barriers and the fence itself. It was a sombre visit.

I experienced an extremely rare event during one of my first operational scrambles from Battle Flight on 21 January 1980, flying XV434. We were regularly launched to conduct a border patrol of the IGB. On this particular occasion we were vectored towards the northern border in the vicinity of Hamburg. It was a clear blue day and the line of the IGB was very obvious from the air as we turned southerly. The sanitised zone cut a swath through the surrounding countryside, with watch towers and the actual fence clearly visible from 25,000 feet. Even though we were under close radar control and receiving vectors from our ground controller, we were confident that we would not infringe East German airspace. As we ran south on our first pass it became obvious that our TACAN, our radio-based tactical navigation system, was not giving an accurate range and bearing to our selected beacon. Somehow, and mysteriously, the radio beacon at Fassberg appeared to have moved well inside East Germany when in fact Fassberg was some miles west of our position. A navigator's map showing the area around Fassburg is shown in Plate 32. Luckily, we were navigating using visual references otherwise the conflicting information would have been extremely confusing. It was readily apparent that we were being jammed, and we now realised that someone was paying rather more attention to our patrol than we had expected. The first run south and the return leg back towards Hamburg was uneventful, but as we turned south for the second time our radar warning receiver began to chirp away and I quickly assessed the incoming signal which had a vector over to the east. It was a 'Jay Band' signal that showed as a five-dashed line on the radar warning display, and the distinctive scan pattern in the headset told me it was a perfect match to a Soviet fighter. I noticed about the same time that the radio frequency was much noisier than it had been up to that time, so my senses were alert. Our route back south took us very close to a distinctive bulge in the IGB in the Kassel area, which extended well to the west of the line of the border. Maintaining a southerly heading from our position would have taken our aircraft directly over East German territory. As we were receiving radar control we waited for the controller to turn us back westerly to parallel the border, but at the critical point his instructions were blotted out by loud rock music on the frequency. Conscious of the rapidly approaching scar that was the IGB, we turned immediately onto a safe westerly heading and switched to our back-up frequency to re-establish contact with our controller. Luckily, we experienced none of the frustrating difficulties with the Phantom radio and the controller was immediately loud and clear and resumed control. With hindsight, a little lapse in concentration or solid cloud cover, which would have complicated the navigation, could have made our life much more uncomfortable and we might have become an interesting news story. I have no doubt that the bleeps and squawks I was hearing on the radar warning receiver was a reception committee in the form of a MiG fighter just over the border. We were briefed later on the details. The actual systems that were targeted against us were very effective. The Soviet controller had employed electronic countermeasures in co-ordination with his air defence assets to lay a credible trap for an unwary crew. Luckily, due to our training, the ruse had failed, but it was a salutary lesson that the game of 'cat and mouse' played out during the Cold War was real and very dangerous. At best it could have been a diplomatic incident. At worst, we could have been forced to defend ourselves against the opposing fighter or, if we had capitulated, enjoyed an enforced stay courtesy of the Stasi or the KGB. Battle Flight took on a much more sinister feel for the remainder of my time at Wildenrath.

Another incident that caused me to think hard about Cold War politics was during the time when the Warsaw Pact satellite countries began to rebel against their Soviet masters leading to Gorbachev's Glasnost policy. Born in the shipyards of Gdansk, the Solidarity movement was a serious challenge to the communist stranglehold. There was much speculation on whether Polish refugees would confront the border guards and attempt to leave for the West. There was also speculation in military circles as to whether any Polish military aircraft would defect. Up to that point, most QRA crews were clear on how to engage an incoming aircraft if ordered to do so. If that aircraft was attempting to defect, a much more complex scenario would be played out. How would a Polish MiG pilot react if intercepted? Which base should the MiG be taken to? Was it sensible to take the aircraft to a frontline base or were there better options? Would the Soviets try to follow the defector in hot pursuit and try to prevent the escape? If so, that would be a clear breach of West German airspace and could constitute a hostile act. Would QRA crews be ordered to intercept and destroy the Soviet fighters but shepherd the Polish aircraft to a NATO base? There were many questions and equally conflicting answers, even among the experts. QRA crews operated under one very simple fundamental principle: the sovereign right of self-defence. If engaged, a crew could legally respond with equivalent force, which gave the flexibility to respond to an attack at close quarters. For other situations, the crew was invariably under the control of a ground agency with direct communications to the Air Defence Commander. Permission to engage a target would be given by that commander and would be authenticated using codes by the crew. It would have been unlikely to be asked to shoot down another aircraft without first having a period of escalating tensions, allowing crews to adapt to the new scenarios. The real possibility of defection, however, challenged that cosy norm. I sat QRA with many different pilots, so it was not possible to sit down as a crew in advance and agree likely reactions. For that reason, I rehearsed various scenarios in my own mind and had an idea of what I would do under each situation. Whether my conclusions agreed with my colleagues I will never know. Add to that the fact that such a scenario would have demanded a pairs scramble, and the other aircraft was flown by crews from the other squadron. The 19 (Fighter) Squadron crews favoured different tactics and may have seen the situation in an entirely different light. Ultimately, tactical situations rarely panned out as straightforwardly in the air as they did in the sterility of one's own mind. A simple defection would most likely have been predictable, but a 'hot pursuit' scenario was impossible to plan precisely

A Flogger 'Bravo' of the Polish Air Force on display at the Aviation Museum at Newark.

and would have taxed the best crews to the limit. In the event, there was no such defection and the discussion remained within the confines of QRA. Events consigned the Cold War to history, but not before it caused much discussion among the crews holding QRA.

CHAPTER 7
The Phantom in Royal Air Force Germany

Three of the four RAF flying stations in Germany were grouped around the Dutch/German border near Mönchengladbach. During my time in Germany in the early 1980s, the group, which was known as the 'Clutch' airfields, was made up of Wildenrath as the air defence base; Brüggen, which housed the Jaguar bombers; and Laarbruch, with Buccaneers. The exception was RAF Gütersloh, some way further east, which was home to the RAF Germany Harrier Wing.

At the height of the Phantom's service, the command structure was reminiscent of that at the end of the Second World War. RAF Germany had command status and was equivalent in importance to Strike Command in the UK. The Headquarters at RAF Rheindahlen was subordinate to NATO under the Second Allied Tactical Air Force. The feeling among Germany-based crews was that we most definitely reported to the Supreme Allied Commander NATO rather than through our own national chain of command. We were a NATO asset.

RAF Wildenrath fitted into a complex air defence structure. Adjacent to the Inner German Border was the LOMEZ (low level missile engagement zone) provided by the Hawk surface-to-air missiles. Behind that, the longer range Nike Hercules missiles provided the HIMEZ (high level missile engagement zone). The Phantoms supplied a third level of defence in a fighter engagement zone positioned in the rear. With the inherent flexibility of manned aircraft, any gaps in the MEZ could be plugged by fighters. Should all that fail and Soviet bombers penetrated into the rear echelons, a final level was provided by anti-aircraft guns such as the Bofors L70 and air defence missiles such as Rapier which secured the bases by providing short range air defence protection.

The station was set on the edge of a forest near the village of Wassenberg, just a few miles from the Dutch border. Driving down the short stretch of road to the Guard Room, there was no doubt as to why Wildenrath was there. Everything was starkly functional and toned down in a dark green colour. The domestic site, carved from the trees to the north side of the runway, provided all the

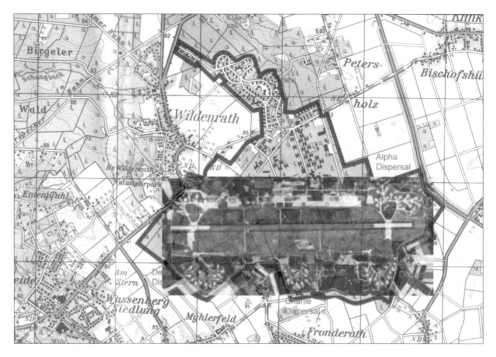

A map of the local area around RAF Wildenrath. Map UK MOD Crown Copyright (1981).

The 92 Squadron Operations Complex on Delta Dispersal.

trappings needed to house the thousands of personnel based at Wildenrath. Even the station's cinema was painted in a low visibility tactical green. This was for real! There were three hardened dispersals grouped along the southern taxiway. Each of the early generation NATO hardened aircraft shelters (HASs) had been built in earlier dispersals that ringed each loop taxiway. A centrally positioned hardened pilots' briefing facility (PBF) housed the main Operations Room for each squadron, and a number of 'soft skinned' buildings acted as peacetime accommodation for the groundcrew.

Both of the main flying units had long histories as fighter squadrons. No. 19 Squadron operated from Bravo Dispersal to the south-eastern corner, with 92 (East India) Squadron operating from Delta Dispersal at the opposite end of the runway. Charlie Dispersal was an identical facility that divided the two but, during the Phantom era, had no resident squadron, although occasionally it acted as a temporary home for squadrons deploying into the area. Ironically, the geographical division of the runway caused a tangible division on the station. The split between the flying community and the administrative personnel was often emphasised by use of the terms 'Northside' and 'Southside' to delineate the communities. It was a constant battle to break down those artificial barriers, but when it came to it, there was no doubt about the aim of the station. A sign at the entrance to RAF Brüggen summed it up: 'The role of this station is to fly and fight. The role of those who don't, is to support those who do' Politically incorrect, probably; harsh, perhaps; questionable, no.

To complete the picture, a surface-to-air missile squadron operated from the northern side. No. 25 Squadron, equipped with Bloodhound missiles, was housed in Alpha Dispersal close to the eastern threshold of Runway 27. The squat surface-to-air missiles were located within the confines of the dispersal and invariably pointed east, giving no doubt as to where the threat lay. The Rapier Wing had its headquarters in a large hangar close to the main flight line, but its normal posture was to deploy forward into the local areas around the RAF airfields and provide a base defence zone when needed. Rapier units comprised a number of fire units that operated the actual missiles. These fire units would deploy in a ring around the airfield some distance outside the perimeter and engage incoming aircraft before they could attack the airfield. In broad terms, the Bloodhounds provided forward area coverage within the HIMEZ whereas the Rapiers were the backstop.

RAF Germany was at the forefront of introducing hardened aircraft shelter operations to the Royal Air Force. Since the 1970s, and well before HAS operations began in the UK, the 'Clutch' airfields had been protected. The UK adopted the NATO standard semicircular HASs, but the original design in Germany was of the older trapezoidal style. Clamshell doors at the front were

25 Sqn Bloodhound Missiles on Alpha Dispersal.

secured with an enormous rotating bar. Once unlatched, they moved remarkable easily considering the weight of the doors, and it was only the resounding clang as they hit the end stops which showed just how heavy they were. Two smaller sliding doors to the rear allowed jet efflux to escape when the engines were running. Although two aircraft could physically fit into a HAS, the wings had to be folded, so it was impossible to operate in that way as the RAF had removed the in-cockpit wing fold controls. For a ten-aircraft squadron there were sufficient HASs to take all the squadron aircraft, so each aeroplane operated from its own shelter. Each HAS was equipped with a winch system that literally pulled the aircraft back under cover, but a tractor could be hooked up to the nosewheel to push the aircraft into its parking slot if needed.

Within the HAS, a small cabin gave the groundcrew a quieter and slightly more comfortable working area. Designed as a refuge to complete the engineering paperwork, it offered a small space for a few seats but no luxuries. After the pushback, the groundcrew would go to work, replenishing fluids, checking pressures, and doing the routine maintenance that kept the sometimes temperamental aircraft flying. Often these turnrounds were completed in full chemical warfare gear, and the groundcrew routinely performed operational turnrounds in 15 to 20 minutes during exercises. Spare external fuel tanks sat on racks at the opposite wall and would be joined by weapons trolleys loaded with missiles during an alert. A small hardened concrete annexe attached to the shelter housed the external power set and although the 'Houchin' could be run inside the HAS, the engine exhaust quickly made the atmosphere unbearable. It was also extremely noisy, so the power set was often relegated to the annexe for comfort. During exercises, air and groundcrew lived in the HAS during the flying day and returned to the PBF only at the end of the shift. Once allocated an aircraft, you stuck with it, assuming it stayed serviceable.

Exercises could be tedious if the flying was scant, so everyone hoped for a swift turnround and an immediate scramble. For the aircrew, the best place to be during an exercise was away from the airfield, preferably in a low flying area. For the groundcrew, once the aircraft taxied, they could relax for an hour before the next turnround. Apart from the flying, the highlight of the day was undoubtedly the delivery of lunch or dinner. The station Messes, normally the Airmens' Mess, delivered meals in large insulated boxes known as hotlocks. Hardly gourmet but the food invariably tasted absolutely marvellous. It was uncanny how often the delivery of a meal coincided with either a simulated air raid or a scramble message. Crews were allowed four sorties in a flying day, and only when they were completed could they return to the PBF.

It was a wonderful contrast moving to RAF Germany from the UK. Exercises in Britain in the late 1970s still had a whiff of the Battle of Britain. Crews would operate from the crewroom and the aircraft would be lined up neatly on the ramp. It was as if we were willing an enemy to destroy the neat lines of Phantoms in one pass. Ostensibly, this was due to a shortage of groundcrew, meaning that dispersed operations around the airfield were difficult to support. In reality, it was a naïvety which the hardened environment changed for ever. The overriding memory on entering the dispersal at Wildenrath for the first time was its bleak appearance. On a typical dark, overcast, and often wet day in north-west Germany, it had a melancholy air. Ringed by the toned down concrete structures and grass covered revetments, barbed-wire prevented unwanted visitors from entering. Even on a normal day, most of the routine activity now went on behind concrete walls. When locked down during a simulated air raid, people were noticeably absent. The whole atmosphere was more serious and focused.

At the height of the Cold War, exercises were a regular feature and the station 'hooter' sounded frequently. Once a recall began, all the service personnel moved quickly onto base and, for collective security, lived and slept there for the duration of the exercise. One of the unanswered questions concerned what would happen to the families in the event of a real escalation of tensions. The presumption was that they would be evacuated back to the UK, but it was a procedure that was never tested and would have caused serious concern amongst service members as the tension mounted. Add to that the number of refugees who would inevitably have flooded west away from the battlefield, and the reality would have been much more complex than the exercise scenarios.

The exercise cycle was directed totally towards the principal event, which was the annual NATO Tactical Evaluation (TACEVAL). To make sure that we achieved the best results, Squadron Commanders began the cycle by arranging small-scale flying exercises. One of these was known as 'Guest Flint' and pitched the Jaguars of Brüggen against the Phantoms of Wildenrath. The flying was intense because how the aircrew performed in their flying roles was the aspect that interested the Squadron Commanders the most. The Squadron Commander had to ensure that the squadrons were effective when airborne whereas the Station Commander would organise exercises to train the wider station personnel. For Wildenrath this exercise was known, fittingly, by the prefix 'Wild'. For example, Exercise 'Wildman' concentrated on making sure the wider elements of the complex station support chain were effective and could keep the Phantoms in the air. Not wishing to be outdone, HQ RAF Germany organised a yet larger event known as MAXEVAL, which brought in the broader command structure and exercised command and control procedures. Only when the cycle had turned full circle would TACEVAL occur, which was the benchmark against which all the other exercises were set. A two-part event, Part 1 was a no-notice generation exercise which checked that serviceable, armed aircraft could be produced within strict time constraints. The 'hooter' would sound, invariably in the wee small hours, and personnel would make their way as rapidly as possible onto base. Personnel lived all around the local area, so pulling them in could take some hours. A complex call-out plan would begin, and everyone was contacted individually by phone if they were too distant to hear the 'hooter'. Even people on leave were expected to turn out, and the regularity of the exercise cycle caused more than a few sharp words among the families who would be woken at all hours as their spouses scrabbled for their exercise kit. In the local area, the call-out was redundant as the low drone of the siren could be heard for miles.

Immediately on arrival at the squadron, the engineers would begin to prepare and arm as many aircraft as possible, and there were strict targets to meet. On a normal day, having less than 50 per cent of the declared squadron strength available to fly was not unusual. One of those was always sitting alert on Battle Flight, so of the ten or twelve aircraft on a normal squadron, maybe only four or five were available to support the flying programme. Lack of spares is not a new phenomenon; they were always in short supply. A limited stock was held forward at Wildenrath, but replacement parts frequently had to be sent out from the UK. Quite often, one aircraft would be nominated as a 'Christmas tree' and spares would be robbed to keep other jets flying. NATO accepted that 100 per cent availability was an impossible target and set the requirements somewhat lower. Despite this, it did not stop the Squadron Commander and Senior Engineering Officer trying for that elusive goal of 100 per cent declared available before 'Endex' was called. Once serviceable, the engineers would fit Sparrows, Sidewinders and load the gun with high explosive ammunition. The crew would accept the aircraft, run the systems, and declare it 'On state'. Once the station had met its target, the exercise would be terminated and the TACEVAL team would retire to draft their report, identifying any strengths and weaknesses.

Part 2 was the flying phase, was pre-planned, and was the focus of the operational year. The huge NATO evaluation team would arrive on site, and as the exercise evolved would begin dissecting the way the station operated. All the elements that made the station tick would be evaluated, from the youngest chef in the kitchens to the Station Commander and his executives. Most exercises followed a fairly standard script. Often, within minutes of the exercise start, a major event would be scripted. On one occasion, a US Phantom was conscripted to act as a defecting Soviet fighter. The plan was to land and shut down on the runway with the crew muttering unintelligible words in Russian. This would check the effectiveness of the Station Defector Contingency Plan by making sure the 'defection' was suitably handled. Unfortunately, no plan survives first contact, and the aircraft, on landing, suffered a nosewheel steering problem and left the side of the runway at slow speed before becoming firmly embedded in the grass. In the event, a new, albeit unplanned, incident was unexpectedly evaluated. The simulated defector became an actual aircraft recovery operation. In the air, missions progressed from the early, low key intervention sorties into intensive flying operations, but always ended with a short, simulated nuclear exchange requiring personnel to operate in chemical protective gear. Other bases would be tasked to act as airborne targets for the Phantoms and would conduct air attacks on the airbase for the benefit of the surface-to-air missile units and ground defence commanders. After simulated air attacks, the ground defence teams would evaluate the simulated damage and prepare contingencies. Personnel would practise operating under the threat of unexploded ordnance or with facilities degraded. Generally, RAF Wildenrath enjoyed a good deal of success on TACEVAL. Units being evaluated were rated on a scale of 1 to 4, with 3 being a marginal rating and 4 being a failure. Despite deficiencies in equipment standards through lack of defence funding, when rated on performance Wildenrath regularly earned the coveted 1 or above-average rating.

Squadron exercises were by far the most enjoyable, as the focus was entirely on the flying. Exercise 'Guest Flint' involved a full week of flying against the Jaguars from Brüggen. Combat air patrols, or CAPs, were established in each of the low flying areas, and multiple four-ship and six-ship bomber formations penetrated the areas during two daily waves. This provided some outstandingly realistic training against large formations that, even in Germany, were not a regular feature. The Jaguar route was constrained to ensure that the opposing formations met in each CAP area. Attacking and defending aircraft engaged in air combat, leading to simulated kills on both sides. Aircrew and aircraft from other Allied nations were invited to join in, not only to operate mixed CAPs with the Wildenrath Phantoms but also to escort the bomber formations. You could never guarantee that you would not need to operate with a wingman from another nation, so much effort went into interoperability training with our friends and allies. A Phantom could take a less capable non-radar-equipped aircraft such as the F5 into an engagement using its pulse Doppler radar and could benefit from having the more agile fighter alongside at the merge. Determining the best tactics when operating with mixed types was always the key to success. The exercise was challenging and culminated in a mass launch of the Brüggen Wing. Each Jaguar squadron generated the maximum number of aircraft and nearly forty Jaguars in a single formation attacked a target on Nordhorn Range, having pushed through the fighter boxes en masse.

Although the scene in the CAP areas seemed like an extract from a Third World War movie, reputations were at stake. RAF Wildenrath had positioned a piano on the Nordhorn Range and each Jaguar pilot had a single practice bomb with the goal of destroying the piano. Such a small target was extremely difficult to hit, but, ironically, the last Jaguar, on the last attack of the last day, managed to put his bomb directly through the target. Sadly, this was one up to the Brüggen Wing. That night, in fine style, the squadrons from Brüggen arrived at Wildenrath on a train that navigated the rarely used railway line between the stations. An epic 'happy hour' in the Officers' Mess culminated in the loss of another piano, this time to a simple box of matches. Piano burning was an old Air Force tradition that had its roots in the earliest days of the service. During the wartime years, it was a stress burner in the literal sense. It was essential, however, to ensure that a 'burner' and not a 'player' was selected. Many a squadron received a large bill on a Monday morning when the Station Commander's treasured musical instrument was mistakenly selected. That night, the correct piano's demise was celebrated in true style with renditions of the squadron songs.

One of the most chilling aspects of the Cold War was the constant threat of chemical warfare. It was widely expected that the Soviets would resort to the use of chemical and, probably, nuclear weapons. Their doctrine referred constantly to such munitions, so the Allies were forced to train wearing NBC kit. The nuclear, biological, and chemical individual protective equipment, to use its more formal title, was worn over normal underwear and comprised a smock, trousers, and bootees made of a charcoal impregnated material. A gas mask topped off by a hood and combat helmet was complemented by rubber

Above: A mixed formation of 92 and 56 Squadron Phantoms over Germany.

Right: A pilot wearing the AR5 and carrying the 'whistling handbag'. UK MOD Crown Copyright (1979).

overboots and neoprene gloves. Although undoubtedly effective at protecting the individual, in use the equipment was uncomfortable and hot. When wearing gas masks, communication was almost impossible. As an example, one devious evaluator rang the crew chief in a HAS and asked a question in a garbled voice. After a few attempts the crew chief gave up and removed his mask in order to hear the voice clearly. 'You're dead,' was the response, proving that short cuts were never a good idea. Just by threatening the use of nuclear, biological, and chemical weapons, the Soviets gained a firm advantage in the 'tit for tat' game by making even simple tasks difficult.

One of the most sinister items of equipment ever developed was the Aircrew Respirator Mark 5, more commonly known as the AR5. Normal military nuclear, biological, and chemical protective equipment was not compatible with aircrew flying clothing, so the boffins designed specialist equipment. The smock and trousers were replaced by a single-piece undersuit that looked similar to a flying suit but was made of carbon impregnated fabric. This was worn under a normal flying suit. The AR5 replaced the gas mask and was adapted from the aircrew oxygen mask but 'with attitude'. It was a single-piece rubber hood with a heavy rubber cowl and neck seal that was worn over the inner suit. The aircrew oxygen mask, topped by an integral transparent visor, was incorporated into the rubber hood. The contraption was pulled over the head and the normal flying helmet worn over the top, connected to the oxygen, the radio, and the mask in the normal way. Once the AR5 had been donned, a portable respirator known colloquially as the 'Whistling Handbag' provided breathing air until you were strapped safely into the aircraft and had transferred to the aircraft's oxygen system. While undoubtedly effective, flying in the equipment was a nightmare. Wearing a rubber layer under the normal helmet was claustrophobic and excruciatingly hot. Add to that the normal gyrations of a Phantom in combat and the discomfort was magnified. Many crews found the experience terrifying, and, for training sorties, pilots were only allowed to fly with a safety pilot in the back seat. That the AR5 picked up a somewhat gruesome nickname was inevitable. The 'Cambridge Rapist Kit' was not politically correct but summed up the sinister look to a tee. Its death knell was sounded during the Gulf War in the early 1990s. With the threat of chemical attack, aircrews were ordered into AR5s. In the high temperatures of the desert it was instantly apparent that the AR5 was a bigger threat to flight safety than a chemical weapon, and it was realised that survival may have been shortened rather than lengthened by wearing the equipment. Not only was the equipment difficult to wear but decontamination procedures were a nightmare. There were areas of the PBF set aside for decontamination. The only thing that was proven to soak up chemical agents was a compound known as fuller's earth, which looked like talcum powder. As the aircrew returned from a sortie, flying equipment and NBC equipment were slowly peeled off through the various decontamination rooms while dusting liberally with the fine powder. A pinhead-sized drop of chemical agent could kill, so the procedure was rigorous and time-consuming. Although crews were thoroughly tired by the time they retired to the cramped bunk beds in the PBF, at least they could sleep in the knowledge that their complexions had been seriously enhanced! The lasting marks from an exercise were the charcoal stains from the NBC suit. It took some days before they could be removed by rigorous scrubbing in the shower.

Chemical warfare aside, a typical sortie in RAF Germany involved intercepting other tactical aircraft operating at low level in the low flying areas. Low flying was essential. Ranged against attacking bombers, the Soviets had a vast array of extremely capable surface-to-air missiles. Engaging a low level attacker, the threat systems faced a huge challenge. Terrain masking could be employed, meaning that by routeing carefully and keeping higher ground between you and the SAM, it would be impossible for the threat to track and engage. Additionally, the missiles had a minimum height below which they were ineffective. Normally this was because the fusing systems were ineffective against very low flying targets, so by flying at low level survival chances increased markedly. A feature of recent conflicts has been the proliferation of portable missile systems or MANPADS. These shoulder-launched threats were largely discounted during the Cold War but their capabilities have since been improved. They may have featured much more prominently had a conflict ever arisen. The Soviet Army embedded MANPADS operators within the combat units, so crews would have faced many of these weapons, such as the SA-7, as they crossed the battlefield. The Soviets were also expected to attack at low level, although the intelligence experts assessed that they would not be able to operate as low as their NATO opponents. Wherever they had chosen to attack, at least the flying training would have been more than adequate to ensure NATO was prepared to meet the challenge.

Low Flying Area 2 in the Münster area was reasonably flat with very few obstructions, allowing good tactical freedom to engage targets. Low Flying Area 3 was well to the east of Wildenrath, but the countryside was much more rolling and hilly. This helped intruding pilots as they could use terrain masking to make the fighters' job much more difficult. One irrefutable fact is that radar cannot see through rocks. Hiding behind a hill, the bomber was safe from interception. The eastern end of the area extended under the Buffer Zone which acted just as its name suggested. The Buffer Zone sat 30 miles to the west of the Air Defence Interception Zone, or ADIZ, and provided a geographical buffer preventing aircrew from inadvertently penetrating the ADIZ. Operating in this area, navigation had to be much more precise, as fighter crews who normally held QRA would have received little sympathy for penetrating the zone and generating a Battle Flight scramble. For that reason, most high intense sorties were planned further west. Low Flying Area 1 was well to the north and although it was a good operating area, the transit to the area took some time. Low Flying Area 5 was to the south of Wildenrath in the stunningly pretty Eifel region, but it was generally quiet as there were few regular military users and, without opponents, training value was limited. For that reason, the area was used only if the weather was poor in northern Germany. However, it was the most popular CAP of all. The CAP datum was over the small village of Gerolstein, but the outbound leg passed over the pit complex of the Nürburgring, and cars and jets were always a great combination. It was also possible to operate with, and against, the Belgians in the Ardennes Low Flying Area, which was the final area that was used regularly. Again this was stunningly beautiful and caused many a pang of conscience, breaking the tranquil calm with our Rolls-Royce Spey engines running at maximum power.

Part of the often recounted folklore concerned a pilot recently arrived at RAF Brüggen shortly after the arrival of the Jaguar in theatre. One of the best navigation features in northern Germany was a large power station sitting in the gap between Hopsten and Münster airfields known as 'Smokey Joe's'. It was a natural choke point between the airfield control zones, so most traffic routeing between low flying areas 1 and 2 passed overhead 'Smokeys'. After a failure of his NAVWASS navigation system, the pilot reported a minor emergency and that he was holding near a large power station. Immediately, every aircraft operating within 50 miles of 'Smokeys' homed in on his position to give 'navigational assistance'. I'm sure that the implications in the cockpit were far more serious than the loss of navigation information, but aircrew never allow facts to get in the way of a good story.

The variety of aircraft operating in Germany during the Cold War was immense. Types ranged from US Phantoms and F15s, German, Belgian and Dutch F104s, Dutch F5s to German Phantoms, and Fiat G91s. RAF Wildenrath nominated Radar Combat Air Patrols (RCAPs) in each low flying area. Normally, a pair of Phantoms would depart from Wildenrath and fly to a low flying area at low level. Outside the LFAs this meant flying at 500 feet, dropping to 250 feet once inside the area. Many of the transit routes were tightly ringed by controlled airspace, so precise navigation was the order of the day. In the Phantom, surprisingly, the pilot navigated to the routine CAP areas, leaving the navigator to carry out a radar search looking for target aircraft, or 'trade' as they were known. Although the turning points could be obscure, such as a Nike missile site, there were few options in order to negotiate the congested airspace, so the routes were standard and became second nature. Once in the low flying area, the game was on. Standard operating procedures allowed any aircraft operating there to be intercepted. Light aircraft remained above 1,500 feet but below 5,000 feet, so were safe from interference. NATO fighters would avoid that band of airspace, but anyone below that height was fair game. The rules were simple. If the intercepted pilot was not cleared to evade, say for example if he was under training, a simple waggle of the wings would indicate that he had seen the attacker but would not react. If the target reacted, operational crews could prosecute the attack up to pre-briefed evasion limits. The training value was exceptional because target tactics were varied and unpredictable. Equally, the bomber pilots benefited because they were under threat of attack from fighters throughout their route and had to balance the need to be 'on track, on time' with the need to negate an air-to-air attack. In operating this way, every sortie was as realistic as possible and emulated what was expected if a real conflict had arisen.

I remember one particular intercept that demonstrated the unpredictability. We had been planned to fly a standard sortie in Low Flying Area 2, north-east of Wildenrath. The standard CAP was at the south-western end of the area over the Reken mast. We had been on CAP for a few minutes when I picked up a formation on the radar and we vectored towards the contacts. As we approached the merge, a pair of Buccaneers passed down the side of the formation. The Buccaneer Force had been grounded after an outer wing panel had detached at the fold point and a crew had been lost when the aircraft crashed. A long engineering modification programme had been initiated, and the first jets were only just being re-cleared to fly. As a temporary measure, the Buccaneer squadrons had been given two-seat Hunters to keep the squadron aircrew current. For that reason we were surprised to see two Buccaneers in battle formation; this must have been one of the first occasions for some time when a pair had flown. As we were about to commit onto the Buccaneers, I realised that there were more targets in a trailing formation. If we turned in behind the lead Buccaneers we would roll out in front of the trailers, leaving ourselves vulnerable to a missile shot. We extended to engage the trailing formation and leave the Buccaneers unmolested. I quickly locked up the trailers on radar and we fired a head-on Sparrow into the mêlée. My pilot called a visual contact and began to press an attack on the other trailer, which proved to be a Hunter. The Hunter was much more agile than the Phantom, and the second aircraft quickly negated the attack by turning towards us and passing close aboard. We entered a turning fight trying to nibble away at the Hunter who was rapidly making ground on us. The rules allowed us to complete two full 360-degree turns before the engagement had to be terminated, but it was becoming hard to decide who

XV500 fitted carrying a centreline tank flying over the North German Plain.

was the attacker and who was the defender as the tables slowly turned on us. Although a type of stalemate continued, the original pair of Buccaneers, not wishing to be left out, had returned and flashed back through the fight. The Buccaneer was an outstanding low level aircraft but, like the Phantom, was no turning machine. It could, however, also carry Sidewinders as self-protection, so by returning not only were we losing out to the agile Hunter but we were now also outnumbered. A rapid disengagement was the only way out of a potentially embarrassing situation.

At that moment the radio burst into life with a call from the Hopsten air traffic controller on the guard frequency asking the formation leader of the formation in the Hopsten Zone to contact him on his approach frequency. That could only be us, so we rapidly waggled the wings, which was the signal to all players to terminate the engagement, and with trepidation transferred to Hopsten's frequency. Infringing a military air traffic zone without clearance was a violation and could cause problems. The normal convention was that in the event of mistakes, a call on the operating frequency would normally placate the controller provided no traffic had been compromised. A quick check showed that we had indeed just drifted into their airspace as the turning fight had drifted north, but in the heat of the engagement we had been unaware and

A guns kill on a Tornado captured on the gunsight camera of an F4F in which I was flying as an evaluator.

the normal courtesy had not been exercised. Extremely apologetic, the lead pilot made various excuses about navigation errors and attempted to extract us from the mire. After a few moments, and with untypical Germanic humour, the controller said quite chirpily, 'Mike Lima 66, Hopsten, this is OK, clear to return to operating frequency and, by the way, did you win?' He had watched the engagement develop on his radar and, like a good policeman, was merely making the point to the over-enthusiastic crews.

Perhaps the strangest intercept I recall was also in Low Flying Area 2. Having found a slow speed target on the radar we prosecuted a very gentle stern approach. The target was at about 1,500 feet, so technically in the low flying area. As we gained visual contact it seemed as if there were two aircraft, yet they were flying in a strange formation. It was obvious that we were closing fast, so my pilot gave the formation a wide berth as we tried to identify the bizarre formation. It proved to be a helicopter carrying an underslung load, but not a typical load. Hanging from a strop was a VAK 191B, which was the German equivalent of the Harrier. Although never operationally deployed, apparently the aircraft was being moved to its new home in a museum by the quickest method available.

Although we expected the Soviet hordes to attack at low level, we still had to keep our skills current in other areas. Most of the medium and high level profiles were flown at night in Belgian or Dutch airspace. European airspace is extremely crowded and, in rather Teutonic fashion, the German GCI sites would allow intercepts only where the fighter and target were at fixed heights, often separated by as little as 2,000 feet. This gave little training value, so we operated in Belgian airspace where the controllers were more flexible. Tactical profiles could be run at all heights and speeds, and even supersonic intercepts were allowed provided the target was above 36,000 feet.

Intercepts often concluded in a visual identification (VID) profile, of which there were a number of types. A Phase 1 VID was flown during daylight; Phase 2 at night, but with the aircraft lights on; Phase 3 at night, but the target's lights were turned off, and so on. Probably the most frightening identification profile was practised overland at night in Germany. The Phase 6 VID was against a target flying at low level, overland, at night, with all external lights extinguished. The minimum height at night was 1,500 feet above ground level. The target aircraft would set up about 40 miles from the fighter and start the run in. The fighter, descending from 5,000 feet, would carry out a stern approach before closing in to conduct an identification profile. With the target's lights extinguished, we relied on the ambient background light from villages and industrial sites to provide a little illumination. It was an alarming experience closing in to 300 yards, only a few feet above another Phantom flying at high speed at low level. Invariably, the aircraft was invisible until extremely short range and it was often the 'black hole' it cast against the ambient light that gave its presence away. Even then, the insanity was not over as the ultimate goal was to move into close formation to allow the target to be identified. Once the pilot had picked out the vague shape, he would ease in gently until sitting on the wing of the target. Funnily enough, few pictures were ever taken during this mission as we were not equipped with low light cameras. At that time, compact night vision goggles, which are now commonly used by military pilots, had not yet been issued and on Battle Flight we struggled with a first generation image intensifier known as a CU19. With its heavy body and a lens with a diameter of about 12 inches, the thought of pulling it from its housing and training it on a target speeding across the North German Plain at low level at night while the pilot eased into close formation was truly chilling.

The reality of operating low level overland was that the weather was invariably marginal. Visual Flight Rules (VFR) set out the weather minima but if crews were to be able to engage any aircraft that might push through at low level, the limits had to be pushed to the maximum and beyond. By training in the poor weather we knew we would always be prepared. The poor conditions in which we operated daily were jokingly called 'Brit VFR' by the pilots of other nations.

I recall a visit by the Mirage F1s from the French airbase at Cambrai. Exercise 'Contact Uniform' was a cross-servicing exercise. Phantom crews would visit

French bases and the Mirage pilots would make return visits. Medium level intercepts were routinely scheduled, but on one occasion the Mirage F1s landed back at Wildenrath for an additional sortie before returning home. As we had already achieved the original aim, it was decided to finish with a low level intercept sortie with the Phantoms opposing the Mirages. The weather to the north was not flyable, with extremely poor visibility and low cloud. The weather in the Eifel was forecast to be clear, but the edge of the poor weather lay just to the south of Wildenrath near the NATO base at Geilenkirchen. The low level departure route threaded its way between Geilenkirchen and the F104 base at Nörvenich and included a few navigation turns to avoid their controlled airspace. We decided that although the initial transit south would be difficult, we would pop out into a nice blue day quite quickly. As we departed from the circuit the visibility was, as expected, poor, so the lead pilot called the Mirages into loose arrow formation which would allow the French pilots to maintain visual contact but the formation could still manoeuvre easily. We expected to pop out into the

56 Squadron Phantoms formate with Mirage F1s of the Cambrai Wing.

blue conditions at any time; the Met Man had promised! As we headed south conditions remained very murky and there were a few mutterings in French on the radio, which suggested that the pilots were not used to operating in 'Brit VFR'. Around 20 miles south of Wildenrath the standard route took a dogleg to the east to avoid a bombing range, and by now the Mirage pilots were hanging in tight. As we turned back south with a Mirage on the wing of each Phantom, I picked up contacts on the radar which were close in range and called them to the formation. Sure enough, within a minute, a formation of British Jaguars passed close aboard, heading north. Whether it was a translation issue, a lack of familiarity with the environment, or the surprise at seeing other aircraft in the murk, at that moment the Mirages pulled up amid various French expletives on the radio, and returned home. Such conditions were typical, and to be able to counter the threat from the Warsaw Pact it was essential to practice in order to cope. It became clear that some nations did, and some did not train to fly and fight in the poor weather that characterised the North German Plain.

It was after a Wildenrath generation exercise on 25 May 1982 when the crew of one of 92 (East India) Squadron's aircraft, XV422, gained infamy after shooting down a Jaguar from RAF Brüggen. It was the first time since the Second World War that a friendly aircraft had accidentally been engaged by our own forces, and the crew members were personal friends. The aircraft in question was 92 (East India) Squadron's 'Oscar', and it served on the squadron for many years. I pictured the aircraft in close formation, shown in Plate 29, during a detachment in Cyprus shortly before the incident. I also flew the aircraft on 17 May 1982 just days before, ironically on a sortie against the Jaguars from RAF Brüggen in Low Flying Area 3. The station had just completed a generation exercise. As was usual, the aircraft had been loaded with live weapons and the crew accepted the aircraft and checked in with the Wing Operations Centre. The norm was to be stood down once the aircraft had been declared, to allow the aircraft to be downloaded before being tasked to fly a subsequent training mission. On this occasion, however, the Station Commander elected to launch the sortie fully armed as he was entitled to do. XV422 and its crew were scrambled immediately into the low flying area to conduct opportunity intercepts. The visual departure from Wildenrath was complex and threaded past a number of areas of controlled airspace around the city of Cologne and the RAF airfield at Laarbruch. On approaching the River Rhine, the airspace became less congested and the rules allowed aircraft to operate at 250 feet above ground level. The navigation feature at the entry to the low flying area was an industrial building known as the POL, which sat on the banks of the Rhine, and flying overhead this feature you would enter the area in clear airspace. On training sorties, weapons switches were made 'live' at the Rhine and the 'game was on'. Other tactical aircraft would be intercepted for training purposes and they would react defensively for the same reason. On recovery, crews could return at low level, but the POL was the point at which aircraft pulled up from low level, contacting Clutch Radar if they wanted a radar service for recovery to their home base. It was that point in the mission where the rules changed. In the area, tactical aircraft were fair game, but at the POL, the fight was over and aircraft could recover unmolested.

The crew of XV422 crossed the Rhine, armed the weapon system, and contacted the control agency. From that point, the chain of events that would lead to the loss of a Jaguar was irrevocably set. As the crew entered the area they almost immediately picked up a target on the radar and began the intercept. To avoid alerting the target's radar warning receiver, they did not lock the radar to the target, so the option of using a Sparrow missile in the front sector was lost. Committed to a Sidewinder attack, they turned in behind the target and the pilot identified the Jaguar, which for exercise purposes had been designated as a 'hostile', simulating Soviet attackers. The Jaguar, XX963, was one of a pair returning from a training mission and was just approaching the pull-up point for recovery. Although the Jaguar pilots spotted the Phantom ahead of them, at that time they would have been looking into their cockpits to change radio frequencies and set codes on their IFF systems, their sortie nearly over, and already thinking about the recovery procedures rather than tactics. As the Phantom pulled hard towards the ill-fated Jaguar, the pilot positioned the pipper in the gunsight onto the target as it began to climb. The Phantom pilot heard the growl of the Sidewinder in his headset, a noise he had heard so many times before on other training missions, and pulled the trigger. With the Phantom below the Jaguar and the pilot faced with a look-up shot that was improving all the time, the missile had few challenges. It struck the Jaguar and the warhead ripped into the fuselage. The pilot of the other Jaguar suddenly realised that his leader's aircraft was on fire. He made an urgent radio call, given that time was precious in such situations. With most fast jets, a fire that was visible externally was almost certainly catastrophic and could occur because of uncontained engine failures or fuel leaks. The risk of explosion was real. Realising something drastic had occurred but not appreciating the full implications, and faced with a bank of emergency captions, the Jaguar pilot knew his aircraft was lost, and ejected. His ejection sequence, thankfully, was perfect and he landed safely in the German countryside and was picked up by a search and rescue helicopter.

Had a Sparrow missile been launched, it would have been possible to turn off the continuous wave radar to leave the missile unguided so that it would have missed the target. Sadly, once launched, the Sidewinder guides on the heat of the jet exhaust or hot tail pipes and tracks its target autonomously. This is a great feature in combat conditions but on this occasion proved terminal for the Jaguar.

In the event, the combat capability of the Phantom had been proven, although, sadly, against one of its own.

There is always some humour to be found in even the darkest of incidents and I remember a few anecdotes related to the accident. I have no doubt, that in true aircrew fashion, they have been embellished over the years. When the pilot reported the engagement to his fighter controller, he was immediately given vectors to further targets flying through the low flying area. The controller, like the crew, was merely following his usual exercise procedures and was anxious for more simulated kills. It took some minutes to make the controller realise that the engagement had been real and that rather than more targets, search and rescue operations were the order of the day. A German pilot who was flying through the area and had witnessed the accident was called to testify at the subsequent court martial. When asked to explain his reaction, he is reported to have said to his wingman, 'Holy ****, the Brits are playing it for real today; we go home!'

The engagement has often been irreverently described as the first kill of the Falklands Campaign which began a short time afterwards. The subsequent inquiry identified many deficiencies in the Phantom design. In order to fire a weapon, the pilot selected his weapon of choice on the missile panel, selected the 'Master Arm' switch to 'live', and fired. The lack of a trigger guard or safety pin meant that, for safety reasons, the navigator pulled the B6 circuit breaker in the rear cockpit, disabling the firing circuit. This circuit breaker was reset only if it was decided that a weapon was really needed, giving two-man consent to use of weapons. Bizarrely, and with hindsight, the only additional safety break was the fitment of a piece of 'bodge tape' around the 'Master Arm' switch. This was the visual clue in the cockpit that the aircraft was armed. For some reason, on that infamous day, the tape had been forgotten, so in every other sense the aircraft, although feeling heavier due to the extra weight of the missiles, showed almost the same indications as if a training load was fitted. To the pilot, he was looking at his displays showing almost exactly the same indications as on every sortie he had flown in the recent past. 'Why?' one could ask. It was important to train as accurately as possible. 'You fight like you train' was the adage drummed into RAF aircrew. We live using motor neurone patterns. These little routines allow us to go through simple actions such as brushing our teeth without thought. In a fast-moving cockpit environment, it is important that aircrew adopt correct routines if they are to be effective. For that reason, training routines have to be as close to the real thing as possible. The inquiry focused on whether the circuit breaker had been pulled as required by normal procedure. The navigator was able to prove that it was possible to reset the circuit breaker by applying pressure with the 'Noddy Guide' which was carried in the lower pocket of the flying suit routinely on exercises. A simple 'fail safe' had been negated.

The court martial placed enormous stress on the crew and their families, but was also felt keenly by the other members of the squadron. It is very easy to blame the crew and to say that such accidents should never occur. With the enormous responsibility that accompanies being in charge of a combat aircraft, and with such severe consequences, this is hard to argue against, but the crew did as they were trained. Aircraft fly armed as a matter of routine; indeed on QRA, live armed aircraft are the norm. Operating with live weapons in the Falkland Islands was an everyday event. In an office environment, mistakes can be worrying or expensive but are rarely fatal. With armed aircraft, actions are far more costly. The crew followed procedures but, self-evidently, mistakes were made, and thankfully the Jaguar pilot escaped unharmed, albeit an expensive aeroplane was lost.

Modern aircraft are now much better designed to ensure that a number of selections need to be made before the weapon system is fully armed. I believe the days of 'bodge tape' around the 'Master Arm' switch are long gone. Many times over the years I have asked myself the question, 'Could it have happened to me?' I would like to say a categorical 'No', but there will always be that nagging doubt, and I have a great deal of sympathy for the crew and, of course, for the Jaguar pilot. XV422 saw out the rest of its time as a gate guardian at RAF Stornoway in the Outer Hebrides, still adorned with a piece of nose art titled *Jaguar Killer*. This might not have been the best way to prove the Phantom's combat capability, but it undoubtedly showed that had the aircraft been called to do its job, it would have performed as demanded.

In 1980, RAF Wildenrath was featured in the respected BBC documentary series *Man Alive* when the reporter Jack Pizzey spent some time on the station with a BBC camera crew collecting material for the programme. The script followed a fictional war from initial alert, through the generation of aircraft, into flying sequences to the inevitable simulated nuclear exchange with the Warsaw Pact. As with any TV programme, there were scenes capturing operations around the station, and personnel were interviewed going about their business. Despite this, to capture the public imagination, some innovative camerawork was needed to record the action in the air, and the film crew made some interesting requests.

A Gazelle helicopter was co-opted to fly down the runway to capture the take-off roll as the Phantoms launched on their missions. The hugely dramatic shots, in the imposing gloom of a German winter day, of Phantoms disappearing into the mist captured the feel of operations exactly. Fundamental to communicating the feeling of flying and operating at low level in Germany was to capture some air-to-air sequences from the cockpit. Video equipment for the amateur was in its infancy and professional video cameras were huge by modern standards.

Using these monsters in the cramped confines of a Phantom cockpit was difficult, even for seasoned navigators used to the environment. To ask a cameraman or a reporter to capture good footage was taxing in the extreme, but the challenge was set. A few squadron navigators were co-opted as honorary cameramen, but it was obvious that even better footage would be needed if the show was to make an impact. A Phantom was specially adapted with a rearward-facing video camera fitted in the tail cone in the place normally occupied by the drag chute. In order to capture aircraft in close formation behind the camera ship, a wide angle lens was fitted to the camera. A formation of Phantoms is wide, so to get all of them into shot the lens was almost a 'fish eye'. The tail camera captured some excellent shots, including some of the landing sequence, giving a view not often seen by anyone, including the crews who flew the aircraft daily. Unfortunately, the very fact that a wide angle lens was fitted in order to produce the impressive pictures was to prove fatal. The facts surrounding the accident were widely reported at the time. Nevertheless, the outcome is a telling testament to the risks of low level operations. It is undoubtedly more distressing, given that the motive was for entertainment rather than for operational reasons.

The fateful sortie was flown on 11 July 1980. A four-ship formation of Phantoms, led by the Squadron Commander of No. 19 (Fighter) Squadron but including crews from both squadrons, launched for the photographic shoot. A 92 (East India) Squadron crew were tasked as number 4. Unfortunately, the original aircraft they were allocated had a problem on start up, not unusually, and they were forced to change aircraft. They quickly moved to an adjacent HAS and accepted Phantom XV418. The main formation departed on time in the company of the camera ship and headed into the low flying area, completing some of the filming en route. The crew of XV418 followed some time later. Once in the planned area, the formation began filming the sequences that had been briefed carefully before the sortie. The crew of XV418 eventually joined the formation, and as they had more fuel than the rest of the formation they were able to remain on task longer. This allowed them to complete some final manoeuvres with the camera ship, which had also used less fuel. The crew was asked to complete a few breakaway manoeuvres from behind the camera ship before being asked to perform what proved to be their last event. The aim was to capture a 'Canadian Break' which, although dramatic, was not a normal operational manoeuvre. To achieve a safely executed break, the pilot would need to raise the nose before rolling the wings through 270 degrees and breaking out dramatically. The problem that led to the accident proved to be nose position. Because of the wide angle lens, in order for the Phantom to be nicely in shot it had to be flown in a very close line astern formation position. The actual formation position was carefully analysed after the event and was about 600 feet behind and 20 degrees below the camera ship. To the pilot this would have looked quite intimidating due to the proximity of the aircraft ahead. In order to execute the manoeuvre successfully, raising the nose was critical as it had to remain above the horizon throughout the rolling manoeuvre. The fact that the sortie was being flown at a relatively slow speed only 1,500 feet above the ground proved telling; the factors were adding up. The Phantom should have pulled gently away from the camera ship, maintaining height before starting the manoeuvre, but the nose progressively dropped. By the time the 270 roll had been completed, the nose was well buried and the aircraft was descending rapidly towards the ground. Efforts to regain control were unsuccessful. The time from executing the manoeuvre to crashing in open fields near Diepholz in northern Germany, killing both the crew instantly, was only 8 seconds.

I lost two good friends that day. As a qualified flying instructor, the pilot was skilled and able, and everyone agreed he had a 'fine pair of hands'. He was probably one of the least likely candidates to have made the fatal error in flying what was a standard aerobatic manoeuvre. I have often analysed the manoeuvre in my own mind to determine my own thoughts and reaction. The navigator was experienced but would have had little opportunity to eject, although he undoubtedly would have tried in the latter stages as it became apparent that the jet was doomed. Whilst the pilot would be aware of his mistake, the time for the navigator to evaluate the unexpected was limited. It would have been apparent that the rate of descent was high, and the pilot's natural reaction would be to pull the nose up to counter that high rate of descent and recover to level flight. In the back, the nose above the horizon would have been reassuring, but the back cockpit lacked appropriate flight instruments to recognise the fatal rate of descent, possibly lulling the navigator into false optimism. I was lucky to have had few truly scary moments despite hundreds of hours at low level. I was under no illusions, though; hesitation in such circumstances could be fatal.

As with many accidents, the supervisors on the sortie in question were criticised. A number of experienced pilots were asked to fly the manoeuvre in the simulator and, even with 20/20 hindsight, many were unable to prevent a crash. The manoeuvre was challenging to the limits at such a low level, but many of us felt the criticism was harsh. It is easy to sit in judgement in the calm of an office, but 'there but for the grace ...'

If any good can come out of loss, the incident is now used as a training vehicle for new squadron supervisors to demonstrate how events can lead to accidents. The various decisions and flaws in the planning are explained and analysed during the Flying Supervisors Course at RAF Cranwell where squadron supervisors are trained. Hopefully armed with that knowledge, such an accident in the future may be just a little less likely. Undoubtedly, a low level 'Canadian Break' will never again be flown for the cameras.

The TV production crew joined in with the wake in the Officers' Mess that evening. They, being civilians, could not believe that such a raucous celebration could follow the loss of a crew. Aircrew are largely fatalistic and live with the knowledge that any sortie might be their last; this was particularly true at Wildenrath during the Cold War. It was a strong tradition that in that sad event, their colleagues would celebrate their contribution and have a last drink on their bar bill to send them on their way. 'Live hard, fly hard, and play hard' would sum it up. The damp eyes came later.

RAF Wildenrath closed in April 1992. For some time the Married Quarters were used by service personnel from RAF Brüggen. A railway line served the base during its active days, and this proved to be the feature that guaranteed a role for the station for the future. Siemens, the German engineering company, bought much of the land and it is now the home of a test track for trains. The track cuts across the runway and through Bravo Dispersal. The former aircraft servicing platform has been taken over by sidings, workshops, and shunting loops. Only the threshold of Runway 09 remains evident at the western end of the former airfield. Most of the HASs were demolished in 1998. One or two remain in use on Bravo Dispersal, including the old 92 (East India) Squadron QRA facility. Charlie Dispersal is almost gone, and only a few HASs on Delta Dispersal, the old home of 92 (East India) Squadron, remain but for how long? The taxiways are derelict and overgrown, and the dispersals have reverted to an almost natural state. Ironically, the facility that survived the Cold War and still carries out its old role is the station golf course, now a thriving private club.

CHAPTER 8
The Falkland Islands

The story of the Falklands War has been recounted extensively, but what is little known is that the Phantom could have been a major player. Only a few years before the outbreak of hostilities, the Royal Navy enjoyed a capability that could have been deployed at the outset of the campaign. A similar story repeats itself today. The demise of HMS *Ark Royal* in 1979 saw the retirement of the last of the steam catapult carriers in Royal Navy service, and the Phantom became shore-based. But for those few years, the UK would have had Phantoms available and ready to deploy to theatre. There can be no doubt that if the UK had been able to deploy a 'look-down shoot-down' fighter such as the Phantom, the air-to-air battle would have been hugely different. Employed effectively and in sufficient numbers, the longer range, all-aspect Sparrow, extra weapons load, and longer range detection would have prevented many Argentinian aircraft from ever arriving over the islands. Combat air patrols could have been pushed further west, intercepting incoming aircraft well out in the South Atlantic before they came in range of the ships. Given that most of the Argentinian tactical aircraft were reliant on dropping 'dumb' bombs, this would have reshaped the operational losses. Ironically, the Navy had retired the capability that was needed when 892 Naval Air Squadron, which had operated Phantoms from the Ark Royal until 1979, had been disbanded and the aircraft transferred to the RAF.

When operations began in 1982, the 'through deck cruisers' of the *Invincible* class were the only carriers available to the operational staff, and the Sea Harrier FRS1 was the only fixed wing aircraft that could operate from this class of vessel. Military planners played with various contingencies to provide additional air defence coverage during the conflict. Borrowing a US carrier was mooted, although the reality of such a move was far more complex than the vision, and would have been barely viable without US assistance in operating the ship. Such a move would also have been politically significant. The appearance of a US carrier, even if it was ostensibly under a British flag would have been a significant escalation. Options to build a temporary airstrip on the islands using AM2 steel matting as a runway were also considered, and the plans progressed beyond conjecture. The Phantom squadrons were put on notice to move south, anticipating the installation of the airstrip, but it never materialised. The temporary runway was lost aboard the Atlantic Conveyor when it was sunk by an Exocet. In the event, the temporary runway was not installed until well after the war.

Although the Sea Harrier acquitted itself well in combat, it faced serious operational limitations. The airframe, based on the original Harrier design, was similar to the RAF Harrier GR1/GR3 airframe, with a small fuel load and limited range. Given that the British carriers were pushed well to the east, the Sea Harrier pilots faced long transits to the combat air patrol areas and had limited time on task over the islands. Like the Lightning, it was originally equipped with a simple pulse radar known as the Blue Fox, which gave very limited capability at low level. Simple analysis showed that the Argentinian A4 Skyhawks and Daggers were also range limited and would be attacking from the west, arriving over West Falkland. Their tactics dictated that their attacks would be conducted at low level using free fall bombs. Only the Super Etendard carried a stand-off weapon in the form of the Exocet missile and could be refuelled in the air. Prior to the war, the Sea Harrier carried only four AIM-9G Sidewinders, although these were upgraded rapidly to the AIM-9L and AIM-9M versions, giving an all-aspect capability. Fortuitously, the Argentinian combat aircraft were also operating at their limit of endurance, which gave the Sea Harriers a huge advantage. Had the Argentinian pilots been able to engage in full combat over the islands without fuel constraints, the RN pilots would have encountered opponents who were aggressive, well trained, and well matched in turning capability. The outcome might have been very different.

With some frustration, Phantom crews sat out the conflict in the UK and the Ascension Islands. It was not until after the war that the Phantom finally arrived at Port Stanley in the guise of No. 29 (Fighter) Squadron, which deployed the aircraft into the South Atlantic in 1983. Known originally as 'Phandet', the squadron was quickly rebadged as 23 (Fighter) Squadron and the Red Eagle, the squadron symbol, began its association with the Falkland Islands. Ironically, the movement of the squadron 'down south' resulted in another significant event for the Phantom Force. The deployed aircraft had to be replaced in the UK to maintain the numbers for NATO declarations. The Rolls-Royce Spey-equipped aircraft were unique and could not be replaced as the production lines had long since closed. As a stopgap, one of the most effective examples of contingency procurement was initiated. A squadron of ex-US Navy F4J Phantoms was reactivated in America and pressed into service in the UK under another famous

An armed 23 Squadron Phantom intercepts the inbound Tristar.

badge, that of No. 74 (Tiger) Squadron. I never served on 74 Squadron so sadly I cannot offer a suitable pictorial tribute, but the aircraft was almost universally praised.

The long journey south to the Falkland Islands affected deployed personnel in different ways. For most Air Force personnel it was the furthest from home that they had served. For many years the only way to reach the islands was by ship or by C-130 Hercules, which extended its range by refuelling in the air. For a few years, the 'airbridge' flight was provided under contract by British Airways before being replaced by the TriStar as the RAF pressed some ex-BA and Pan American aircraft into service. Most who arrived in that bleak landscape would probably have preferred taking the next flight out, but that was not the military way. Deployments to the islands lasted for four months. The first sight of a Phantom for most new arrivals deploying to the Falklands would be as the TriStar came within range of the islands. It was a squadron tradition that, whenever possible, the inbound flight was intercepted by a 23 (Fighter) Squadron aircraft. Although designed as a morale booster, showing that we could protect the air corridor, there was a serious reason for the presence, as an attack on the 'airbridge' by a marauding Argentinian fighter was not out of the question. Inevitably, those first pictures snapped from the window of the TriStar were grainy, but, in retrospect, that added to the impression. Other than the daily drone of Phantoms launching from the main runway, that might be the only time that some personnel saw the real reason for their being in the South Atlantic.

After the war, it was important to establish an integrated air defence system as soon as possible. The risk of rogue attacks by unwelcome Argentinian aircraft could not be tolerated. From personal experience, discussions proved that the islanders had been traumatised by events during the war, and their security was paramount. The islanders are not displaced Argentinians despite the Argentinian rhetoric. They are as British as any farmer who you would find in any rural community in the UK. As British citizens, they wanted to be, and deserved to be, protected. While some might have questioned why we were fighting a war in such a remote location, once you had met a Falkland Islander there could be no doubt as to their loyalty.

The Falkland Islands Air Defence Ground Environment, or FIADGE, was the air defence system that was rapidly introduced after the war. Using the mobile capability of the UKADGE, a Sector Operations Centre (SOC) was set up on the inhospitable summit of Mount Kent just outside Stanley. This unit controlled two reporting centres located on West Falkland at Mount Byron and Mount Alice. Two C-130 tankers, based initially at RAF Stanley and later at RAF Mount Pleasant, provided air-to-air refuelling and a rudimentary maritime patrol capability. Search and rescue and logistics support was provided by Sea King and Chinook helicopters of No. 78 Squadron and civilian S61s. The SOC controlled the fighters, tankers, and a squadron of Rapier missiles that provided airfield defence. A Royal Navy air defence picket ship was stationed routinely in the South Atlantic. The specialist ship, a Type 42 destroyer, had a comprehensive radar capability that could be linked into the recognised air picture at the SOC, providing extended radar cover to the west of the islands. The UK was not well served for airborne early warning capability in the years immediately after the conflict. It was too far to deploy the ageing Shackleton, and the Boeing E3D had yet to replace the ill-fated Nimrod AEW aircraft. For that reason, the coverage provided by the ship was a vital capability. Together, this mixture of aircraft, radars, missiles, and ships provided the safeguard to make sure that Argentina was not tempted to press its claim to the islands again.

Stanley airfield on East Falkland, a ramshackle collection of temporary accommodation cobbled together to house the military force, grew rapidly after the conflict. Centred around the original 4,000-foot runway, the airfield was designed to operate small civilian aircraft that moved people around the islands. Although adequate for the short take-off Harrier GR3s that initially provided a rudimentary air defence capability armed with AIM-9G Sidewinders, the undersized strip was inadequate for air defence Phantoms. To allow operations to begin, a temporary runway using AM2 matting was laid over the original concrete. The matting consisted of sections of interlocked metal planks strong enough to take the weight of a Phantom or a C-130. The hastily prepared overrun area extended the available runway length to 6,000 feet, but this was still barely adequate for a high performance aircraft, so, in addition, hydraulic arresting systems (RHAGs) were installed onto the short tactical strip. If memory serves, there was a cable at each end of the airfield and one at the midpoint of the runway. These wires, similar to those installed on aircraft carriers, were normally used to stop the Phantom in an emergency. On the short Stanley runway they were brought into action on a routine basis and all landings were arrested. With limited diversion options, the aircraft landing back at RAF Stanley were heavy. Typically, extra fuel was required to hold off in the event of bad weather, so as much as 4000 lbs of fuel could remain in the tanks, plus the added weight of the war load of eight missiles and the gun. After each sortie the aircraft was landed into the approach end cable. During the early days, a Phantom deployed the chute as it engaged the cable but the parachute rigging wrapped itself around the rear fuselage, causing major damage to the aircraft. The QFIs therefore investigated other options, and it was decided to deploy the drag chute before touchdown. The chute could safely be deployed at speeds of up to 200 knots, which was faster than the normal landing speed. In the unlikely event of missing the approach end wire and then the midfield RHAG, the chute could still be jettisoned if a go-around was needed. The pilots who had completed tours with the Royal Navy aboard HMS *Ark Royal* had used the technique in the past, and I recall it being demonstrated to me at RAF Wildenrath by a carrier qualified pilot well before using it in anger at RAF Stanley. The Phantom was remarkably stable with the chute deployed and it redressed some of the balance of the weight penalty. After landing, the pilot held the aircraft in position using power but keeping the cable taut. By chopping the power quickly, the aircraft would begin to roll slowly backwards under the tension of the cable, at which time the hook could be retracted, allowing a gentlemanly disengagement from the cable. The fire and recovery crews became adept at re-rigging the cable in record time to allow other members of the formation to land. There were surprisingly few problems operating from the metal runway; however, the constant pressure of heavy Phantoms thumping down onto the strip caused the AM2 planks to shift down the runway. Typical Air Force ingenuity came to the rescue as the C-130 tanker was co-opted to make fast taxi runs in the opposite direction. By braking hard, the heavy aircraft was able to shift the metal matting back in the opposite direction. The scream of a C-130 aborting a 'fast taxi run' at Stanley became a regular feature of life.

In the north-eastern corner of the airfield a group of temporary hangars, nicknamed 'Rubs', because they were literally made of rubber, had been erected to protect the Phantoms from the worst of the South Atlantic weather and to offer shelter for the maintenance personnel as they worked to fix the everyday snags. The aircraft were pulled outside for normal operations as shown in Plate 40. Number 23 (Fighter) Squadron had taken root on the southern side, and a collection of temporary buildings sprang up to form the main operations complex centred around the QRA aircraft and their crews. As with the rest of the airfield, facilities were basic and creativity was needed. Mains water was at a premium, but an inventive engineer, after brief negotiations and the inevitable bartering, acquired a water tank which was hoisted onto the roof. A few rickety pipes and a tap with the occasional top-up from a water bowser provided the luxury of running water.

Around the airfield small communities, looking more like a travellers' camp than a military base, provided the numerous support functions vital for a functioning airbase. One of the few permanent structures, the air traffic control tower, was a small two-storey structure with slab-sided, drab green walls and a temporary signpost 'Royal Air Force Stanley' fixed to the front. The C-130 tankers operated by 1312 Flight had pride of place on the main dispersal in front of ATC. The Flight enjoyed palatial accommodation next to the tower, although the term 'palatial' was relative.

To complete the air of a war zone, hulks of Argentinian Pucara fighter-bombers dotted the airfield in varying states of disrepair. Most bore the signs of retribution exacted by disgruntled troops at the end of the conflict. Representing the spoils of war, a complete Pucara had already been shipped back to the UK for evaluation, along with a captured Skyguard radar and Oerlikon guns. Although the Pucara was dismissed by experts at the time, it may have proved extremely useful in later conflicts such as Afghanistan. In the event, it made a few appearances at air shows before being placed in the RAF Museum at Cosford where it is still displayed. The Skyguard, however, was put to good use guarding UK bases for many years after the war. It was initially operated by an Auxiliary Air Force unit to provide short range air defence protection for RAF Waddington, eventually being transferred to the Electronic Warfare and Training Range at RAF Spadeadam where it undertook a policing role and was deployed into the low flying areas to monitor the height of aircraft operating in those areas. It is still used to develop countermeasures to be programmed into UK electronic warfare equipment.

Above: The
23 Squadron
operations complex
with hastily rigged
'running water'.

Right: RAF Stanley
Control Tower.

1312 Flt with visiting C-130K Hercules transport aircraft.

A wrecked Pucara on the airfield at RAF Stanley.

The 'Coastel' Accommodation Barge in Stanley Harbour.

To house the mass of military personnel, converted oil accommodation barges were shipped from the UK and moored in an inlet adjoining Stanley Harbour. Two of the barges housed the Army units and a third was allocated to the RAF. In comparison to the original tent city, the 'Coastels' provided luxurious civilisation. Although bleak in appearance, the small rooms were warm and comfortable compared to a tent and camp bed, which had been more typical immediately after the conflict. The individual accommodation containers could house four people and offered shower and toilet facilities. A makeshift Officers' Mess provided dining facilities and a bar. The challenge was to reach the public rooms via an outside walkway, which meant braving the howling South Atlantic gales. Ironically, once their role in the South Atlantic was complete, the barges were returned to the UK and pressed into service as a prison. Before they could be accepted, they were extensively upgraded. It was a source of some amusement to the members of the services that, apparently, accommodation standards were higher for prisoners than for serving personnel.

Flying from RAF Stanley was an intriguing experience, totally unlike operating from other RAF bases at the time. The aircraft flew fully armed on every sortie and, under strict guidelines, we were cleared to use the weapons against any potential maverick Argentinian pilot who chose to press the claim on the newly liberated British enclave. The contrast with training operations in the UK could not have been starker. The easterly threshold was close to the beach, so the approach to the runway was over the sea. Standing on the austere airfield, it was possible to hear the noise of the rollers crashing in from the Atlantic on the occasions when they were not drowned out by the noises of aircraft being prepared to fly. The westerly departure ran directly down Stanley Harbour before it narrowed at the western end, rising into the steep gulleys in the hillside that flanked the town. Those peaks had names that had become famous during the conflict: Mount Longdon, Two Sisters, and Mount Kent, the highest.

The flying in the Falkland Islands was outstanding. Low flying was allowed throughout the islands, and the locals were extremely happy to be visited by a Phantom. In fact, they were positively insistent that the crews conducted regular flypasts of the settlements. With the constant threat of air attack from the mainland, crews trained hard and knew the operating area intimately, and the islanders were overtly grateful. They would quite happily host visiting squadron aircrew for an overnight stay, which provided a welcome break from the military routine of RAF Stanley. If the Argentinians had rekindled their territorial ambitions they would have found a well-motivated and aggressive opponent. The sortie profiles were varied and all types of interceptions were conducted regularly. In the years immediately following the war there were only a handful of low flying restrictions allowing full tactical freedom within the airspace. Most sorties were day tactics leading to aggressive combat manoeuvring that maintained a fighting edge. The other deployed aircraft provided opponents, and it was one of the few areas where day tactics against targets as diverse as a C-130 and a helicopter could be flown daily. One of the more unusual restrictions was to avoid the many wildlife areas such as penguin colonies and seal sanctuaries, although a visit to see the llamas, introduced to Weddell Island many years ago, proved irresistible.

Accidents were rare, but I lost good friends in one mishap. XV484 was one of a 'three-ship' from 23 (Fighter) Squadron that launched on 17 October 1983 to carry out practice interceptions over East Falkland. The crew had been nominated to act as target for a pair of fighters manning a combat air patrol over East Falkland, but despite good weather, cloud covered the tops of the hills that ran down the central spine of the island. The Phantom had already been intercepted by the pair and turned back to the west for another run. Once it turned inbound on an easterly heading, the fighters had a brief radar contact that faded and never reappeared. After losing radio contact, the fighters alerted their controller and a search and rescue operation began. The wreckage was found on the slopes of Mount Usborne. Tragically, neither of the crew had tried to eject. The members of the Board of Inquiry could not identify a sound reason for the loss. They reported that the aircraft had not suffered a technical failure, and that it was in controlled flight when it struck the ground. They reasoned that because the inertial navigation system had been found to be inaccurate, the crew may have been unsure of their position and let down into cloud and struck the high ground. The report stressed that there was absolutely no suggestion that the crew were doing anything other than flying the briefed profile in their normal professional manner.

In the crewroom the accident caused much debate. Aircrew always like to understand the reason for an accident in order to be able to prevent a similar situation and prepare themselves mentally. The facts were indisputable; it was only the 'why' that remained a mystery. There was something about the conclusions which troubled many of us who had operated at low level in poor weather, particularly given the undoubted skills of the Germany-based crew.

We rarely needed the inertial navigation system in the Falklands when flying in good weather. There were plenty of excellent navigation features, which meant that we knew exactly where we were at all times. The geographical features over East Falkland were predictable. The ridge line was unbroken, and even if the upper slopes were shrouded in cloud the lower slopes would have been clearly delineated. The ground to the south was relatively flat, with nothing in the area above 100 feet. The start point would have been in the area to the north of Goose Green, which is close to Falkland Sound and is easily recognisable. For such exercises we would navigate to a known start point from where we would aim towards the nominated CAP position and carry out evading turns around a mean heading. The best way to avoid detection was to turn away from the fighters through 90 degrees, using a manoeuvre known as 'notching'. This made it very difficult for the navigator in the fighter to see the target in pulse Doppler mode as it would be 'on the beam' with very little closing velocity. Holding the diverging heading for a short while would guarantee that the fighters lost contact, which would not be regained until the target turned back towards them. Equally, if a fighter locked on, the manoeuvre would also break that lock, so it was a very effective tactic. There appeared to be no reason to fly towards the high ground above cloud, and, particularly, not to descend into that cloud. This was also a Germany-based crew who were used to operating at low level every day. Over East Falkland a turn to the south would put the target over the flat plain. Unfortunately, a turn to the north would quickly put the target in the vicinity of the high ground. With cloud on the slopes, a northerly heading could not be held for long and a turn back would be needed to avoid entering cloud. Timing that turn would be critical. From personal experience I know that cloud can cause powerful sensory illusions. I remember flying a ground controlled approach into Wattisham in a Phantom many years ago. Mendlesham Mast sat at about 10 miles on the final approach. On this particular day, a shallow but dense bank of fog covered the countryside. Our decision height was 240 feet and we flew the whole approach in bright blue conditions and overshot because we could not see the runway as we were still above the fog layer. The ground was less than 250 feet below us, but all we saw throughout the approach was a solid deck of fog. Only Mendlesham Mast poking up through the fog bank gave any perspective of reality. No one will ever know what happened that day, but I know for certain that the crew were professional to the last.

My first stint on the island had a very specific purpose. Our role was to return two aircraft to the UK to undergo major servicing, and we were to be responsible for the first roulement of the Phantoms. A four-month detachment was physically and mentally demanding, and crews felt drained at the end of their time 'down south'. For flight safety reasons, fresh crews were nominated as each of the two legs home were over 8 hours in length, including five air-to-air refuelling brackets. Either the take-off at Stanley or the landing at Ascension Island would be in the dark, so our first task was to get night current in theatre. For the first time in months, the squadron was tasked to night fly. As the seasons are reversed in the South Atlantic, although it was late June, winter was approaching in Stanley. The unpredictability of the weather characterised the operations in this barren area over 400 miles from the nearest land. To experience weather of all four seasons in a single day was not unusual.

The first night sortie proved to be an eventful affair. The wind was strong but straight down the runway. At night, it was normal to plan for a stream take-off. Each aircraft would roll individually, with the second aircraft following after 30 seconds. The wingman would follow the leader about 2 miles behind, using the radar to maintain contact until the formation was in clear air. The wingman would then call a manoeuvre to put the pair into battle formation and then hold station on the leader's navigation lights. This was to be the plan for our first night sortie. Things immediately went wrong, and the leader aborted his take-off after losing the reheat on one engine. This caution was unique to the Falklands as, for normal operations in the UK, we could continue the take-off with reheat on only one engine, and the Phantom was quite capable of that. On the critically short Runway 26 at Stanley, attempting to get airborne with only one reheat, particularly at night, was fraught with risks. An abort was the only real option, as the overrun area was rocky and there were some unforgiving ground at the western end of the runway. With such a short stopping distance, using the arrestor gear was essential after an aborted take-off, as there was insufficient runway length remaining to use the drag chute. Normally, the smooth surface of a UK runway was predictable, but the surface of the metal planking was far from smooth and the hook had been known to bounce. In the event of the hook skipping the arrestor cable, the aircraft would go into the overshoot at the far end of the runway and ejection was guaranteed. The rocky overrun was far too unpredictable to risk staying in a jet still travelling at up to 100 knots. So it was with trepidation that I waited for the call that they were in the cable. The wait seemed like an eternity but eventually it came, and I remember breathing a sigh of relief. The fire crews quickly removed the aircraft from the runway and re-rigged the cable. After a short wait we were cleared to launch by Squadron Ops and instructed to operate with the C-130 that had departed ahead of us.

'Albert' was the local nickname for the C-130 tanker, or 'Fat Albert' to be precise. The standard Hercules had been modified rapidly to give it an air-to-air refuelling capability, and an electronic surveillance suite had been added for operations in the South Atlantic. The refuelling equipment was rudimentary and consisted of a standard Victor hose/drogue unit (HDU) strapped to a cradle in the rear cargo door. The doors were literally cracked open to allow the refuelling hose to be trailed. Although slow and limited in height, it had a useful fuel giveaway and, more importantly, it could operate easily off the short metal runway at Stanley unlike its larger jet stable mates, the VC10 and Victor. We hadn't briefed intercepts with the C-130 tanker, as we had planned to carry out routine intercepts with the other Phantom, but we had been authorised for 'Ops Normal', which allowed us to intercept anything in the airspace.

The lights of Stanley town slipped away quickly, and the most obvious feature that characterised night flying in the South Atlantic was immediately apparent. The feeling of isolation was heightened at night because there was no ambient light in the vast areas of ocean. It was extremely dark. We were handed off to the GCI controller at Mount Kent who was briefed to control our intercept sortie and we headed north away from the islands. The C-130 had been airborne for some time, so the controller had already set up the intercept profile. I immediately picked up a contact on the radar and dropped into the well-practised routine. The target was slow, as expected. We knew it was a C-130, so I wanted plenty of lateral displacement. Eight miles' separation would allow me to roll gently round the final turn and carry out a nice controlled stern intercept. All hopes of an easy time evaporated as the target immediately evaded, and this went on for the whole run. As soon as I established my intercept geometry the target turned, negating the planned attack. At 10 miles from the target, the controller would make a safety call to check that the weapons switches were safe. When the call came, all my carefully planned displacement had disappeared and the target was pointing directly at us only 2,000 feet above. This was, without doubt, the worst place to be on a dark night. With no turning room, I resorted to the old trusted technique called 'short range procedures'. We had a set of last-ditch figures, or 'keys', which would resurrect the intercept. If I could put the blip to a particular point on the radar scope, a 4G turn would result in a vaguely presentable roll out. Turn too soon and we would roll out in front of the lumbering tanker; too late and we would roll out way behind him. As we pulled hard around the corner I expected to get an early visual pick-up on the lights of the tanker, but despite my calls to the pilot trying desperately to talk him on, neither he nor I could see it. This meant that I would have to earn my keep and control the intercept using radar all the way. Sometimes pilots would keep quiet when they picked up the target to make the navigators work a little harder, but on an operational sortie there would be no such in-house tricks. Our brief was to carry out some night tanking, so I was looking to put the tanker about 2 miles ahead. As we rolled out, remarkably at the correct range after the fraught attack, I locked up the radar by designating the blip and squeezing the acquisition trigger on the hand controller. This commanded the scanner to centre its tracking beam on the location of the target ahead giving precise readings of target heading, height, and speed. The identification routine that followed should have been a carefully choreographed geometric profile which we had practised hundreds of times before. The approach was from below, climbing up an 8-degree approach angle, directly behind the target, keeping the approach speed under control. In this position we were invisible to the tanker pilot as we were below the belly of the large transport aircraft. As we closed, there was still no sign of the navigation lights and the surrounding airspace was still as dark as I had ever seen.

On normal training sorties, lights out visual identifications, or visidents, were flown against another Phantom and the pilot would hold a rock steady heading. The C-130 crew were obviously oblivious to the effort involved, and the target drifted off in heading a number of times, making the approach much more difficult. Although this is what we trained for, it didn't normally happen this way – but this was an operational sortie, after all. Doing 'lights out' intercepts over the North Sea we would see a reflection from an oil rig stack, or a flash reflection from the moon bounced back off the target's fuselage. Here in the pitch black of a moonless South Atlantic night there was nothing. As we approached our minimum radar range of 300 yards the pilot eventually picked up a dull glimmer in the blackness. It proved to be the beta lights, the small lights that ringed the refuelling basket. Normally they were visible only in the final few feet as you closed to make contact with the refuelling probe. On this dark night they were a dull beacon. Although the tanker was still 300 yards away, the basket on the end of its 100-yard hose was much closer and trailing well below the belly of the still invisible C-130. We had to be aware of its proximity as we manoeuvred into position, but I could do nothing to help as we had moved inside the minimum range for the radar, so it was down to my pilot to ease in visually. Edging closer,

34. XV437 in full afterburner over an overcast North Sea.

Overleaf: 35. XV500 flying over Suffolk.

36. XV486 over a Norwegian Fjord.

37. XV426 carrying a load of drill missiles.

38. A 92 Squadron Phantom fires the gun. Flames are visible from the barrel and spent cases are being ejected overboard.

39. A 92 Squadron Phantom dumps to get down to landing weight after experiencing an emergency. Both photographs were taken by the squadron QWI.

40. The 23 Squadron 'Rubs' and two of the squadron's Phantoms at RAF Stanley.

41. 23 Squadron QRA Phantoms protected from the extremes of the Falklands' climate by cockpit covers.

42. XV474 tanking from the C-130 Tanker at 10,000 feet during the first refuelling bracket abeam Uruguay.

43. Ready for contact.

44. XV433 over the main dispersal at RAF Coningsby.

45. XV486 and Stavanger based Northrop F5s in close formation after an air combat sortie.

46. XV469 on a snowy ramp at Keflavik with XV466 taxiing past.

47. XV466 over ice floes within the Arctic Circle.

48. XV466 at Low Level off the Icelandic Coast.

49. XV500 in the HAS Neck on Delta Dispersal at RAF Wildenrath.

50. XV500 pushing back into HAS54 on Delta Dispersal at RAF Wildenrath.

51. XV465 with its undercarriage travelling after take-off carrying no external stores.

52. A 56 Squadron Phantom in formation with a 92 Squadron Phantom during Exercise Bold Pointer.

53. XV435 deploys its drag chute at RAF Akrotiri.

54. XV490 in a hard turn over the Suffolk countryside.

55. Tanking from a VC10 over the South Atlantic.

56. Phantoms XV490 'G' and XV464 'B' waiting to refuel from a KC135A.

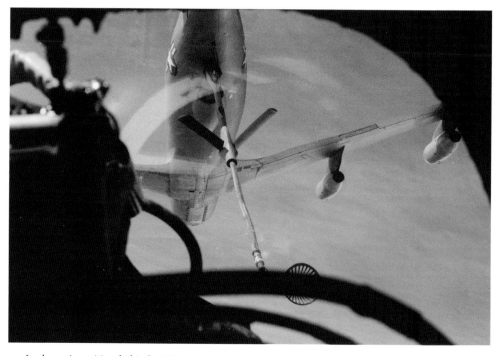

57. In the wait position behind a KC135.

58. XV490 refuelling. The short hose section is looped once in contact with the basket.

59. 56 Squadron Phantoms en route for Cyprus to refuel from a Victor tanker.

60. XV471 in a hardened
aircraft shelter at RAF
Wildenrath.

61. A 92 Squadron Phantom
deploying to Cyprus for
armament practice camp.

62. XV433 in a vertical climb carrying a drill missile load and a gunpod.

63. XV464 on the flightline at RAF Wattisham.

64. A Phantom on alert in the Wattisham QRA Hangar. The aircraft is finally armed and the crews helmets and lifejackets are positioned at the base of the stairs ready to scramble.

65. XV426 carrying a practice missile load.

66. A Sparrow missile being loaded onto XV468 during Operational Turnround Training.

67. Sidewinder Missiles on a weapons trolley ready for loading on XV468.

68. A SUU-23 Gun fitted to XV424 at the RAF Museum Hendon.

69. The Phantom Gunsight.

70. XV437 on finals to RAF Coningsby with gear travelling.

71. A Mig 21 Delta of the Hungarian Air Force.

72. A Sukhoi Su27 Flanker of the Soviet Air Force.

73. The Thrust Vector Control system on an AA11 Archer.

74. A Mig 29 Fulcrum of the Soviet Air Force.

75. XV424 begins its take off roll en route to the Victor tanker for the airborne media pictures.

76. XV424 taxies past a cameraman.

77. XV474 testing the prototype air defence grey but fitted with a black radome carrying only a centreline tank.

78. XV474 in the interim configuration with the smaller but darker RAF roundels.

79. XV408 displaying the Commemorative Blue Colour Scheme at the Squadron Disbandment.

80. 92 Squadron at RAF Akrotiri. Both camouflage schemes can be seen along with the prototype 'Grey Ghost' XV418.

81. A pair of clean wing 56 Squadron Phantoms, XV468 and XT897 in Echelon Formation.

82. In the RHAG after a double utilities failure with the cable stretched out along the runway.

83. A dusk take-off at RAF Akrotiri.

84. XV409 in close formation over Suffolk

85. XV464 being prepared for a combat sortie at RAF Alconbury.

86. XT897 in loose formation during the 56 Squadron handover flight.

87. A night take-off.

88. XT891 taxies in after a gunnery sortie at RAF Akrotiri.

89. A 56 Squadron Phantom on short finals at RAF Akrotiri.

90. A 56 Squadron navigator being welcomed by a resident pilot on the ramp at Stavanger Sola.

91. XV437 at low level over Norfolk.

92. XV465 during a turnround at the Danish airbase at Skrydstrup.

93. XV497 outside the 8 Squadron Headquarters at RAF Waddington.

94. XV468 in the sun.

95. A Phantom in full afterburner at dusk.

the lights on the HDU mounted on the ramp of the C-130 suddenly burst into life above our heads as the crew activated the refuelling system, temporarily killing our night vision. There was a brief flash of reds as the unit charged with fuel before the yellows flashed simultaneously, clearing us to tank using silent procedures. After the intense darkness, the light from the drogue unit was, paradoxically, disorientating, but the tanking from my perspective was otherwise uneventful. After we left the tanker, we completed a few more intercepts before returning to Stanley.

We thought by then that the drama of the evening was over, but not so. As we approached the islands, our air traffic controller asked us if we would make a practice diversion to Mount Pleasant airfield, which had recently opened. Although it had been used for trooping flights during the day, this was the first occasion when aircraft had operated at night, so it offered a good training opportunity for the controllers. After the sweat and toil of the intercepts this should have been a breeze as we were vectored west towards the new airfield. At 10 miles finals, we were handed over to the talkdown controller. The white lights of the centreline and the distinctive crossbars of the approach lighting were easily visible, even from that range. The aircraft flew precisely down the approach, with my pilot following the gentle patter from the controller. I took the opportunity to see how the airfield looked on radar in case I ever needed to find it without assistance. As we approached our minimum descent height, at about 300 feet above the ground, I heard an expletive from the front cockpit, which was not what a navigator wanted to hear. At this height just above the threshold of the new runway at Mount Pleasant, gear and flaps dangling, Wireless Ridge just a mile to the north, turbulence from the ridge tickling the jet, it had just gone very dark again and the bright approach lights had disappeared! As the burners immediately bit, my pilot initiated an overshoot as the controller announced that they had just experienced a total power failure. As the speed built back up to 230 knots, the wheels retracted slowly into the wheel wells and the flaps retracted. The altimeter increased rapidly through 1,000 feet, safely clear of the surrounding terrain, and the rush of adrenaline faded. Even dropping the wing for a good look, it would have been impossible to know that just below us was a new airfield capable of housing a squadron of fighters and over 2,000 people. Just a few solitary lights flickered in the otherwise darkened countryside and the Falklands had taken Mount Pleasant airfield back. Despite so much fun already, the night wasn't quite over yet.

Recovering to Stanley for a visual join, we arrived at 'initials', a point about 5 miles from the threshold on the extended centreline, and the short strip at Stanley was clearly visible. The runway lighting consisted of omnidirectional lights spaced 1,000 feet apart down the length of the strip. These were interspersed by unidirectional lights that could be seen only from the approach direction. The normal rejoin for a Phantom was to fly over the upwind runway threshold and break into the circuit before carrying out a circuit to land. From our break height of 500 feet the runway looked very short, probably magnified by the surrounding darkness. The speed washed off quickly as we turned downwind, bringing the aircraft back to approach speed. As my pilot dropped the landing gear, finished his landing checks, and looked for the runway, I heard yet another muttered expletive, but this time I was well aware of the reason. As I looked to the right where the runway had glowed just moments before, it had been replaced by a pitiful series of barely glimmering white omnidirectional lights and Stanley had descended into virtual blackness. This was becoming a theme. The squadron had not flown much at night except for QRA missions and as the Argentinians did not fly often at night, a night scramble was rare. No one had warned us about this feature of Stanley airfield, and we could see only a fraction of the normal runway lights. Once again we were plunged into a black abyss, although at least this time we were 1,000 feet above the ground in a planned pattern. The Phantom operated from a minimum strip of 7,500 feet in the UK. With 6,000 feet of metal matting, we ordinarily planned to make an arrested landing at Stanley, taking the approach end cable with the arrestor hook. The tiny runway, now barely visible, seemed woefully inadequate. Even on the average day, placing ten tons of screaming Phantom on the designated concrete was exciting. As we completed the downwind leg, just the six meagre omnis glowed bright. The jet committed nose down for the final turn, and only as we passed 500 feet in the descent did the full splendour of the approach lighting reappear, almost as if someone had hit a switch. The landing run at Stanley was brutal at the best of times. I braced my neck and turned gingerly to watch over my shoulder for a successful 'trap'. With insufficient care the navigator would be 'listening to the radar' as his head was whipped forward by the retardation, and I had almost made that mistake on my familiarisation sortie on arrival.

The standard procedure was to pop the chute just before the wheels hit the runway and apply a tad of power. If the Phantom didn't catch the cable, reheat was needed straight away for a go-around, so it was good to have the engines spooling up. Sodium lights marked the position of the cable 1,300 feet into the runway. There was a tell-tale ripple of the tapes that marked the end of the cable when the hook snared the wire, which should have been visible even at night. When it came, the vicious retardation of the hydraulic arresting gear dragged the aircraft to a shuddering halt in just 600 feet of runway – half the distance of UK cables. It was good to have your head firmly planted on your shoulders at that point, but you knew you were back down on the ground. After the thrills of the first night sortie at RAF Stanley we were night current and ready to redeploy the jets back to the UK. It was only later I learned that my pilot had never tanked at night from a C-130!

As the day for the tanker trail approached, the lead navigator for the trip had been refining the planning after receiving the air-to-air refuelling plan from the tanker planners. It was to be a double hop via Ascension Island, which lay just inside the Southern Hemisphere very close to the Equator. After a forty-eight-hour rest, we would press on for the final leg home. On the first leg the Phantoms would launch from RAF Stanley at first light and rendezvous with four VC10s which would depart from the new airfield at Mount Pleasant. We would take on our first fuel as we passed abeam Uruguay from the first VC10. It would then carry out buddy-buddy refuelling, topping off the other tankers before returning to Mount Pleasant. The formation would complete all the refuelling brackets over open ocean; so-called blue water operations. Our en route diversions would be in Uruguay and Brazil as the Argentinians still did not accept visits from British fighter jets. After the final bracket, the Phantoms would accelerate ahead to be safely on the ground at Ascension before the remaining VC10s arrived. If there were any problems with weather at the destination, easily possible in the tropics, there would be insufficient fuel to loiter. Decisions would have to be taken during the final refuelling bracket by the tanker mission controller who controlled the entire operation, and a diversion to South America was the most likely option.

The forecast headwinds for deployment day were stronger than expected, leaving little flexibility in the planned fuel offload. Furthermore, one of the VC10s had been declared unserviceable at Ascension Island and would not be available for the deployment, leaving us critically short of fuel against the plan. The remaining VC10s, due to arrive that morning, represented every available tanker in the RAF. Even if another precious airframe became available, it would take at least four or five days to position it from the UK. This would mean further delay, which everyone, particularly the crews, was keen to avoid. The lead navigator, who was an extremely experienced friend and colleague, worked hard at the figures but could still not make them work within the planned offload. Eventually he came up with an alternative plan, but had to convince OC 23 Squadron, the boss of the Falklands Phantom Squadron, that it was viable. The commander at the time, who eventually rose to the highest levels of command in the MOD, was renowned for being extremely cautious and risk averse, so it was not expected to be an easy sell. To make up for the higher fuel burn, the revised plan had the Phantoms launching at the same time as the VC10s and carrying out a rendezvous in the climb, known as an 'RV Echo'. In the meantime, the C-130 would be pushed ahead onto a tactical towline about 100 miles up-route. Unfortunately, as the C-130 cabin was unpressurised in the tanking role, the maximum height it could operate was 10,000 feet. The VC10s were committed to climb to the planned height of 25,000 feet or they would burn yet more fuel, thereby defeating the object. This meant that the Phantoms would have to leave the VC10s and descend in order to rendezvous with the C-130 tanker. After the additional fuel had been taken on, the Phantoms would climb back to 25,000 feet to chase down the VC10s before the start of the second refuelling bracket off Rio de Janeiro. The C-130 tanking bracket had to be short – just long enough to get the essential fuel but not long enough to allow the VC10s to extend too far up route or the Phantoms could not catch up in time. An orbit by the VC10s was out of the question as they already had insufficient fuel to waste. The Phantoms could not use reheat to close the range quicker as that would also waste precious fuel. In any tanker plan, each refuelling bracket had a critical point that was pre-planned and known as the Mandatory Diversion Point (MDP). At this point, unless the refuelling aircraft had taken on its fuel, there was insufficient fuel to make the destination and there was no option but to divert. However it panned out, the Phantoms had to be back in formation with the VC10s before the MDP for the second tanking bracket or it would be a diversion to South America.

The rendezvous procedure with the C-130 was a complex manoeuvre at the best of times, and was known as an 'RV Delta'. It began by setting up a 180-degree intercept, tanker and receiver pointing at each other from over 100 miles away. A piece of onboard electronics known as air-to-air TACAN displayed the range between the two co-operating aircraft. In theory, a radio direction finder on the tanker allowed the two formations to point directly at each other until the fighters made radar contact with the tanker. The tanker navigator activated the DF equipment when the Phantom navigator transmitted on the radio and could point directly at the incoming Phantoms. Unfortunately, the hastily modified C-130 was not equipped with a DF set. In this case, the initial vector would follow the planned track towards Ascension Island, hoping that the C-130 was flying the return heading accurately. Once in radar contact, the lead navigator would run an offset intercept to about 12 miles range, at which time he would turn the tanker through 180 degrees to head in the same direction as the fighters. The tanker had to turn at a very precise rate to achieve the airborne choreography. Often, the tanker crew could destroy the manoeuvre by turning too hard or too gently, spoiling the carefully crafted geometry. The Phantom navigator had to assess the progress of this turn and manoeuvre aggressively if it seemed to be going awry. Hard manoeuvring cost fuel, which was already scarce. It was an ambitious and complex plan but had been planned well and it had the potential to save the day. There was little to lose. If the rendezvous with the C-130 was unsuccessful, or we failed to catch the VC10s by the MDP, we were returning to Stanley. All we would lose would be the fuel consumed by the formation, although that was not insignificant. If we didn't try, we were staying for an extra couple of days, or even weeks, until the winds were more favourable, or the broken tanker at Ascension Island could be fixed and flown on to the Falkland Islands. In the meantime, the engineering programme in the UK would be on hold.

On the morning of the mission, the sun was just rising as we crewed in. The aircraft were positioned in adjacent 'rubs' on the Northern Dispersal and had been carefully prepared for the long journey. The fuel tanks had been topped off, and the various oil and hydraulic reservoirs filled to the brim for the eight-hour flight. These were the two aircraft that had to return to the UK, so, for once, there were no spares. We had a plan to cope with a delay during the start sequence, but if either of these two jets failed to start it was at least a twenty-four-hour delay.

Travelling anywhere by Phantom was a bleak event. The aircraft was fitted with a baggage pod which was a converted napalm tank. Although the capacity was reasonable, the two hatches through which the bags were loaded measured only 24 inches square. A lightly packed air force kitbag would fit, but only if inserted diagonally and manoeuvred roughly into place. Lunch consisted of a pack of dry sandwiches. Butter was flammable, so didn't mix well with the oxygen that pumped from the oxygen mask at height. A couple of pieces of fruit and some chocolate biscuits completed the meal. Oranges and sausage rolls were certainly not edible at 25,000 feet. To make matters worse, my pilot was a smoker, so he faced a rather tense few hours between cigarette breaks. Mistakes by Catering Flight were legendary, although how often did we take the time to explain? On the deployment down to the Falklands, the 29 Squadron crews had been given a bottle of orange squash to be shared equally between the crews. This proved difficult, as they were split equally between four aircraft! In my case, there were plenty of small packs of fruit juice to drink. The compromise was that too much liquid too early in the flight would guarantee one of two things. Either I would make use of the airborne 'piddle pack', or sit uncomfortably for the last few hours of the transit.

I took much more care than normal when I aligned my inertial navigation system that morning. A plan that put us thousands of miles from the nearest coast for much of the sortie before landing on a tiny outcrop of rocks on the Equator made it quite important to know where I was. As we started engines and checked in, the tower was already relaying that our tankers had started and were ready to taxi. The launch sequence would be carefully timed. The VC10s had to allow a gap between take-offs, so would launch individually and make one orbit overhead Mount Pleasant to allow all three to join loosely before heading north. We would hear a call on the radio when they set heading, and would launch from Stanley and set a converging heading to join up in the climb. The departure worked perfectly, and despite the lack of fuel, we flew a tight turn to the south of the airfield before completing an obligatory flypast over Stanley airfield and setting our northerly heading. As we checked in on the GCI frequency, the captain of the lead tanker had already set about marshalling his formation. We immediately found the large blips on the radar and began closing for a join up. With the lead navigator in the other Phantom controlling the join up, I started searching on radar for the C-130 which was established on the tactical towline at the appointed height. I didn't expect to see him until he turned onto a southerly heading as he was still over 150 miles north of our position, which was way too far for a radar contact. We had nominated a reference point by which time we had to be in formation with the VC10s. Once we descended for the first refuelling bracket the tankers would slow to their minimum airspeed, which would leave us about 25 miles behind the VC10 formation once we had taken our allotted offload from the C-130. Nothing could go wrong.

Our heading was taking us rapidly away from the Falkland Islands Protection Zone that marked the patrolled territory around the islands. For this trip, however, the aircraft were unarmed, but it was still only a few years since the retaking of the islands and tensions were still high. It was not inconceivable that some Argentinian commander still bearing the scars of a defeat could target a lumbering formation of aircraft in transit. We would be relying on QRA to watch our backs. Later, as we passed 35,000 feet and climbed into the contrail layer it was a nervous moment, but both our GCI controller and the radar warning receiver display were reassuringly quiet and by then we were well north. As we hit the reference point, we accelerated ahead of the tanker formation and began to search in earnest for our C-130 tanker. The faster we could go at this stage would be a help later. Hearing our call, the C-130 tanker captain had timed his turn to perfection; as we descended away from the VC10 formation, he had begun his run back south. Almost straightaway, the lead navigator in the other Phantom announced that his radar transmitter had failed, which meant that he was unable to track any targets. The tanker join with 'Albert' and the subsequent rejoin with the VC10s was suddenly all down to me. Success and we would be enjoying a forty-eight-hour layover on a sunny beach in the Ascension Islands. Failure and it would be another pint of Penguin Ale on the 'Coastel'.

Luckily, the tense wait for a radar contact was short and the familiar blip appeared exactly on the nose. There was nothing tactical about that intercept. Everyone knew the plan, and locking up allowed the C-130 navigator to see our radar signal on his electronic surveillance equipment. That way, even if the intercept was less than perfect we might see each other visually and be able to salvage a join up. Sixty miles was a healthy detection range, even against the

XV474 refuelling from the 1312 Flight C130 tanker.

VC10s in transit formation en route Ascension Island.

lumbering C-130. We descended to 12,000 feet, which was our planned intercept altitude, approaching the tanker from above, and once we had the tanker in sight we would descend further. It was a bright blue day, but we had to pick up the dark grey camouflage of the C-130 against the dark grey background of the South Atlantic. As the critical range of 12 miles approached, I made the call for the tanker to turn northerly onto our heading. It was the most important call of the day, and success and failure of the whole mission hinged on the next 2 minutes. I heard an acknowledgement from the tanker pilot and immediately the blip began to track away from the nose as the tanker turned. This was probably the same pilot who had given me such a hard time on the night sortie a few days before. That day, I knew he was doing everything in his power to ensure we succeeded. Monitoring the progress around the turn, the numbers checked out and the blip followed precisely the path I wanted. I held radar contact as we eased slowly back towards the tanker, and as he rolled out we were perfectly placed. Much to my relief, my pilot saw the tanker at about 5 miles. As we closed in on the ugly old 'trash hauler' with its droning props and dangling basket, I could safely say that it looked positively beautiful. We ran quickly through the tanking checks and extended the probe ready to take on fuel. Our leader dropped in astern the single hose and began the first joust of the day with the basket.

As we climbed away with our tanks topped off, we rocked the wings in an exaggerated message of thanks. The key question was whether we could catch the VC10 formation in time. I had regained radar contact with the tankers and we were climbing back through 20,000 feet to level at 24,000 feet, just 1,000 feet below the formation. The range showed 25 miles to the VC10s, and the needles on the Attitude Direction Indicator showed 60 miles to run to the start of the next refuelling bracket. The radar was showing that I had about 120 knots overtake, which meant that I was running them down at 2 miles a minute, meaning that we would catch them up in just over 12 minutes. Travelling at 6 miles a minute would put me 12 miles into the refuelling bracket once joined up. It was tight, but we could still refuel both jets before we hit the MDP. At least the formation was too far from Stanley to return and the diversion by now was Montevideo. With 30 miles to go to the bracket, the range was down to 12 miles, so the plan was working. More speed meant using more fuel, so as the miles ticked down it was difficult to avoid the desire to pop in the burners to close the range quicker. As we finally joined, the two massive ex-airliners were already in contact as one VC10 topped off the other, transferring its spare fuel to allow the remaining VC10s and the Phantoms to reach our intermediate destination. Although it was an amazing sight, the mutual bracket should have been finished before we rejoined. We were already pressed for time and the delay was pushing us further into the tanker bracket, cutting down our own time for refuelling. As the VC10 cleared to the right-hand side of the formation we were impatient, prompting the tanker leader to allow us to slot in behind. Once cleared, the lead Phantom dropped immediately astern the left-hand wing hose, followed closely by us behind the right-hand basket. As fuel began to flow, a quick check of the watch showed that there was still enough time to top off the tanks.

All seemed to be going smoothly until the radio burst into life with our leader announcing that he had a problem with the centreline tank and only 20 miles remained to the diversion point. The problem was that the tank had failed to feed its contents into the fuselage. We had no idea whether it was a failed valve or an iced up pipe, but fuel trapped in the external tanks was useless, so, as things stood, the aircraft was carrying the dead weight of the trapped fuel all the way to Ascension. The calculation was critical, as being 4000 lbs down, there might be insufficient fuel onboard the tankers to make Ascension Island. Failure to take on the full fuel load meant that the aircraft with a problem should divert, but the diversion plan was that we should keep all the aircraft as a formation. We needed all the fuel to make the destination, so pressing on was risky and would need an impromptu top-off from the tanker that was now serviceable at Ascension Island prior to landing. I glanced over at the lead Phantom. There had been a lot of nervous banter between the Phantom pilot and navigator and the tanker mission commander concerning fuel flow rates, contents, and distances to the MDP. Eventually the sums seemed to work out and the leader was cleared to disconnect. The formation pressed on northwards with just a hint of disappointment, as the diversion airfield had been Rio de Janeiro!

The remaining brackets passed without incident and we remained in company with the tankers, watching the miles to Ascension Island tick down slowly. A normal cruise descent began at 50 miles, so we were keen to be released by the tanker leader. Eventually, for whatever reason, the release came late at 40 miles, so we had to lose height more quickly than normal. By now it was dark and it seemed like a lifetime since we had launched from Stanley. The TACAN was winding down in range through 30 miles and we were only just passing 20,000 feet. Sensing that we were too high, the leader popped the speedbrakes and I felt the pull on my shoulder harness as they bit into the airflow. Still the altimeter wound down too slowly. The airfield at Ascension reminds me of a disused coalmine rather than an equatorial island. The massive volcanic mountains rise on both sides of the runway and look surprisingly similar to slag heaps. Being charitable, I could call it a lunar landscape, and it is no surprise to learn that Ascension was the place where NASA tested the Lunar Rover before sending it to the Moon. More relevant to an aviator is that a circuit is impossible as the mountain peaks are far too high and flank the runway. A straight-in approach was definitely the order of the day … or night. As we approached, 'initials' we

Left: XV474 flies in loose formation framed by the VC10 fin.

Below: XV474 refuelling from VC10 K2 ZA140 off the South American coast.

were still at 5,000 feet, which was too high, so we needed to orbit to get rid of the remaining height. Although we were still some miles from the runway, the orbit would take us below our safety altitude, meaning that the tops of the hills would be above the height of the aircraft. Landing at an airfield like Ascension hemmed in by volcanoes, this fact was highly significant. I recall glancing out of the darkened canopy, knowing that the mountains were not too far away. It seemed like an eternity as we hit safety altitude and levelled off, now heading away from the runway. Deciding we were well clear of the island, we continued the turn onto final approach with the glow of the runway lights a welcoming sight. Seven hours down; nine to go.

The second leg was uneventful in comparison with the first, although it started badly. Ascension Island was a fascinating change to the Falkland Islands, and the beaches were certainly warmer. After a welcome break between sorties, we prepared the aircraft under clear blue skies, the only problems surfacing during crew in. Immediately prior to strapping in, we had to don bulky immersion suits as we would be passing over miles of empty ocean with only limited search and rescue coverage. To have any chance of survival in the event of an ejection, an immersion suit was vital. Unfortunately, with an outside air temperature in excess of 30 degrees Celsius, heat stroke during the first minutes in the cockpit wearing the heavy rubberised suits was a definite danger. Things didn't improve, and the inertial navigation system was reluctant to align. With take-off rapidly approaching, we knew that it had aligned sufficiently to give attitude for the flight instruments, so decided that others could do the navigation for this trip and I placed the system into 'Nav'. With that decision taken, the remainder of the trip passed quietly, albeit boringly. Another long sortie took us past the southern coast of West Africa, past the Azores and the Canary Islands before entering the more familiar airspace of Western Europe. We eventually coasted-in across Cornwall, arriving unceremoniously at RAF Coningsby in the early evening to a welcome beer. The inertial navigator was somewhere over Europe and had been for most of the sortie. My log book records those two sorties. The first leg, on 24 June 1985, was 5 hours flown in daylight and a further 2 hours 20 minutes at night, with the second sortie, on 26 June 1985, showing exactly 9 hours. The total flight time of 16 hours 20 minutes spanned the globe from the cold Antarctic waters around the Falkland Islands via the equator to the UK.

The Phantom that I delivered back to the UK that day, XV464, completed its major service and remained with me on 228 Operational Conversion Unit, so we were reacquainted briefly during my remaining time on the Phantom Force. Later, it moved to 56 (F) Squadron at RAF Wattisham and spent a number of years in active service. In the early 90s, following the end of the Cold War, it was decided to withdraw the Phantom from operational service. It met its fate in 1992 when it was moved to the Wattisham 'graveyard' and was rendered unflyable before being reduced to scrap. The other Phantom involved in the mission, XV474, fared better. It served on 56 (F) Squadron at RAF Wattisham from 1986 to 1991 before transferring to 74 (Fighter) Squadron, serving until the squadron disbanded in 1992. It was to record a highly significant final milestone when it was flown to the Imperial War Museum at Duxford for permanent display.

CHAPTER 9
Life as an Instructor

After the heady days of flying in Germany, the logical career progression was to train as an instructor. That meant a posting back to RAF Coningsby in Lincolnshire in 1982. Number 228 OCU and, particularly the OCU syllabus, had changed little since I had completed the course in 1975. In the intervening years, the unit had gained a reputation for being tightly controlled by the 'Old Guard', with the average instructor approaching pensionable age. A number of us had been identified as being young enough to bring some recent squadron experience to the OCU, and at the same time lower the average age. There were a number of types of specialist instructors at the OCU, and new arrivals slotted into one of the disciplines. Qualified Flying Instructors taught the pilots to fly the aircraft. Qualified Weapons Instructors were weapons specialists and taught how to employ the weapons. Radar Tactics Instructors taught intercept techniques. Air Combat Leaders taught the skills of air combat. Finally, Instructor Pilots, although not qualified to teach the handling skills, were checked out in the rear cockpit and taught tactics, particularly during the air combat phase. At various times during the course, the different types of instructor were called upon to pass on their knowledge.

The first task on arrival was to complete an instructor work-up. I admit to being disappointed at the time. My initial impression was that too many of the old school wanted to demonstrate their prowess rather than pass on the techniques of how to become a good instructor to the new kids on the block. It was one thing to run through the profile for a basic radar sortie and ensure that my technique matched the approved OCU method. It was another thing altogether to understand the nuances of instructional technique and how to give both the student navigator and the student pilot a good understanding of how the Phantom ticked. Even though I had two squadron tours under my belt and over 1,500 flying hours on the Phantom, after six brief sorties, during one of which the radar was unserviceable, I was cleared to instruct. Of the other four sorties I flew in my first month, one was an air combat staff continuation ride and three were with a staff pilot for a station exercise. This was not how I had envisaged being taught to be an instructor.

My first instructional ride, fortuitously, was with a very experienced ex-Lightning pilot who was about to command 29 (Fighter) Squadron. I suspect that he was too much of a gentleman to comment on my embryonic instructional skills. The very next sortie was a fist solo for an ab-initio pilot. This felt like going from the sublime to the ridiculous, and was a real baptism of fire. Luckily, he became a good friend in later years, so the sortie must have passed without event. A further four sorties early in the following month saw me qualified to instruct air combat, which was an equally meteoric rise to fame. I vowed at that time to rectify the deficiency in this staff training, and eventually inherited the staff work-up cell in my final months on the OCU. I quickly learned that squadron techniques such as 'that looks about right' would not work in the controlled environment of the OCU. Intercept techniques in the Phantom were an art, not a science. It was unfair on the students to be exposed to many differing techniques used by the frontline squadrons that were regurgitated as gospel by well-meaning instructors, so the OCU syllabus had to be rigid and standardised. Using the approved procedures and techniques, there were a certain number of elements that the student had to demonstrate before he was allowed to progress to the next stage. Meeting the sortie aims could not be allowed to rest on the personal views of individual instructors, so specific learning objectives were rigidly enforced. Even so, allowance had to be made for the sometimes poor serviceability of the radar. It often required an amount of tender loving care to get the best from an errant radar set, and struggling by with a poorly performing radar could often separate the stars from the duffers.

There was a rigid order in which training was conducted. Firstly, the student crew was introduced to a new intercept profile in the Air Intercept Trainer. This was the same instructional aid on which I had trained when I went through the course many years earlier but was still giving sterling service. The majority of the training time was devoted to the student navigator, and I was looking for him (still no female aircrew on the Phantom as yet) to demonstrate that he understood the concepts and techniques in the quiet of the classroom. An hour session allowed somewhere between six and ten intercepts to be completed and debriefed, and at least three good runs were needed to pass the session. The emphasis at this stage was on teaching the basics and establishing a routine that would work in the cockpit. The pilot would be given at least one run where he could practise the geometry, but if the navigator was producing good results, more emphasis could be placed on the pilot. During pilot controlled runs, the navigator would merely lock up the radar and sit back. Barracking was positively encouraged. To be fair on the navigators, it could be a handful at this stage just operating the radar controls and doing the mental arithmetic. The pilots were guaranteed a blip on the radar scope to play with, so it took some pressure off; although, in their defence, they did have to fly the aircraft and do the sums simultaneously.

Once the students had passed the AI Trainer sortie, the student crew would fly the same event in the simulator. In addition to the intercepts, the simulator staff would throw in some equipment failures and some practice emergencies to make life more difficult. Only when the crew had passed this stage would the event be flown in the air. It was a well-known fact that most of us left around 50 per cent of our brain capacity on the ground once the wheels were in the well. For some aircrew that left precious little spare capacity to play with. It was not uncommon for a crew to 'ace' the trainer and simulator events but totally flounder once airborne. I am sure psychologists have good explanations for this phenomenon, but it could be frustrating. It was very frustrating for the student who failed the event, but could be equally frustrating for the instructor to explain why. The event was flown first as a split crew, with a staff instructor in the other seat, allowing the instructors to monitor closely how the student was performing. At various stages of the course some events were flown as a crew ride, with the student crew in one aircraft and the instructors watching from the target aircraft. The concept was that this sortie, although much harder to analyse, gave the crew confidence by being less supervised. As always, the films of the intercepts were carefully scrutinised and the film debrief was critical. The measure of success was the award of a DCO, or 'duty carried out', by the instructors. The staff pilot would have a good idea during the sortie that all was well, but the staff navigator's assessment of the film confirmed it.

Standards were important, and a cell on the OCU monitored instructional sorties and ensured compliance with the syllabus. Shortly after I arrived, the new OCU weapons instructor set about producing a comprehensive guide to intercept theory. This document was invaluable to the students, who inherited a ready reference on how to complete basic intercepts and all the theory that supported the profiles. It was also devoured by many of the staff instructors, who realised that their theoretical knowledge might not have been as good as they hoped. It was many years since most of us had sat wide-eyed through the same lecture, and we had learned too many bad habits on the squadrons during the intervening years. Everything considered, the OCU instructors were hard but fair, and, with few exceptions, extremely professional. Occasionally, during an AI Trainer session, one of the experienced instructors who made up the Standards Cell would appear at the back of the room and watch quietly. Normally, a quiet reminder of a few key points meant all was well.

Student abilities and characters varied wildly. Some were over-confident and needed the 'stick' approach to keep their feet on the ground; others were quiet and needed a 'carrot' approach to coax them along. There were ebullient characters and there were the quiet ones. As the students progressed, different problems required different solutions, and instructors would be carefully selected to ensure that an appropriate style of instruction was given. In an academic environment it can be easy to identify and fix learning deficiencies. In the detached and isolated environment of a fast-jet cockpit, solutions could be more elusive as it was difficult to see exactly what mistake was being made. The radar film showed the outcome, but it was harder to understand and correct the error.

With the massive training costs – a single sortie in a Phantom cost tens of thousands of pounds – progress had to be quick and consistent. A failure to pass an event resulted in a short remedial package of training on the ground followed by a refly. A second failure placed the student on review. After another short remedial package, the second refly was a 'chop ride'. Failure meant recourse, if the student was lucky, or more likely a wash out. Recourse to a subsequent course was expensive. The 'chop rate' was high, as much as 20 per cent on some courses, and it was always a challenge for the Flight Commanders and Course Mentors to decide when to pull the plug. Throwing away a potentially useful asset who might just be a slow learner was not done lightly, particularly considering the cost of taking a pilot or navigator to this stage of training. Literally millions of pounds had already been spent by the time crews converted to the Phantom. There was a tendency to press on just that bit further to try to graduate a student, but this could meet resistance among the staff officers at HQ 11 Group, and there were serious implications in doing so.

The squadrons had fewer staff trained to conduct the final combat ready work-up. Generally this was done by the small cadre of weapons instructors or perhaps ex-OCU instructors now on the squadron. By passing on a training risk, the OCU was overloading an already finely balanced process. To fail on the squadron was even more costly in terms of effort and actual money. It was also harder for a squadron to justify 'chopping' aircrew if the OCU had passed them on with a seal of approval. The ultimate question was, 'would the student become combat ready within six months?' For a navigator it was somewhat easier. It was unlikely that a navigator could ever cause the loss of the aircraft. The jet would be ineffective in combat if he failed to deliver, but would return home safely – unless he talked his pilot into flying into the ground. The problem of passing a weak navigator to the squadron was the extra effort and sorties needed to achieve combat ready status. For a pilot it was more complex. Low level overland operations in Germany were perhaps the most demanding environment. To conduct what actually constituted air combat at low level demanded consummate pilot skills. A poor pilot could place the aircraft in danger very quickly and potentially kill his navigator. It was this litmus test that ultimately determined the fate of a marginal pilot. Trust was paramount. Navigators flying with weaker pilots became quite nervous when the safety of the aircraft was in question. The lucky ones who failed the OCU were transferred to other, perhaps easier, types such as the Canberra or C-130 where things occurred at a more gentlemanly pace. Occasionally, the only offer on the table was to transfer to the air traffic control branch or the administrative branch, which was a devastating blow to aircrew who had almost achieved their goal of becoming operational.

Exercise C5 was one of the more exciting sorties for the staff navigators, as this was the student pilot's first 'solo' in the Phantom. With just 5 hours on type, the pilot was cleared solo by his Qualified Flying Instructor, or QFI, and given into the tender care of the staff navigator. The new Phantom pilot might be an experienced ex-Lightning pilot, or a pilot returning to flying after a ground tour, but could also be a brand new trainee with only a few jet hours on the Hawk trainer, which was a lot more forgiving than a Phantom. The exercise repeated a basic handling profile that had recently been demonstrated by the QFI. After a short transit into the North Sea airspace, the pilot ran through his new-found skills including aerobatics and a supersonic run down the North Sea. If an ad hoc target could be found to demonstrate the radar modes, that was a bonus, but the profile was deliberately gentlemanly. Later, a short low level navigation exercise was included. Coasting-in at Skegness, a ground controlled approach into Coningsby finished in the circuit. Normal circuits, flapless circuits, and every variation of boring circuits known to the QFIs was the penance for the instructor navigators as the new pilot honed his technique. C5s were normally flown in a two-stick phantom that had dual controls in the rear. This was not to suggest that the navigator would ever take control uninvited; that was one of the taboos, unless the pilot handed over control to give the back-seater 'stick time'. The two-stick version of the aircraft had additional instrumentation, which helped the navigator to monitor flight parameters more closely and allowed him to offer additional advice when relevant. Advice to pilots on flying techniques was always received with a frosty silence, even though many navigators were qualified pilots and had much experience. What many pilots forgot was that the navigators flew with all the squadron pilots, ranging from good to not so good. The pilot's skill level was very clear, and evaluating his capabilities became second nature. The same could of course be said of navigators by pilots, but perhaps this explains why navigators were generally more diplomatic ... It was a fascinating pastime comparing skills. As an example, and admittedly a stereotype, while the QFIs were often not the most aggressive pilots in air combat, their technique was a positive advantage in air-to-air gunnery where smooth flying and precise tracking was needed. Interestingly, a young pilot with 5 hours on the Phantom

XV433 over the North Sea.© Andrew Lister Tomlinson.

was the captain of the aeroplane and ultimately responsible for its safety, despite the fact that his staff navigator might have thousands of hours on the jet with much more experience. Surprisingly, this rarely caused any issues, and problems were normally resolved by gentle discussion. Good crew co-operation was vital, but often contained a good deal of fatherly advice from both cockpits.

OCU Training sorties for the staff navigator were generally not as much fun as squadron flying, but the emphasis in the cockpit changed. Rather than concentrating on your own performance, the emphasis switched to making sure the pilot flew safely and effectively, and in demonstrating how to conduct 'perfect' intercepts and tactics by the book. During target runs, thoughts turned to how the student navigator was coping with the intercept in the other aircraft. Needless to say, when considering your own performance, perfection was not always guaranteed and honesty tended to be the best policy. A badly executed intercept could be used as a teaching vehicle and showed that even with many hours in the

XV433 on approach to RAF Coningsby. © Andrew Lister Tomlinson.

aircraft, mistakes occurred. Despite their inexperience, real scares when flying with the ab-initio pilots were rare, as those selected for the Phantom tended to have graduated from their courses at the Tactical Weapons Unit in the top half of the rankings. It was accepted that the best pilot at TWU would be offered a posting to single-seat aircraft such as the Harrier. It was demanding to fly and, as a single-seater, the aircraft gave the pilot a heavy workload in the cockpit. In the Phantom, the load could be shared, meaning that experienced navigators could help weaker pilots until they gained experience on the aircraft. Some pilots sent to the squadron as training risks eventually proved to be exceptional pilots once they were mentored by their more experienced back-seater and fellow pilots and given time to develop. Without doubt, taking a weak pilot or navigator under your wing and watching them improve until they graduated from the course was one of the most rewarding experiences as an instructor.

The OCU schedule was relentless, and 'all work and no play' is an apt description. Uncharitably called the 'sausage machine', a course of up to twelve students arrived at Coningsby about every eight weeks. The output was controlled tightly by HQ 11 Group to ensure that the crewing levels were maintained on the squadrons. Keeping a mix of experience was always a delicate balance, so feeding the front line with a combination of newly trained aircrew and experienced aircrew returning after ground appointments was the key. The progress for each course was monitored by chasing the inevitable line up the chart in the Flight Commanders' office. Course graduation dates could, of course, be delayed, but this did not mean delaying the arrival of the next course. Flying effort was dictated by the number of available aircraft, so backlogs meant poor continuity for the newly arriving courses as the emphasis remained on graduating the senior course. During my time on the OCU from 1982 to 1986, a total of forty-one courses passed through the unit, feeding the squadrons with new crews to keep the Phantom flying. In hard numbers, this was a phenomenal volume of aircrew cycling through the Phantom Force. Such a volume could have repopulated the Force many times over.

At an individual level, each student's progress was logged in a progress folder and each trip was evaluated and numerically scored. At the end of the course, the inevitable trophies were presented. The accolade was to be awarded the best pilot or best navigator, but there was an additional prize. The 'Dogger's Trophy' was presented to the pilot or navigator who showed either the best performance or the most improvement during the air combat phase. The prizes were normally presented on 'Postings Night' when the students found out which squadron they were posted to. Germany postings were the prize, but inevitably there were a few commiserations as well as celebrations when the news was broken.

One of the significant milestones for an instructor was to be nominated as Course Mentor. This was perhaps the most important role during an instructor's tour of duty. The Course Mentor took the course members under his wing throughout their time on the OCU. He looked after every aspect of their training from daily programming, through progress reports, to discipline. It was one of the proudest moments in my career when 100 per cent of my first Long Course of ab-initio students graduated from the OCU. Many of those aircrew went on to achieve great things during their careers, including a Red Arrows pilot and a Squadron Commander. That one officer eventually emigrated to Australia and joined the Royal Australian Air Force was nothing to do with his treatment under my supervision …

With the normal stresses and strains of the training task, continuity was vital. Weather was a constant battle, particularly in Lincolnshire in winter. Student pilots had a 'white' instrument rating, which meant that they could not operate when the cloudbase was below 400 feet or when the visibility was poor. In addition, many sorties needed good weather in the operating area, particularly if planned at low level. The last thing anyone needed was a problem with the airfield. It was a gloomy day when we learned that RAF Coningsby would be closed for up to six months to allow the runway to be resurfaced. The cynics said that as soon as a runway resurfacing was scheduled, it was guaranteed that the station would close within a few years. Luckily, the decision had already been taken to base the new air defence Tornado F2 at Coningsby, so its future was assured, and the work was to prepare for the F2's arrival.

A long detachment away from base could cause stresses, not just domestically but with the engineering and logistics chain that would be needed to maintain up to twenty-four aircraft away from home for an extended period. It was with mixed feelings that we heard that the jets would be detached to RAF Waddington for the 'Bolthole'. Although nearly 30 miles from Coningsby, with planning, a daily commute was possible, and spares could be sent quickly when needed. It was greeted with positive enthusiasm by staff members who lived near Lincoln, as it would actually cut down their commute to work. It also meant that students could be based at Coningsby when not scheduled to fly, and would still have access to the Air Intercept Trainer and simulators to continue their ground based studies. After an on-site inspection, the OCU was offered Alpha Dispersal, the site now occupied by the E3D Sentry Force. Rather more austere than the present-day accommodation, the dispersal still had its old post-war buildings, which were large enough to act as makeshift briefing rooms for the flying events but not big enough to take the OCU en masse. Being close enough to Coningsby meant that only briefings and debriefings for the flying events would be conducted at Waddington and the rest of the training would still be concentrated at Coningsby. Rather than the usual private cars, fleets of buses made the trip between the two bases at regular times during the day. Ironically, working to a strict timetable with limited space made the routine somewhat more predictable than normal, although the crewroom was eerily quiet at times. It meant that the programmers had to be more careful, as it was harder to schedule the phase brief that had been forgotten or the AI Trainer session that had to be repeated. However, once a routine was established, the 'sausage machine' ran like clockwork and the time away passed remarkably quickly.

As always when flying high performance aeroplanes, there was an incident during the detachment that brought home the realities of life on a fast-jet squadron to the students. Two Phantoms were scheduled to conduct a routine instructional sortie over the North Sea. This was to be a crew ride for the students, so a staff crew in one aircraft would lead the student crew into the area. Having briefed and walked to their aircraft, the crews taxied out to the holding point of the main runway at Waddington. In XT891, the staff crew lined up for what they assumed would be another routine take-off. As the burners bit, the aircraft accelerated normally and sped down the runway. Almost immediately the pilot felt a violent pull on the rudder pedals and the nosewheel canted sharply to the right, causing the aircraft to leave the runway. It was nothing the pilot had done that had caused the problem. A random nosewheel steering fault had occurred at the most inopportune time. Luckily, the pilot had the forethought to cancel the reheat, but with the aircraft travelling at high speed across the grass and a number of buildings and obstructions ahead, the crew felt vulnerable as it was inadvisable to collide with a fixed object at Phantom take-off speeds. They decided to eject. After perfect ejection sequences, both crew members floated down safely onto the airfield, having spent only a few brief moments in their parachutes but watching their aircraft continuing on a diverging heading across the grass.

Crews from No. 29 (Fighter) Squadron were operating from an old building adjacent to the main aircraft servicing platform on the north side of the runway. Hearing the distinctive 'bang, bang' of a double ejection, a few aircrew raced outside to see what was amiss and were immediately faced with the sight of a Phantom, at high speed, bearing down on the building. They scattered, literally fearing for their lives. Fortuitously, the aircraft veered back towards the runway, missing all the obstructions, and most importantly the 29 Squadron building, coming to rest adjacent to the short disused runway. As it slowed to a halt it buried itself up to its axles in mud, having ploughed a furrow across the grass. With the crash alarms blaring across the airfield, the emergency services reacted immediately and sped across to the crash site. The fire crew closed down the engines and made the cockpits safe. Having survived its experience, XT891 looked forlorn. The seat rails that guide the ejection seats safely from the jet were sticking up into the air, and the missing canopies had landed elsewhere on the airfield. Once the initial crash actions were complete and the site secured, the engineers began to work out how to recover the aircraft. A tow bar was attached to the nosewheel and a tractor began to pull the aircraft from the mud. A crowd of aircrew had formed and those of us watching groaned inwardly as the nosewheel flexed and strained under the pressure. We had visions of an almost perfect Phantom being dropped onto its nose as the nosewheel broke under the stress. Luckily, good engineering sense prevailed and as the aircraft stubbornly refused to move, a crane was brought in to lift the jet the remaining few feet onto the taxiway. Remarkably, the aircraft was almost undamaged, and after new canopies and seats were fitted it was returned to flying in just a few months. It now sits proudly on the gate at RAF Coningsby, but few people are aware of its 'off road' capability. Ever the comedian, the navigator logged 5 seconds of captain time in his log book, which was rare for a navigator! This represented the few moments after the pilot had ejected and he was alone in the aircraft before his own ejection seat fired.

Having kept the courses roughly on schedule during the 'Bolthole', yet more challenges faced the unit on its return to RAF Coningsby. During our absence, as well as a new runway surface, the hardened aircraft shelters and hardened personnel shelters had been finished. The decision had been taken that HASs were the way of the future for Phantom operations, and Leuchars and Wattisham were being equipped with similar facilities. In order to train the crews in the new procedures, it was agreed that the OCU should operate from the newly completed Foxtrot Dispersal on the south side of the airfield. The facilities were outstanding. A large briefing facility contained the operations and engineering desks, briefing rooms, a vault, decontamination rooms for chemical operations, and storage rooms. Next door, a brick-built annexe housed offices and the crewroom. Although purpose-built for a squadron, the buildings were quite snug for the OCU, which had twice the number of aircraft and four times the number of aircrew. Operating from HASs also brought with it many additional problems, which meant processes and procedures had to be adapted, for both aircrew and groundcrew. Rather than the aircraft being lined up neatly on the ramp, they were now dispersed in the individual shelters. While not a huge problem for aircrew; in fact crewing in during a rain shower became much more comfortable, it caused huge problems for the groundcrew. Turnrounds took longer; people and equipment were spread thin. It was inevitable that the hydraulic rig needed to fix one aircraft was some miles distant across the dispersal. Rather than pull broken aircraft into the hangar and allow a tradesman to work a number of problems simultaneously, it could take 15 minutes to move people and tools between HASs before work could even begin. It had all been done before in Germany, but for UK crews it was a whole new way of working.

One of the difficult conundrums was the fact that No. 64 (Reserve) Squadron, the OCU shadow squadron numberplate, was a squadron in its own right and shared the station with another operational squadron, No. 29 (Fighter) Squadron. It was declared to NATO with an A1 status, which meant that there were no concessions for its role as a conversion unit. The squadron was expected to react to the 'hooter' in just the same way as any other operational squadron and generate crews and aircraft to meet its commitments. In later years, the OCU was released from its A1 commitment, meaning that student flying could continue during exercises. Often this meant deploying away from home base, as the Station Commander was quite rightly concerned more with his operational role rather than his training commitments. There were many strains as 64 Squadron sought to keep its operational edge in the new HAS environment yet continue to push out the courses on a regular basis.

By then I had been a programmer for some time. Having programmed the squadron flying effort in Germany, it was a surprise how complex the OCU programme could be. There were only enough personnel on strength to support an extended day shift. In order to night fly, the flying day had to slip to the right or fewer events could be planned for the morning hours. The engineering staff was normally the limiting factor. Course Mentors planned their course flying programmes and submitted their requirements to the main programmer who put the disparate threads together. Although unpopular, it was vital that all the course inputs were received by mid-afternoon to allow the main programme to be constructed. This was despite the fact that some sorties were not complete at that time and debriefs could stretch into the early evening. Staff instructors with appropriate skills had to be allocated to individual students. Instructors had to be carefully programmed to cycle from one event into the next, as an instructor who had only one event planned for the day was a wasted asset. There were strict limits on crew duty time, and not only for the staff. It was not sensible to programme a student with three events over a twelve-hour day and expect him to produce the best results in the early evening after a long day. The jigsaw had to be put together, and every day saw the latest drive to achieve a quart from a pint pot. And all this had to be finished by 17:00 before people began drifting away, to ensure that everyone knew what they were doing in the morning. Inevitably, there were days when heads were still being scratched many hours after the bar had opened, or a failed sortie produced an unexpected re-plan well into the evening.

Shortly after returning to Coningsby, one of the more bizarre incidents occurred. The unit was regularly asked to provide a flight of aircraft to give a flypast at graduation ceremonies at the Officer Training Unit at RAF College Cranwell. As the reviewing officer received the general salute from the Parade Commander, a pair of Phantoms in close formation would fly over the top, providing the perfect motivator for the new RAF officers. It was a well-practised routine. The run in heading was fixed, as the aircraft had to approach from behind the dais and fly over the parade at a fixed time. I was the Duty Authoriser on the Operations desk one particular morning and I out-briefed the crews who were nominated for a parade flypast. The details were entered into the authorisation sheets and the crews walked for the sortie. Although I was the Duty Authoriser, each aircraft carried a staff instructor who self-authorised the specific sortie to be flown. Despite hearing the details, I had no inkling of what was about to unfold. Although a conventional flypast had been briefed, the aircraft flew low over the parade, scattering people and blowing hats across the parade square. The sound of the Spey engines at maximum power was literally ear-splitting. I had handed over as Duty Authoriser before the phones began ringing, so I missed much of the immediate fallout. My Squadron Commander, whom I respected immensely, convened a mass briefing at 07:30 the following day. He left no doubt as to the consequences should anyone try to emulate the performance. It was one of the few 'bollockings' I received during my flying career where the boss was wearing his No. 1 uniform whereas I was wearing a flying suit. His next port of call was to be the Station Commander's office. It did, however, demonstrate how difficult it was to supervise flying operations, even in the strictly controlled environment of an OCU when surrounded by hugely experienced aviators.

The OCU did not enjoy routine landaways as the programme relied on the rigid AI Trainer, simulator, flying cycle. Occasionally, when bad weather was forecast for an extended period, the Course Mentors would schedule a series of AI Trainers and simulators, leaving just the flights to conduct. A small detachment would then depart, searching for areas of better weather, such as Leuchars in Scotland, and fly intensively for a few days. This was ad hoc at the best of times, but despite these constraints the HQ 11 Group staff was persuaded that winter training detachments to Cyprus were a sound logic, given the much better weather in the Mediterranean at that time of year. The air combat phase was well suited to a detachment, as it was less heavily reliant on the ground based aids. Again, the courses were primed with a series of trainers and simulators before leaving for Cyprus on the regular trooping flight. A newfangled computer based training aid called the MAIT, or Micro Air Intercept Trainer, which replicated the Phantom radar, was hurriedly deployed to fill the gap. By cycling the courses through Akrotiri, it was possible to maintain a steady progress when we might otherwise have been sitting waiting for the weather to clear in Lincolnshire.

My last trip in the Phantom, ironically, was flown not from Coningsby but from the RAF station at Akrotiri, as my departure from the OCU coincided with one such training detachment. I had already received my posting to the Tornado F2 and to 229 Operational Conversion Unit which was soon to re-form. The trip was a fitting finale. On 10 February 1986, after flying the Phantom for over eleven years, my close association with my first aircraft came to an end. The sortie was a 2 versus 2 dissimilar air combat sortie against a pair of Hawk trainer aircraft that had been supporting our detachment. I flew with Sqn Ldr Paul Day, an exceptional fighter pilot, who was, and is, famous in the flying community for his time flying Spitfires and Hurricanes on the Battle of Britain Memorial Flight. His latest mount is the two-seater Spitfire, MJ627, which now lives at RAF Waddington, ironically sitting alongside the Piper Cherokee Warrior that I now fly as a private pilot. The Phantoms were clean wing, in other words not fitted with external fuel tanks, so we were able to fly the jet to its 'G' limits in free airspace close to base. The weather was fine and the combat area was just off the coast to the south of the island. In all, it could not have been a better way to end my association with the Phantom. I have little recollection of whether we won or lost the engagements that day, nor is it particularly relevant. I do, however, remember a spirited flypast over Golf Dispersal, which the boss approved to mark my last sortie. It was a sad day to think that my time flying the beast was over. I vaguely remember overdosing on brandy sours that evening to celebrate the move onwards. I may even have taken a short route to ground level from a bar stool, given the volume I consumed. My return to the UK the following day was aboard a TriStar transport aircraft, feeling a little jaded. A sad day, indeed, but I left with many happy memories. With the aircraft apparently in demise, it was a good time to move on, although my love of the aircraft would never fade.

CHAPTER 10
Squadron Deployments

Squadron deployments broke the monotony of the daily routine and performed a vital function. Occasionally, tabloid headlines prefaced articles describing drunken aircrew rampaging through 5-star hotels. It would be insincere to suggest that the odd beer was not consumed during such trips away, but they were a vital part of the education process. Operating in northern waters on QRA missions took the aircraft close to the Arctic Circle and well away from the UK mainland. This meant that in the event of bad weather in the UK or in the event of a problem, a diversion to an unfamiliar base in Norway or Iceland was highly likely. For that reason, aircraft were regularly sent on landaways to familiarise the crews with procedures at the airfields that they might have to use in an emergency.

Imagine the situation on QRA. It is a midwinter night and the QRA Duty Force Commander has declared 'Mandatory', meaning that because of weather or other operational conditions, scrambles should only be ordered in extremis. Despite the restrictions, the 'hooter' sounds and the scramble message is for a QRA mission into the Iceland-Faroes gap. Two hours into the sortie chasing a Soviet bomber that has descended to low level just off the Norwegian coast, the 'Master Caution' caption illuminates, alerting the crew to a problem. It is a double utilities failure, meaning that some essential services, such as the normal operating modes for the refuelling probe, the flaps, and the normal operation of the hook, have failed. The stability augmentation system has also failed, as have the speedbrakes, the ailerons, and spoilers. The aircraft is seriously sick, and thoughts of past accidents when inexperienced pilots lost control come to mind. The flight reference cards say land as soon as practicable for an approach end cable engagement. The aircraft still has the power controls providing limited manoeuvrability, but any further problems could be critical. It is too far back to Lossiemouth or Leuchars – the nearest diversions on the mainland – so it is the nearest diversion. Stavanger Sola is 50 miles away down the coast and is

XV486 over a Norwegian glacier.

the safest bolthole with an approach end cable, so the decision is taken: divert to Stavanger. Suddenly, the familiarisation detachment to Stavanger Sola was a sound idea. Instead of an unfamiliar approach into a strange airfield at night, the key features that were reconnoitered during the trip are easily recalled.

Exercise 'Whisky Troll' was the topical name for the familiarisation sorties in Norway. In addition to the opportunity to conduct navigation exercises around the fjords, the locally based Norwegian Air Force crews were always available to act as opponents for interception sorties or air combat. The Norwegians were highly capable operators, although at that time they were operating the Northrop F5, shown in Plate 45, armed with early generation AIM-9 Sidewinders. Some of the early Sidewinders had severe limitations as to where they could be launched, so the F5 really did have to be 'in the saddle' to take a shot. Typical of the era, the rules of engagement for the 2 versus 2 air combat sorties discounted the beyond visual range Sparrow shot, ensuring that the Phantoms were dragged into a turning fight. Employing the correct tactics, it was still possible to survive the close fight, taking shots when they were presented. To add balance, there was much discussion at the debrief about tactics to defeat a head-on missile, such as the Sparrow, stressing that it had done its job before the F5 pilot had even seen his opponent. The Soviets operated similar weapons, and false lessons about capability could be dangerous.

Another potential diversion destination was the US Navy Base at Keflavik in Iceland where the USAF's 57th Fighter Interceptor Squadron operated the F4E Phantom. Apart from providing defence of the island, which had no indigenous air defence capability, the other reason for being based in Iceland was to intercept Soviet Bears and Badgers operating in the northern waters. The US Phantoms also held QRA supplementing Phantoms based in the UK. The 'E' model was significantly less capable than our own aircraft, as it had only a pulse radar. This limited its ability to find the Soviet aircraft if they descended to low level to carry out their mission and, unless assisted by another radar site, the F4Es could lose contact. That said, even for a PD-equipped British Phantom, searching such a vast area was a problem. To plug this capability gap, the Americans regularly deployed E3A AWACS aircraft from the continental US to help find the intruders in the vast expanses of ocean. The E3As had a long range surveillance radar and could search large sea areas much more easily than a fighter. It had significantly greater capability than the UK Shackleton, which was approaching obsolescence.

Exercises were arranged on a regular basis to practise air defence procedures simulating an attack on Iceland. Iceland was a strategically important base in the battle against submarines operating in the North Atlantic waters, and its loss would have been critical in a Third World War. Normally a pair of British Phantoms would deploy and operate with the American crews to practise procedures and to conduct interceptions with the 57th FIS. Sadly, the scenarios were extremely scripted and provided little real training value in contrast to most of the deployments around Europe. Air combat was forbidden, and defensive manoeuvring was restricted to one 90-degree turn, which was a far cry from the free-wheeling tactics in the UK. It was also in stark contrast to other US squadrons with whom we worked on a regular basis.

The role of the squadron was QRA and it concentrated almost exclusively on that role. Operated on an extended detachment basis, crews were not expected to take on diverse tasking, so their role was deliberately restrictive. Even so, the operation was impressive. The weather in Iceland in winter could be truly horrific, and there was a well-regimented effort to keep the base clear of snow and open for QRA, despite the conditions. The base was very well equipped with all the usual US facilities such as the base exchange, and was run with true, albeit pedantic, American precision. The QRA facility was palatial, with huge living areas equipped with TVs, a pool table, a coffee bar, and a dining facility. As usual, we felt slightly awed at the money the US lavished on the complex in support of its personnel. One of the highlights of a visit to Keflavik was the chance to visit the American squadron bar, 'The Whifferdill', which was perhaps one of the best fighter bars in Europe. To explain, a 'whifferdill' was a badly executed basic combat manoeuvre. The correct manoeuvre was a lag pursuit roll in which the fighter completed a full rolling manoeuvre behind the target in order to reposition for a kill. A 'whifferdill' was flown in the wrong sense, was completely useless, and invariably put the offending fighter pilot in a worse position than he began. The bar, known locally as 'The Whiff', was stuffed with memorabilia from the squadron's history. A control column from an F102 adorned the bar and was wired up to a box below the counter, which allowed random buttons on the stick to be wired to a bell. In a game of Russian Roulette, victims had to work through the buttons until the bell rang. The loser downed the inevitable shot as a penalty. One thing was certain: the hospitality was second to none, and no one forgot a trip to Keflavik.

Squadron exchanges where nominated NATO squadrons worked together for a week were the highlight of the year. Not only was the flying guaranteed to be challenging but the social events were a key factor in building relations with our allies. The announcement of the location and squadron with whom we would exchange was awaited eagerly every year. Exchanges were set up on a 'Home and Away' basis. Each squadron would be divided into two, with half the squadron hosting the visitors at home and the other half being hosted at the overseas venue. The exchange ran simultaneously, with each squadron deploying to the other's base during the same week. The flying was always impressive, but it was equally educational to have the opportunity to fly in other aircraft operated by the home nation. Normally, air defence squadrons were matched with a squadron tasked with a similar role, but it was not unknown for our Phantoms to be matched with a ground attack squadron. The role of the host squadron dictated the type of flying, and if the match-up was with a fighter squadron, air combat was most likely. Crews fought hard in the air and played hard on the ground. It was always wise to have a flying team and a drinking team to ensure compliance with the 8 hours 'bottle to throttle' rule. Tactics were studied carefully to give the best chance of success when pitted against the hosts. Sometimes mixed formations were flown to assess the strengths and weaknesses of the other aircraft. All this analysis helped to build a picture of how we could operate as an effective fighting force if ever called on to do so. After such an exchange, a formation of that type checking in on frequency became less daunting. During exchanges, lifelong bonds of friendship were formed.

In reality, the social events could generate as much, or even more, one-upmanship than the flying. I recall one exchange with a famous German Phantom fighter squadron. The inevitable drinking game was rolled out by the visitors in which a sequence of drinks and titbits had to be downed in a particular order. The game was similar to the salt, lemon, tequila game that many university students will have suffered as a rite of passage. Unusually, one of the items was a

A USAF F4E of the 57th Fighter Interceptor Squadron Keflavik.

USAF E3As on the ramp at Keflavik Airbase.

XV466 at low level inside the Arctic Circle.

XV466 over the ice floes.

XV466 pulls up from low level.

XV466 on a training combat air patrol south of the Icelandic coast.

A 56 Squadron Phantom over the Mohne Dam.

small piece of rolled up bread. Thinking the aim was to provide a 'blocker' that would make the subsequent alcoholic drink more difficult to swallow, most of the brave British crews sailed through the challenge. The following morning, however, there were a number of shifty looks and nervous discussions after a visit to the 'little boys' room'. Unbeknown to the Brits, the bread had contained a small pill used to track problems with 'the waterworks' that had been provided by the German squadron doctor. It was some hours before the hosts stopped producing bright blue water!

Although the RAF operated Phantoms from both UK and German bases, UK operations were significantly different to those on the Continent. At the simplest level, the hardened aircraft shelters were of a different generation and required different procedures. The standard operating procedures for RAF Germany were modified to reflect the airspace control procedures in the Central Region. Most significantly, unlike the UK where the combat air patrols were flown at medium level many miles out over the North Sea, the CAPs in Germany were flown overland at a height of 1,500 feet. In the event of heightened tensions with the Warsaw Pact, UK crews might have been tasked to reinforce the forward bases in Germany, so an exercise named 'Phantom Leap' was introduced to allow UK-based Phantom crews to operate from the hardened facilities at RAF Wildenrath and to conduct overland interceptions in the German low flying areas. UK Phantoms would deploy on a Friday morning to receive briefings from the resident squadrons and fly a mission in the afternoon. On Monday two further missions would be flown before recovering to the UK. For UK crews it was a radically different way of operating, given that the whole sortie was conducted at low level. Techniques were radically different, CAP procedures were different, and the targets that were intercepted used different tactics. These short detachments could never hope to produce crews who were operationally capable in the Central Region, and it took many months to work up to combat ready status for Germany-based crews. Like any detachment, it could give only an insight into how the other squadron operated.

Exercise 'Ample Gain' was an exercise for the benefit of the groundcrew. NATO nations would deploy their aircraft to other bases to conduct cross-servicing training. To improve NATO interoperability, groundcrew had to be able to service any NATO type that landed at their base. On arrival, the aircraft was parked with the host squadron and handed over. A training package might be arranged using qualified local experts to demonstrate the do's and don'ts to less experienced colleagues of how to service a Phantom. Sometimes the aircraft were merely turned around in less than an hour and sent on their way without fuss. The favourite venue was a US airbase where a visit to the Base Exchange (shopping mall) and a touch of retail therapy was essential. Most of the other nations had a much more austere existence, although each was fascinating in its own right.

It was after one such 'Ample Gain' mission that one of the most potentially serious incidents occurred. Returning home on my bike after a couple of beers in the Officers' Mess, I followed my normal route via the main Guard Room and down the well-marked cycle path alongside the road that led to the adjacent village where I lived. The cycle path crossed the westerly threshold of Runway 27 at Wildenrath, and as I approached the extended centreline I heard a Phantom overshoot sounding somewhat noisier than normal. Using afterburner for a single engine overshoot was perfectly normal and ensured that the aircraft had sufficient power to climb away safely. The engine noise from this Phantom sounded different and attracted my attention. As I watched the jet climb away in the gathering darkness, it was clear that it was trailing something behind. Unable to identify the weird sight, I could see sparks falling away as the heat of the reheat plume burned the trailing mass. Thinking my beer count might have been under-estimated, I took the rest of the ride back to my married quarter extremely carefully. Something was clearly amiss, so I called Squadron Operations to report what I had seen. From the curt response I received from the Duty Authoriser, it was clear that he had already received more than enough inputs, and that there was little I could add.

Over the coming days the story unfolded. RAF airfields were equipped with two types of arrestor gear. Cables stretched across the runway, so that in an emergency, fast jets equipped with a hook could catch the wire, with the hook slowing the aircraft to an immediate stop. Aircraft not equipped with a hook did not have that luxury. Should an aircraft be at risk of leaving the end of the runway at speed, it had to be stopped before it broke through the airfield perimeter and risked the lives of passing civilians. To provide this last-ditch solution, a barrier or a net arrestor gear was positioned at each end of the runway. This literally enveloped an overrunning aircraft in a net, stretched between steel cables at the top and bottom, which brought the aircraft to a halt. The standard configuration for normal operations was for the arrestor cables to be rigged, the barrier in the undershoot to be lowered, and the barrier at the overshoot end of the runway to be raised. On this ill-fated day, a mistake by the duty air traffic controller had left the upwind barrier, namely the one in the undershoot, in a raised position. The side supports for the barrier are extremely heavy pieces of ironwork and stand over 10 feet tall. Set in concrete, they were designed to restrain twenty tons of reluctant Phantom, but only when it had slowed to a running pace after its landing roll. On a standard approach, a Phantom passed just feet above the upwind barrier even in its lowered position. On this occasion, the pilot had made a normal approach, but just as he was about to touch down he felt a huge impact under the aircraft and it began to snake uncontrollably. Thinking he had hit a large bird or even a deer (which roamed the airfield) his immediate thought was to stay down, but the aircraft was gyrating so badly that he thought that he may go off the side of the runway. He quickly decided to go around for another circuit to sort out the problem and selected full power for the roller, but the aircraft bucked violently and he realised he would need reheat to get airborne. What he did not know was that with the barrier having been left in the raised position, the aircraft had struck the top wire which had wrapped itself around the external tanks and embedded itself, cutting deep into the gun pylon. The net that was designed to stop the aircraft had come adrift from its mount but was also tangled around the airframe. Designed to work at slow speeds, the inertia of the Phantom striking the barrier while still flying had been enough to rip the supports out of the ground along with the heavy concrete foundations. As the crew rolled down the runway, this mass of wreckage was being towed behind the aircraft, causing the abnormal movement that was being felt through the controls. Luckily, the heavy concrete came adrift quickly, leaving just the wire wrapped around the jet, and it was this fact that almost certainly averted an accident. As the Phantom lurched into the air, with the wire and net trailing behind, it was the molten globules of wire being torched by the heat of the reheat plume that was visible from the ground, magnified by the gathering darkness.

The pilot coaxed the still unstable Phantom into the circuit, concerned that he might lose control at any time, and he warned his navigator that they may have to eject. Fortunately, he maintained control and flew a very gentle circuit to land back into the approach end arrestor cable. To recover the aircraft safely was without doubt an unparalleled feat of airmanship and piloting skill. When the aircraft was inspected, it was discovered that the thick upper wire of the barrier had sliced into the pylon that attached the gun to the centreline station. The wire had caused significant damage as it had flailed against the airframe at 200 mph, although it proved repairable. Other than a number of wasted heartbeats, and a significant dent in air traffic control's reputation, there was no other harm done.

As always with such incidents, there's a funny story. During an 'Ample Gain' turnround, once the aircraft was turned over to the local engineers to do their 'engineering stuff' the aircrew were at a loose end. Mission planning had been completed at home base, so a leisurely lunch was often possible. At American bases, the most obvious pastime was to visit the Base Exchange shop and the food court. The navigator, who was well known as a gadget aficionado on the squadron, had taken the opportunity to buy the latest 'can't do without' piece of audio equipment. Unless the aircraft carried a baggage pod, storage for personal items on transit sorties was limited in the Phantom and items had to be arranged around the cockpit as best as possible. On this occasion, it was late in the day by the time the aircraft was released from its commitment, so it had been agreed that the crew would return directly to Wildenrath without flying another mission. With no hard manoeuvring expected, the navigator felt safe to sit the box containing his new purchase in one of the normal stowage positions in the cockpit. The return trip had been uneventful until chaos ensued as the aircraft struck the barrier. As the pilot wrestled with the sluggish aircraft, he quite rightly warned his back-seater that in the event of losing control they might have to eject. This allowed the navigator to adjust his seating position and tighten the straps, guaranteeing the best posture for an ejection. In his inimitable sardonic style, the navigator later explained that, far from being concerned about the fact he might have to eject, he had been more worried about not being able to save his new audio equipment if he had been forced to leave the aircraft. It would have been an interesting insurance claim.

For many years, France was not a full member of NATO, but it was important to retain interoperability. For that reason, aircraft from each nation would detach to each other's bases for co-operative training under the banner of Exercise 'Contact'. In the Phantom Force, the Mirage F1's base at Cambrai was the most common destination, although there were also Mirage squadrons at Colmar and Reims. The Mirage F1 was a capable fighter, but the French operated mostly at medium to high level, which was not the best regime for the Phantom. The aircraft we generally trained against was armed with two internal 30-mm cannons and a single Matra R530 semi-active missile carried under the fuselage. The main armament, however, was the R550 Magic infra-red missile, two of which were mounted on rails on the wingtips. The preferred French tactic was to drag the Phantom into the upper air. Invariably, the engagement would begin with the Phantoms loitering at about 15,000 to 20,000 feet, with the Mirages sitting at 35,000 feet plus, and it took an enormous amount of encouragement to bring them lower. In theory, the Matra R530 had a similar performance to the Sparrow, but there was a marked reluctance for the French to adopt true front hemisphere tactics and they seemed to favour a beam attack into a stern conversion for a Magic missile shot. When I asked a French pilot to explain this anomaly, he was extremely dismissive of the weapon. His actual words, delivered in a very French way, were that the R530 was 'a stupid missile' and that his tactic was to jettison it into the river after take-off! Presumably this performance deficiency was rectified when the improved Matra R530F appeared in the 1980s. When we managed to drag them down to lower level, the scales were much more weighted in the Phantom's favour. It was even more evident on the few occasions we persuaded them to fly at 250 feet that, other than pure navigation, they were not comfortable fighting at those extremely low heights. Some of it was explained away by the restrictive low flying regulations in France, but lack of practice would account for the trend. It was always fun to visit the French bases, as the aircrew had a much more relaxed approach to life. Lunch was an event, and the pace always seemed so much more 'gentlemanly', unlike the hustle and bustle of an average Brit squadron. One habit I never adopted was the apparent concession of a glass of wine with the lunchtime meal well before the hangar doors had been closed. I am sure those days have gone, given recent world events.

Perhaps one of the less enthusiastic welcomes I received on a deployment was after landing at the German Air Force base at Wittmundhafen. A squadron exchange was planned for later in the year between 56 (F) Squadron and 711 Squadron, from the famous 'Richthofen Wing'. I was in the back seat accompanying one of the Flight Commanders as he conducted a pre-detachment reconnaissance. We flew a few intercepts over the North Sea against another Phantom before heading east for the German base, which sits on the north German coast to the west of Hamburg. It was the height of winter and, coasting in, we could see a solid covering of snow blanketing the countryside. As we broke into the circuit as a pair, the runway was clear of snow, the snow ploughs having done a great job of clearing the whole width of the runway and a centre strip down the parallel taxiway. The landing was uneventful, and we turned off and began the long taxi back to the dispersal at the opposite end of the airfield. Normally, the after-landing checks were completed on a challenge and response basis between the two cockpits, immediately after turning off the runway. Unbeknown to the pilot, the chute had not jettisoned properly but had collapsed behind the aircraft as the speed dropped to a walking pace. Of course, being an intrepid Flight Commander, there could have been no way that he could have forgotten to pull the jettison handle ... Unfortunately, we were dragging the still-attached chute behind us, and a slight crosswind had blown it to the side of the taxiway where it was trailing on the ground out of sight from our position in the cockpit. As it followed in our wake, it was methodically decapitating the taxiway lights that were mounted on short poles to raise them clear of the snow. It was some time before the local controller spotted our exploits and advised us to hold on the taxiway to allow the German groundcrew to pull the chute clear. For some reason, I detected a less than enthusiastic tone from the local controller in the tower as he said in a very strong local accent, 'Velcome to Vittmund!' The sarcasm was tangible.

One of the most important training deployments for squadron crews was the NATO Tactical Leadership Programme (TLP). Originally based at the German air base at Jever, it moved to Florennes in Belgium during the 1980s before moving to its present home at Albacete in Spain. The course, which is designed to give NATO aircrew the opportunity to develop airborne leadership skills and tactical flying capabilities, starts with a week of groundschool discussing NATO capabilities and looking in detail at potential adversaries and their equipment. It also allows concepts and doctrine to be discussed before moving into a flying phase. The remaining three weeks are devoted to flying one or two missions per day. Aircraft arrive at the end of the first week, with each course made up of twelve ground attack aircraft and six air defence aircraft. The core members were usually reinforced by specialist support aircraft providing reconnaissance capability and air-to-air refuelling. In the final week, external squadrons provided additional aggressor fighters so that the core members could act as escort fighters for the bombers.

Every mission begins with the nomination of an overall mission leader who then retires to scope out a rough plan using all his available assets. A leader for the opposing air defence assets is also nominated, but the enemy forces brief separately. The TLP staff set a challenging target that has to be attacked using the forces at the mission leader's disposal. Detailed mission planning is followed by a mass briefing where the leader explains his plan and briefs the timings and procedures. At the nominated time, the combined air operations package fires up and the plan unfolds. The old adage that 'No plan survives first contact' is almost always true, and the challenges of sequencing large numbers of tactical aircraft

A USAF RF4E on detachment to TLP at the Jever Airbase.

to meet a carefully choreographed sequence over the target are enormous. The plan needs to follow a minimum risk route in to the target, avoiding hostile forces as much as possible and arriving within seconds of each other so that the defenders are swamped. Once airborne, it is the role of the aggressors and the surface-to-air missile forces to disrupt the carefully crafted plan. Not only do the TLP staff assess the plans but afterwards they debrief each individual engagement between the opposing forces and decide how well the individual players reacted to the challenges that were set. Other than the famous 'Red Flag' exercise, TLP offers some of the most complex scenarios available in peacetime training and is universally praised. In many ways TLP is more demanding than live operations, as the scenarios are carefully crafted to be difficult but not impossible to achieve. If a TLP graduate can say on his first operational mission that it was easier than TLP then the staff have succeeded in their aims. For that reason, the award of a coveted TLP badge is an accolade.

CHAPTER 11
Air-to-Air Refuelling

The Phantom was a predictable aircraft to refuel in mid-air and most pilots adapted quickly whether it was their first time refuelling or whether they had flown other types on the tanker. To get the best from the aircraft, air-to-air refuelling was essential. The Phantom had enough fuel to deploy into Europe, and bases as far as Decimomannu could be reached unrefuelled by fitting the centreline tank. To reach bases in the eastern Mediterranean, tanking was needed. In the UK, air-to-air refuelling (AAR) was practised on a daily basis. Towlines were positioned around the coastline close to the intercept areas. For the southern air defence bases, Towline 5 was positioned over the North Sea overhead Dogger Bank. A tanker slot would be annotated on the daily programme against one of the intercept sorties. Typically, a pair would join the tanker and practise refuelling techniques for about 30 minutes, plugging and unplugging a number of times. Only 6,000 lbs of fuel was allocated for each thirty-minute slot, so the small amount of fuel would be used during the time spent on the tanker. Not surprisingly, if the tanking slot was programmed later in the evening, fuel suddenly became abundant as tanker crews began to sense the call of the bar. During the early days of Phantom operations in Germany, the squadrons were not AAR qualified. It was only in April 1981 that HQ RAF Germany decided that the Germany squadrons would be trained in AAR techniques. For most of the crews who had operated in the UK it was an easy transition, needing only a quick refamiliarisation sortie. For some new Germany-based pilots and navigators who had never tanked, a full AAR work-up was needed. Up to that point, Germany squadrons had deployed to Cyprus via NATO bases in Italy, refuelling on the ground before continuing down route. Unfortunately, the Phantom could be temperamental, and it was well into the second week of a gunnery deployment before one crew finally arrived at RAF Akrotiri, having been stranded in Brindisi for a week. AAR prevented such delays and avoided the risk of aircraft going unserviceable during a turnround en route.

Tanker towlines are enormous holding patterns controlled by the Control and Reporting Centres. Fighters nominated to refuel are vectored towards the tanker and conduct an intercept before joining alongside. Normal towlines are flown at 15,000 to 20,000 feet in the UK, which was a comfortable height for the Phantom. For transits or QRA missions where large distances had to be covered, the height could be pushed up to 25,000 feet. For a heavily loaded Phantom this was about as high as you would want to operate during refuelling. At and above this height, particularly carrying a centreline tank, minimum reheat would have to be used on one engine to maintain height.

The whole refuelling procedure was controlled by the tanker captain who would give commands on the radio to 'the chicks', as receivers were known. Fighters chopped across to a dedicated tanking frequency and joined the tanker formation on the towline. The new arrivals would hold to the side of the tanker until any aircraft already refuelling had taken their offload. Once cleared in behind a basket, lights on the hose/drogue unit (HDU) would show the status of the refuelling equipment. A red light meant hold position, an amber light meant clear for contact, and a green light meant fuel was flowing. The scariest signal was flashing reds which signified an emergency breakaway and that it was time to move clear of the hose. On those rare occasions, the breakaway manoeuvre was done with all due haste. Throughout the process, one of the crew monitored the activity using a video camera in the cockpit of the tanker.

To tank, the receiver pilot would trim the aircraft and move into the wait position about six feet behind the basket and in line with the trailing hose. The basket could be quite lively when it was flying in free air. Just enough power was added to start a slow overtake of about 2-3 knots. The navigator would pick up a commentary, which would sound familiar to those old enough to remember the TV programme *The Golden Shot*. 'Right a foot; up a foot', and so on. The pilot was encouraged not to look at the basket, as it was very easy to over-control the aircraft and end up in a pilot-induced oscillation, always chasing but never catching the rapidly moving basket. In the Phantom, the best technique was to formate on the tanker and make small corrections based on the navigator's commentary. The aiming point was a position at about 2 o'clock on the rim of the basket. As the Phantom moved in from the waiting position, the airflow around the nose would trap the basket and it would become much more stable. The basket would rise and drift outwards slightly as the probe got closer, and a gentle approach would invariably end in a solid contact down the centre of the receptacle. After feeling a reassuring 'clunk', which indicated a positive contact, the pilot eased forward a few more feet and matched speed by closing the throttle just a tad. It needed a solid prod with the probe to ensure the coupling connected. It was possible to be too gentle, known as a soft contact, in which case the probe did not lock into the receptacle and fuel would not flow.

The hose was marked with a large amber section at the top of its reach. Once in contact, by pushing this section of hose back into the HDU, valves opened in the tanker aircraft and fuel would flow down the hose and into the Phantom's tanks. Throughout the time fuel was transferring, the pilot would fly formation on the tanker and the hose would reel in and out of the HDU to allow for relative movement between the two aircraft. It was readily apparent if the pilot failed to hold a good formation position, as the hose would be forced from its natural trail position and you could almost feel the stress on the hose and the couplings. While in contact, the pilot merely followed any navigation turns, albeit precisely. Disengagement was straightforward. The pilot would close the throttle gently and the aircraft would back out slowly. As the limit of travel was reached, the clamps that had held the probe in contact would release and the basket would separate. It was important to follow the natural trail of the hose when backing out. Any misalignment would cause the basket to whip dramatically after it broke free as it fought to find its natural position in the airflow. It was not unknown for the heavy metal of the basket to rap the cockpit canopy quite firmly, which was always a scary moment. There was often a healthy slug of fuel discharged before the valves in the basket closed and shut off the flow. Invariably this excess fuel was deposited down the side of the rear canopy, causing a distinct reduction in visibility. The equivalent would be to throw a small glass of petrol over your car windscreen and then try to drive without wipers. It was a good few minutes before a clear view was restored as the rapidly moving air washed the sticky aviation fuel from the canopy. Accidents were rare, but, in extremis, probes could be broken off by the weight of the hose and basket. I remember my first Flight Commander, an experienced Lightning pilot, being presented with the remnants of his probe mounted ceremoniously on a plinth by a Victor crew after a less than perfect disengagement had induced a whip in the hose.

Fortunately, accidents were rare but not unknown. I remember hearing stories when I was going through training of a Buccaneer that had come to grief making an emergency disengagement. Tangled in the drogue after a failed attempt to connect, the pilot pulled back on the stick and the Buccaneer sliced through the tail of the Victor tanker which broke off, causing the jet to crash into the sea. Only the co-pilot of the Victor survived after ejecting from the doomed aircraft; the rest of the crew was tragically lost.

The Phantom probe was mounted internally on the right-hand side of the fuselage behind a long retractable door. The operating switch had three positions: 'extend', 'refuel', and 'retract'. In the 'extend' position the probe could be extended but the fuel tanks remained pressurised. To refuel, the tanks had to be depressurised, which was done by selecting the 'refuel' position. This gave the flexibility to sit behind a tanker with the fuel system operating normally but

Astern the port hose of a Victor tanker. The reflections in the canopy of the pilot's helmet could be very distracting.

with the checks done, the switches made, and ready to tank on demand. There were also procedures in place to allow silent refuelling. 'On the lights' was the only call that was needed from the tanker captain; the rest would occur without chat. The receiver would drop in behind and watch while the lights flashed in various sequences as the hose was primed. Eventually the reds would go out and the ambers would light, at which time the pilot would move to the 'wait'. After contact, the green lights would show that fuel was transferring. Flashing greens meant 'you've had your fuel but stay plugged in if you want more'. Flashing ambers meant 'you really have had your lot'!

The fuel in the Phantom was stored internally in seven fuel tanks located down the spine of the aircraft. A further two tanks were located in the wings. The aircraft could also carry up to three external tanks, two wing tanks known as 'Sargent Fletchers', and a larger centreline tank that could hold 4,000 lbs of fuel. A quick sum shows that a clean Phantom with no external tanks had 13,522 lbs; 18,420 lbs with two small wing tanks fitted; and, with all three external

The refueling probe extended.

tanks, a very respectable 22,383 lbs. The whole system was pressurised. Electric transfer pumps moved the fuel from the external tanks first, followed by the wing tanks and, finally, the fuselage tanks. It was always a surprise to see the fuel tanks when a Phantom was stripped down. The tanks were rubberised bladders connected together by some fairly agricultural pipework and sat in cradles within the airframe. Another surprising fact was that there was no fuel gauge in the rear cockpit, yet fuel management was a crew responsibility. It led to a lot of unnecessary nagging from the back cockpit, particularly when afterburner was being used. The fuel was managed by the pilot. One of the 'gotchas' was that if any fuel was trapped in the No. 7 tank it could give a dangerously aft balance to the centre of gravity of the aircraft, making a 'departure from controlled flight' a distinct possibility. Ensuring that No. 7 tank transferred was important.

Fuel was measured in pounds weight, so any calculation was unintelligible to a layman. The key figure to remember was that an RAF Phantom had to land with 2,000 lbs of fuel, plus enough reserve to get to a nominated diversion airfield. This could be a local crash diversion in good weather conditions, or a

A 56 Squadron Phantom refuelling from a Victor tanker.

more remote weather diversion if the weather was marginal. I remember feeling distinctly nervous when, after a particularly spirited air combat sortie with a very experienced weapons instructor, we landed with 600 lbs of fuel. As the gauge was only accurate to within a couple of hundred pounds, that was rather less fuel remaining than either of us would have preferred. We both kept a reasonably low profile as the refuelling figures were entered into the aircraft log book after that turnround. The normal fuel flow was 90 lbs a minute for medium level cruise settings in a normal training fit. Using reheat, the Phantom could guzzle fuel at the crazy rate of 2,000 lbs per minute. Typically during an air combat sortie remaining close to base but using reheat most of the time, the mission lasted 20 minutes or less. Fuel could be 'dumped' or jettisoned in case of emergency from two vents at the back of the wing fold hinge. A fully loaded Phantom could not land immediately after take-off as it was too heavy and trying to do so would over-stress the airframe and undercarriage. It was rare to need to dump, and the only time you might wish to do that would be if an emergency occurred immediately after take-off. In this situation, fuel had to be dumped down to a safe limit. Dump was selected from the front cockpit, but the Phantom was not selective and if the pilot forgot to turn off 'dump', every last pound of fuel could be unceremoniously jettisoned overboard until the tanks were dry and the engines stopped. Once 'dump' was selected, the pilot kept his hand on the switch and watched the fuel gauges extremely closely. The Phantom had a 'Buddy Fill'

Looking across at the port HDU of a Victor tanker over the southern Alps.

capability, although the RAF never bought tactical refuelling pods. A refuelling pod could be attached to the centreline station so that the Phantom could pass its own fuel to another aircraft. This capability was a throwback to its carrier days where the only AAR capability might be mutual refuelling.

The Phantom was cleared to tank from all the RAF tanker types plus a few other NATO tankers as well. The Victor was designed as a strategic bomber but adapted well to the tanker role, proving itself in combat during the Falklands Campaign. Airflow behind the Victor was smooth, and with a centre-mounted HDU and two wing-mounted HDUs it was a flexible platform. The early K Mk 1 Victor had problems, as it was underpowered for the new role. With upgraded engines and a few additional modifications, the K Mk 2 was an immediate success. If memory serves me correctly, the later version offered a healthy 109,000 lbs of fuel to be offloaded to its 'customers'. Fuel was transferred from the Victor at 4,000 lbs per minute from the centreline HDU and 1,250 lbs per minute from the wing HDUs. If operating as a single aircraft, the higher fuel flow offered by the centreline meant that fuel could be taken on more quickly, which was the preferred method. Operating as a pair, it was normal procedure for both aircraft to be refuelling from both wing stations at the same time, making the transfer quicker overall.

Tanking was not always straightforward, and crews could face a conundrum. Use of minimum reheat in a very heavy QRA fit aircraft or tanking at 25,000 feet or above meant that the fuel burn rate was high. On a wing hose, fuel was feeding at 1,250 lbs per minute. With one engine at maximum 'cold power' and the other in minimum reheat, fuel was being pumped out of the back at up to 300 lbs per minute. Topping off took much longer than normal.

The VC10 was the mainstay of RAF tanker force for years. Like the Victor, the original VC10 C Mk 1 tankers were equipped with a centreline HDU and two wing stations. In theory, triple point refuelling was possible. But it was a little busy down the back end with three Phantoms plugged in, and it was rarely if ever seen. Additional VC10 airframes were added to the fleet over the years as the RAF acquired ex-civilian airframes retired from airline service. The K2/K3 and K4 versions all had three point refuelling, but during the early 1990s, the original transport C Mk 1s were also equipped with wing-mounted HDUs but no centre HDU and were designated as VC10 C1Ks. The VC10 is probably still one of the most graceful aeroplanes ever designed, and, like the Victor, it adapted well to the tanker role. The airflow below the fuselage was smooth and all the baskets flew well and were stable when moving in for contact. Most importantly, the formation references were clear and the tanker was well lit at night, making for an undramatic experience, which was always welcome. Perhaps the only criticism I would have was that there was a slight dihedral on the wing when it was loaded in flight, giving a slightly false horizon. In wispy cloud it could be a little disorientating, but not unduly so. Apart from night exercises at 02:00, I can safely say I was always happy to see a VC10 tanker.

A small number of C-130 Hercules were converted to act as tactical refuellers in support of operations in the Falklands. The fit was not particularly pretty. A standard HDU was mounted on a pallet bolted onto the C-130 loading ramp. The HDU was plugged into the C-130 fuel tanks to allow fuel to be dispensed. Some of the piping literally ran through the cargo bay. An 'Orange Crop' electronic surveillance system was added at the same time to give the aircraft some form of electronic protection in the rather more dangerous South Atlantic airspace. It also allowed the tanker to double up as a surveillance platform, and it would often be tasked to inspect fishing vessels operating within the Falklands Maritime Area. The modified aircraft could be recognised by the large pods added below the wingtips, which housed the receive antennas.

When tanking, the C-130 tended to operate at lower levels than its peers, and tanking at 5,000 feet in the Falklands was not unusual. This was mainly due to the nature of the installation, as the cabin was unpressurised when the AAR equipment was in use. This limited the height at which the aircraft could operate unless the crew went onto oxygen. Whilst very tactical, the greater turbulence at those lower heights meant plugging in could often be more by luck than judgement, as the basket could be extremely lively. The navigator's commentary

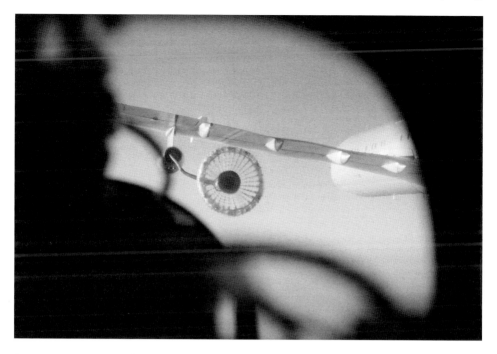

A navigator's eye view of the basket from the wait position.

XV474 tanking from a Victor K3 over the South Atlantic.

could sound extremely contradictory as the crew jousted with a gyrating basket. A regular chant of 'in line' could closely be followed by 'missed at 6 o'clock' as the basket took umbrage at the final stages of the plug, frustrating the pilots no end. Dare I say, for fear of insulting the very professional Victor and VC10 crews, that because the C-130 operators were not dyed-in-the-wool tanking specialists, they proved to be extremely flexible, and no task was too difficult. Outrageous requests for offbeat tactical towlines were greeted with barely a comment and executed without drama. Perhaps this is unfair criticism, as all RAF AAR crews were universally acclaimed by crews from other nations in every recent conflict and were invariably flexible and professional.

The Vulcan, like the Victor, served most of its life as a bomber. Immediately following the Falklands War, the demands on the tanker force were huge and Victors supported the C-130 transport fleet that were conducting refuelled 'airbridge' sorties to the islands. At that stage, without the AAR fleet, operations to the islands would have been impossible. A few Vulcans were hastily converted to the tanker role and operated for a few years by No. 44 Squadron in the UK. The fit was outrageously simple, with a basic HDU scabbed under the tail to provide a single point tanker. Like its more numerous predecessor, the Vulcan proved to be a very capable AAR platform, and was well liked by those who used it. Sadly, few photographs survive of this short period in the Vulcan's service history.

The KC135 was adopted by the US Air Force, so KC135s were by far the most common tanker available on operations, given the greater numbers. Despite the old adage 'Never turn down a tanker', the difficulties of tanking from a KC135 were not insignificant. At night it was poorly lit and gave the crews a significant challenge, even when it was operationally essential to use it. Clearing RAF crews to tank proved difficult, and there was much soul-searching at the test establishment at Boscombe Down as the test pilots tried to clear RAF aircraft to operate from the aircraft. Unlike the RAF system, the KC135 was fitted with a boom refuelling system, and the technique was entirely different to the RAF method. For USAF aircraft, a boom operator in the tanker literally 'flew' the boom into a receptacle on the spine of the receiver, using a control stick. This did not work for a British Phantom, which had been adapted from the US Navy system and used the probe and drogue method. It was in 1977 that we were asked to conduct the first evaluation of an adapted KC135 fitted with a drogue unit. The test pilots at Boscombe Down conducted some hasty trials and offered some basic advice to the squadron. At this stage we were tasked by HQ 11 Group to venture onto the towline and add a squadron perspective. The problem with the KC135 was that to fit a drogue, a short section of hose was attached to the end of boom. The basket was much smaller than the comparable RAF basket and, to compound the problem, once contact was made, the pilot had to move gently to the left and set up an 'S-shaped' kink in the hose to allow the valves to open before fuel would flow. Once this delicate operation was complete, at best the unfortunate pilot had to fly a precise formation position holding the shape of the 'S' in the pipe or the valves would close. At worst, the hose would disconnect rather dramatically if the stresses on the short hose became too great. In clear air, there was generally no drama, but tanking in cloud or in turbulent air became exciting, particularly if the tanker captain forgot that he was not towing a USAF Phantom, which was much more firmly attached to the boom.

Tanking took on comic proportions if the boom operator ever decided to help out by flying the basket onto the probe. An 'aerial joust' would not describe the chaos adequately. For RAF pilots, the tanking technique was the same to make contact, albeit aiming for a smaller basket. As the pilot made the corrections from the navigator's commentary, there would suddenly be a double correction if the boom operator intervened. Although, with experience, pilots became more used to the KC135, it was never easy, and crews breathed a sigh of relief when allocated to a VC10 on operations.

The TriStar was deployed operationally in 1986, so it was not available through most of the Phantom's early operational service. Although a fine tanker,

Phantoms XV490 and XV464 waiting to refuel from a KC135A.

'On the Starboard'.

XV464 alongside the KC135 tanker.

The boom operator's view of XV490. UK MOD Crown Copyright (1977).

it was fitted with only a single HDU mounted under the tail after problems were encountered fitting wing hoses. This meant that although the fuel flow rates were higher, only a single aircraft could refuel at any one time, so tanker brackets were longer. It was always a risk that both of the two baskets in the dual HDU could be lost or damaged, trapping the fuel onboard. As an alternative, the TriStar often topped up VC10 tankers on a trail, returning to base and leaving the VC10s, with the more flexible three point fit, to go down route.

I learned the practical challenges of NATO interoperability when I was deployed to the Balkans Combat Air Operations Centre in Vicenza, Italy. My role was to control the daily air tasking order and ensure that the programme that the NATO planners had put together was executed correctly by the individual aircrew. It was a massive operation involving hundreds of aircraft deployed to forward bases, with some flying daily from home bases as far away as the UK and Germany. The main holding area was in the Adriatic Sea and was known colloquially as 'Main Street'; it was here that most of the tanker towlines were situated. The main operating areas in Bosnia and Kosovo were accessed through Albanian airspace. Aircraft routeing into the area would refuel

A Tristar tanker.

to ensure that they had a full fuel load before entering the operational airspace. To aid me in the task I had a dedicated tanker controller sitting next to me on the Operations floor. He or she would keep a close eye on the specifics of the AAR missions, ensuring that tankers were en route, serviceable, and had the offload and capabilities to fulfil the mission. Given that USAF aircraft used the boom refuelling system and that many other NATO nations used probe and drogue, it was a challenge to ensure that tankers with the correct fit were on task and allocated to the correct towline. A probe-equipped Harrier would have no joy trying to refuel from a KC135 equipped with a boom.

For squadrons deploying overseas, the planning was conducted by a specialist cell at HQ 1 Group. An Air-to-Air Refuelling Co-ordinator, or AARC, was nominated who flew the actual sortie with the tanker crew. The original plan was passed to the deploying squadron, and although it was reviewed for accuracy, the planners were extremely good. Back at the squadron, crews were briefed and they prepared maps and charts for the sortie. For a trip to Cyprus, about twice the amount of fuel the Phantom carried was needed for the four-hour transit. It would seem logical that a single tanking bracket would be planned at the midpoint of the sortie, after which the fighters could proceed alone. That type of plan was rare, and in ten years on the Phantom I saw only one such tanking operation. For a normal deployment to Cyprus, three or four brackets were planned, topping off the tanks with smaller amounts of fuel as the mission progressed. Although more complex, such a plan was more adaptable. A typical plan would see the fighters conduct the first refuelling bracket over central France, with a second on the leg off the southern French coast, and a final bracket approaching Crete. About 100 miles from the destination, the fighters would be cleared to depart the formation and complete the journey at a higher speed ahead of the tankers. Such a plan would need about three or four tankers to refuel a squadron-sized detachment. Not all tankers would continue on to the destination. After the first bracket, the first and perhaps the second tanker would transfer the remaining fuel to another tanker and return to the UK. This made best use of the available AAR aircraft by keeping most of the fleet in the UK.

Tanking plans could be incredibly complex and, perhaps the most famous was the plan for the 'Black Buck' raids on the Falkland Islands. For those missions, eighteen individual Victor sorties were needed to give a single Vulcan enough fuel to complete the 8,000+ miles round trip to Ascension. A complex rolling refuel, with successive Victors performing mutual tanking in addition to topping up the Vulcan, resulted in one of the longest ever strategic bombing missions.

Not all NATO nations treated AAR in the same way as the UK. One quiet evening in the NATO Operations Centre, the majority of the flying had finished and I had just one pair of F18 fighters from a European NATO nation still flying over Kosovo. As they began their recovery and handed off to the Italian Air Traffic Control agency, one of the F18s declared a problem, although he was reluctant to declare an emergency. Despite this reticence, it became obvious that one of his engines had failed and he was returning towards Italian airspace. Based at Aviano, the pilot faced a long transit back to base with only one engine operating, so I immediately passed messages via the ATC liaison officer in the CAOC advising him that the nearest diversion was Brindisi, which was open and operating. To my surprise, not only did the pilot not divert but passed his intention to conduct AAR with a C-130 tanker as had been planned before the mission. I watched the operations plot, horrified as the pilot plugged in using his remaining working engine and took on fuel. The F18 then remained with the tanker, which towed him all the way back up the Adriatic to Aviano airbase. This might seem reasonable at face value, but older heads may not have been quite so bullish. My experience told me that tanking is not without risk. Years earlier I had watched as my pilot had struck a basket rim quite hard and it had broken up in mid-air, with some parts going down the air intake. The engine had ingested the debris and began to protest as the fan blades became unbalanced. We closed down the affected engine and returned to the nearest diversion airfield, which luckily was quite close. On inspection, the engine turbine blades had been badly damaged. We had already felt vibration before we shut down the engine, but a catastrophic failure was not impossible had the damage worsened. I was not the operating authority for the F18, so I had no power to divert the aircraft, although I was sorely tempted. All I could do was highlight the issue to the relevant national liaison officer. When quizzed, the liaison officer from the F18 detachment merely shrugged and said that the F18 had plenty of power to tank with only one engine. True, but imagine the embarrassment had the pilot damaged the basket and caused a failure of his one remaining good engine. It would have led to the loss of a vital NATO asset. I certainly learned about both tanking and airmanship that night, and realised that not all nations have similar standards.

CHAPTER 12
Weapons

The Phantom carried a series of weapons over its RAF service career. Normal fit for the aircraft was four AIM-7E-2 Sparrow III missiles carried under the fuselage, four AIM-9G infra-red guided missiles carried on LAU--7 launchers on pylons under the wings, and in service in RAF Germany, a SUU-23 gun pod on the centreline station. For UK QRA the gun was replaced normally by a centreline fuel tank to give the extra range.

During the early years, the AIM-7E-2 Sparrow III missile, used in conjunction with its AN/AWG-11/12 pulse Doppler radar, gave it a true look-down shoot-down capability not matched until the introduction of the F15A by the US Air Force in the early 1980s. The Sparrow had its roots firmly embedded in the 1960s, and by 1980 it was becoming obsolete. It was therefore replaced during the early 80s with the British Aerospace Skyflash missile. Similar in design concept to the Sparrow, the Skyflash incorporated a significant number of improvements aimed at keeping the F4 weapon systems credible. Regrettably, it was never equipped with an active missile such as the American AIM-54 Phoenix, which was probably too large to be carried. A UK modification called Active Skyflash was proposed by British Aerospace but was never funded by the MOD. The Phantom had already retired before the AIM-120 AMRAAM was deployed in RAF service.

The AIM-7E Sparrow was the main armament for much of the aircraft's life. The cylindrical missile body contained the various elements of the missile. Fixed triangular fins at the rear provided stability, with a further four fins at the midpoint of the missile body providing steering. A small radome at the front protected the electronic seeker head, making the missile aerodynamic. The main components were the seeker head, the missile guidance section, the autopilot, a fuse, a warhead, and the rocket motor. The missile, weighing in at 510 lb, was 12 feet long and 8 inches in diameter. Classed as a medium range missile, the maximum range varied with height. In the upper air, launch ranges of as much as 25 miles were theoretically possible, although, typically, medium level shots were taken much closer at 10-15 miles. At low level, this maximum range was reduced to as little as 5 miles. There was also a minimum range. The safety and arming mechanisms needed time to be primed, so it was possible to be too close to a target. There was also the obvious risk of being struck by debris if a short range shot proved effective and the target aircraft broke up.

The semi-active missile was guided by a continuous wave radar integrated into the main radar of the Phantom. CW radar signals transmitted through the Phantom's main radar bounced off the target and could be received by the Sparrow missile. With the radar in the search mode the CW transmitter was disabled in order to avoid alerting the warning systems of any potential target aircraft. Once the main radar was locked on, the CW transmitter was enabled and a rear reference antenna transmitted priming signals so that the missile could 'tune' to the CW frequency sent from the Phantom. On trigger press, data was fed to the missile via an umbilical plug giving it spatial coordinates for the target, and a 'speedgate' was set in the missile guidance control to a value representing the target's closing speed. Once launched, the Sparrow's homing head followed the reflected CW signals and the autopilot gave commands to the control fins guiding it to the target.

The Sparrow launcher was semi-recessed under the fuselage, so that when the missile was fitted only the lower half of the body was visible. This design feature greatly reduced drag from the missile's appendages and minimised the effect on aircraft performance; this was of great value when carrying four missiles weighing over 2,000 lbs. With this configuration, clean separation from the aircraft was a concern, particularly at high speed, and the risk of collision during launch was real. Once the pilot pulled the trigger, two strong hydraulic rams built into the launcher pushed the Sparrow away from the lower fuselage and out into the airflow. Using technology more akin to the Napoleonic War than a Third World War, a lanyard attached to the missile was pulled out, allowing the motor to fire. The missile motor powered the weapon towards its target at around Mach 2.8 above the launch speed. In the cockpit, the sound of a missile accelerating away, reaching three times the speed of sound almost instantly, sounded like an express train.

Once launched, there was a safe and arm mechanism to protect the Phantom and its crew. The warhead was armed by a simple mechanical device that rotated as the missile accelerated. Once it had exceeded a minimum acceleration value for a minimum time the warhead was enabled. This simple device had the great advantage of being robust and reliable. Due to the acceleration needed to perform the arm function, the missile was well ahead of the launch aircraft before the warhead could explode. If fighter crews were in any doubt as to whether they would see an air-to-air missile targeted against them, those thoughts were quickly dispelled as the massive smoke trail advertised the missile's presence and marked its progress towards the target. The missile quickly accelerated to its terminal velocity during the boost phase, after which the motor burned out and the missile coasted for the remainder of its journey to the target.

The missile being semi-active, the Phantom had to track the target with its main radar for the flight time of the missile in order to maintain the CW radar signal required by the missile. The seeker and guidance system never actually knew where the target was in space. The seeker head was moved by the missile's electronic brain to follow the returning CW radar signal, whilst the guidance system simply moved the fins to put the missile on an exact collision course with the target. This simple but effective guidance method proved robust and effective. Unfortunately, the need for the Phantom to keep illuminating the target with the CW radar meant that for long range firings, where the missile flight time could be up to 25 seconds, the attack had to be prosecuted to within visual range, making the less agile Phantom vulnerable if the missile failed to kill the target. Although an enemy would have been at a psychological disadvantage having just survived the passage of a 'smoking telegraph pole' (as missiles were colloquially known) if the missile failed, the attacking pilot had the opportunity to capitalise on the consequently more vulnerable Phantom. The terminal phase of a missile attack was clinically brutal. Although the designers hoped that the missile would fly into a target causing kinetic damage, it was more likely to achieve a close miss, hence the term 'missile'. They designed a fuse and warhead to cope with this most likely scenario. As the missile passed within close proximity of the target, a radio frequency fuse detected the bulk of the enemy airframe and commanded a detonation of the warhead. Inside the warhead a ring of hard metal rods were packed around an explosive charge. When the fuse detected the target the explosive was initiated, explosively ejecting the rods, which formed an expanding ring of metal. This ring had two ways to disable the target. If the ring hit the target while it was expanding, it would rip through the aircraft skin in a similar way to the structure being subjected to a band saw: structural failure was inevitable. However, the miss distance could be greater than the diameter of the expanding rods, and, in this case, the ring split into tiny fragments. These would penetrate the thin skin of the target aircraft, playing havoc with sensitive airframe components and avionics. Lethal damage was almost guaranteed.

Because of the high cost of missiles, crews were allocated only one shot per operational tour. My only Sparrow shot came in 1977, on the Aberporth Range in Cardigan Bay. The target was a pilotless drone called a Jindivik, operated by the Royal Aircraft Establishment from Llanbedr airfield. Our Phantoms deployed to a little-known unit called the Strike Command Air-to-Air Missile Establishment or STCAAME for short, located on the far side of the training base at RAF Valley in Anglesey. The staff at STCAAME supervised all the operational aspects of the firings, assisting the squadron aircrew and groundcrew. This included briefing and debriefing, through the preparation and loading of the weapons, to co-ordinating with the drone staff at Llanbedr to make sure that the target was in the right place at the right time. The base at Valley was infamous for poor weather, particularly in winter. Horizontal driving fog, which in meteorological terms is impossible, was not uncommon. Suffice it to say that anyone who attended a missile practice camp at Valley would remember endless days waiting for the weather to clear sufficiently to allow the Jindivik to launch. The Jindivik was very susceptible to crosswinds as well as low cloud, and the runway at Llanbedr was not well orientated. The airfield sat on the windward slopes of the Welsh mountains, with a northerly facing runway leaving it exposed to the harsh Atlantic weather. At least with the endless delays, there was no excuse not to be fully prepared for the planned missile shot.

In the early days of the Phantom's service, the missile firing profiles were extremely procedural and were designed to investigate and understand the limits of the operational envelope of the weapon. Firings at the edges of the radar coverage, at high 'G' levels, or at the extremes of the aircraft's flight envelope were conducted to refine how far the limits could be stretched. As the missile performance on the Phantom became better understood, the profiles became more operationally representative and were adapted to give more training value to the crews. Profiles that mimicked the head-on attack profiles that the Phantom employed operationally were designed. Because they were more realistic, success rates were much improved and it led to an improvement in confidence in the weapons among the crews.

Operations at STCAAME were monitored by the constant presence of a Soviet 'trawler' that was always on station in the waters of Cardigan Bay. Surprisingly, little fish was ever landed from the boats, but the host of aerials sprouting from the superstructure must have guaranteed excellent radio reception. For that reason, it was a constant challenge to ensure that loose talk on the radio did not give away information about our operational capabilities, and any signals transmitted from the aircraft were electronically protected against the collectors.

The test missiles were specially adapted by removing the warhead and replacing it with a telemetry pack that collected the essential data from the missile and transmitted it back to the ground. This meant that every electronic command executed by the missile during its short life was recorded and could be analysed later in excruciating detail. It also meant that when the fuse demanded the warhead to detonate, only a simple electronic pulse was transmitted and, without a warhead, the Jindivik would live to fly another day. Well, almost always. A crew on my first missile camp were given a fairly exacting profile that seemed to have little chance of success. The execution to the firing point was flawless and the Sparrow sped to its target perfectly. It was so perfect that it took off the tail of the Jindivik, sending it tumbling in a ball of flames into Cardigan Bay. Despite the lack of a warhead, a Mach 2.8 Sparrow punching a hole through the tail of the hapless drone proved enough to achieve an unplanned kill. To underline the fickle nature of aircrew, and despite the loss of an expensive drone, there was a raucous celebration in the bar of the Officers' Mess that evening and a 'zap' celebrating the 'kill' appeared on the Phantom which had fired the missile. There was another firing that caused rather more consternation. Just at the time when it cleared the nose of the firing aircraft, the missile demanded an immediate maximum deflection on the control fins, rose dramatically from below the nose, and aimed towards the stratosphere. Clearly unguided, it caused the crew a good deal of concern as it looped over the top of the aircraft and began to aim back towards the firing Phantom. A squadron joker suggested that as it made its vertical ascent, the missile had caused an alert by the Ballistic Missile Early Warning System at RAF Fylingdales, but we were never quite sure if this was true. The missile passed harmlessly behind the firing aircraft before diving into Cardigan Bay. The failure proved the value of having a robust safety margin during these firings.

Losing a Jindivik was not typical, and most firings were much more mundane. A detailed briefing was conducted by the firing crew to explain the profile in great depth, working through the procedures and radio calls, and, most importantly, what to do in the event of a missile 'hang up'. A firework that fails to go off on Bonfire Night is easily neutralised. A Sparrow that fails to fire and sits fizzing under the aircraft as it flies around the Welsh coastline is somewhat more problematic. Safe headings, to ensure that an armed aircraft always pointed away from populated areas, and armament safety procedures were briefed endlessly. The crew walked out to the aircraft as if conducting a normal training sortie, but the routine safety checks took on far more significance with a live weapon on board. The pilot paid much more attention to the weapons check, and the navigator made absolutely certain that the radar tested out fully serviceable using the built-in test. Armament safety errors were not tolerated. There was a widely reported incident at RAF Leuchars in the late 1970s. A QRA aircraft was being prepared and the aircrew were carrying out an acceptance check, making sure the missiles were serviceable. As the pilot selected the continuous wave radar to tune the Sparrow missiles, there was a flash and a Sidewinder left the missile rail, much to everyone's surprise. The CW switch was totally unrelated to launching a Sidewinder, so the reason for its unexpected departure was not immediately clear. Luckily, although the launch was dramatic, and undoubtedly expensive, the safe heading was accurate and the missile bounced on the grass at the far side of the airfield, tumbling harmlessly into a small river. The incident was investigated and it seemed that a fault on the weapon system had allowed a stray voltage to remain on the firing circuit. When the CW radar had been activated, the Sidewinder, which needed only a simple 28-volt pulse, had been given a launch command. There was little logic to the fault, but it underlined the dangers of operating with live weapons onboard. Suddenly, the squadron armourers paid much more attention to the 'no volts' checks, knowing that the gremlins could strike easily.

Two aircraft and crews were always briefed for a firing, and if the primary firer was unable to conduct the shot, the secondary firer was always happy to substitute. The type of missile that had been nominated for the firing was loaded onto each of the firing aircraft and prepared in exactly the same way. In addition to the missile, each aircraft carried a missile monitoring pod that would photograph the firing, using high speed cameras. A third aircraft was loaded with camera equipment and would fly behind the primary firer in a loose formation position to photograph the launch. After engine start, if it was a Sparrow shot, the missiles were tuned to the radar frequency and checked to make sure the electronic data was being received by STCAAME. In the case of a Sidewinder, a small infra-red torch was shone into the seeker head to ensure it was receiving the IR energy. This was always a nervous time for the crews, as even the smallest fault could result in the secondary firer stepping into pole position. After take-off it was only a short transit to Bardsey Island, which was the visual entry point to the range. The primary firer and the chase aircraft would then carry on into the range while the secondary aircraft held off, acting as an airborne spare. The range controllers positioned the Jindivik and the Phantom on separate tracks leading to an intercept point in the range. Timing countdowns ran down as the run progressed.

Firing a medium range air-to-air weapon required a great deal of attention to detail. The controllers mapped out a safety trace within the range airspace, and it was vital that both the Phantom and the Jindivik stayed within this boundary. It was also vital that, once launched, the missile would follow a safe heading away from land and fall harmlessly into Cardigan Bay within the range boundary and away from any stray shipping that might have penetrated the range. With a few seconds to go to the firing, flares were ignited on the Jindivik. These would aid visual acquisition, as despite the fact it was painted bright orange, the drone was extremely small and could be difficult to see. Even though a Sparrow missile would track its target with the CW radar beam, the chase pilot would follow the Jindivik visually to record the shot, so the flares ensured that the target was as visible as possible. As the Phantom closed on its target, the calm words from the controller would be a prelude to mayhem:

'5–4–3–2–1; punch; clear to fire.'

The trigger was wired to a pulse tone generator, so immediately following the trigger press, the crew would hear a short beep transmitted over the radio. Whilst the beep was sufficient to enable the tracking systems on the range to prepare to track the missile, it was not sufficient time for the photo chase crew to start their cameras. Therefore, the pilot of the Phantom was expected to call:

'Firing, firing, now';

the 'now' being coincident with the trigger press. Adding another series of actions to the requirements of an already hardworking crew was occasionally just too much. There were several cases of:

beep, whoosh, 'Firing, firing, now.'

Whilst this did not affect the performance of the weapon system or the collection of the data, there would be no photo chase film and a fine of many beers. In addition, there was a 2-second delay while the missile was ejected from the launcher and before the motor fired. Invariably, although the delay was anticipated, it still caused doubt. Had the missile fired? Should I press again? All things being equal, the beep was followed closely by an almighty whoosh from the rocket motor, and the aircraft was enveloped in white smoke. At that point, the firing aircraft broke away, allowing the photo chase to track the missile all the way to the target. Despite procedures, I was unable to find a single pilot who could resist the temptation to drop the wing as soon as he was clear to watch the missile snake away.

What you would not want to hear was:

'5–4–3–2–1; punch; clear to fire.' 'Firing, firing, now' – beep – whoosh – beep – whoosh!

This sadly happened to an exchange officer who, either through enthusiasm or doubt as to whether he had pulled the trigger hard enough, proved that pressing the trigger twice results in two Sparrows leaving the aircraft. Most pilots were well aware of this limitation, and many would recite a short verse when taking a double firing:

'Fox 1, one thousand and one, one thousand and two, Fox 1.'

Fox 1 was the radio call to announce a Sparrow firing. This made sure that the delay was anticipated, but it also gave separation between missiles in the event of a planned double Sparrow firing.

After the firing, the data that was collected was analysed and translated into procedures that were published in the tactics manuals to ensure that any missile fired operationally would have the best chance of success. In the split-second decision-making that characterised an air combat engagement, the less that could be left to chance the better. STCAAME firings added much to the knowledge base, and made the risk of errors in combat just that little less likely.

A Sparrow missile on the front station.

The AIM-7E Sparrow Seeker Head.

Above: An AIM9G missile at
Newark Air Museum.

Right: An AIM9L Seeker Head
and umbilical which attached
the missile to the missile
launcher rail.

The gyros or 'rollerons' on the rear fins of the Sidewinder.

A Sidewinder is launched from a Phantom on Aberporth Range. Picture courtesy David Lewis. UK MOD Crown Copyright (1979).

Above: The onboard missile monitoring pod captures the Sidewinder missile as the motor fires. Picture courtesy David Lewis. UK MOD Crown Copyright (1979).

Right: A Skyflash Missile and the eject launcher showing the hydraulic rams which pushed the missile into the airflow.

The nose cone on the Suu23 Gun gun to the left has been removed showing the 6 barrels of the Gatling gun. Clips of 20-mm shells are laid out. The board behind was used for sighting the gunpod.

XV437 with a drill weapons display.

The RAF Phantom operated two versions of the Sidewinder: the AIM-9G and the AIM-9L. In the early days, the AIM-9G gave only a stern hemisphere capability. To ensure the target would be seen by the seeker, the Phantom had to be manoeuvred into the targets rear hemisphere or '6 o'clock'. The later AIM-9L had a much improved seeker and offered all-round capability. It was much more effective to shoot an enemy in the head-on sector and fly through the engagement avoiding the need to stay and turn with a potentially more agile opponent. In training, opponents often turned sharply in behind, claiming a kill. In reality, the smoke trail from a head-on Sidewinder coupled with the defensive reaction that would have been necessary would have probably negated the possibility of such a manoeuvre. This artificiality was difficult to avoid and had to be dissected at the debrief to gain an accurate analysis of the effectiveness of the tactics. Smaller combat missiles such as the Sidewinder were generally less effective against a target that was opening rapidly, and shots were taken when the missile would have little chance of success. To avoid this, it was important to match the opponent's speed as you turned for the shot, or preferably gain some overtake. This gave the missile a better chance of success. Although almost identical, the AIM-9G had a straight leading edge on the forward control fins. The later AIM-9L could be distinguished by the double delta forward canard configuration and small glass windows immediately behind the canards that housed an upgraded laser fuse.

Until it left the aircraft, the Sidewinder seeker head was cooled by liquid coolant from a bottle that fitted into each LAU-7 missile rail. The front section of the launcher could be moved forward to give access to the coolant bottle, which was changed by the groundcrew during every turnround. A switch in the cockpit initiated cooling and the coolant was fed to the missile head, lowering the temperature of the seeker and ensuring that the seeker head was sufficiently responsive to detect the minute amounts of infra-red radiation of a target engine against the background environment.

The Sidewinder was quite different to the Sparrow, being a heat-seeking missile that tracked the infra-red radiation from the target aircraft's exhaust plume or airframe. It had a much shorter range and was optimised for close combat. The four movable fins on the forebody were the control surfaces that steered the missile in flight. Four larger fixed fins at the rear provided aerodynamic stability, assisted by small spinning gyros on each fin. Like its larger brother, the Sidewinder had a seeker head, a guidance control system, an autopilot, a warhead, a fuse, and a motor. A small revolving disc, called a reticule, spun away inside the seeker head behind the glass dome. The reticule was a complex design that sensed the angular displacement of the heat source away from the missile's centreline. Once the target exhaust had been acquired, the missile generated a warbling tone in the crew's headsets, known as the Sidewinder 'growl'. For the AIM-9G the noise literally was a growl, but because of the way the modified AIM-9L head worked, the noise sounded more like a 'chirp'. This told the pilot that the missile had locked to its prey and could be fired. Unlike the Sparrow, the Sidewinder literally drove off the launcher rail and aimed towards the target. The reticule provided commands to the autopilot and on to the control fins to point at the target throughout the missile flight time. This quite agricultural method of control generated a distinctive type of flight path. The early marks of Sidewinder up to the AIM-9M had an annular blast fragmentation warhead as the killing power. Small metal particles were wrapped around an explosive charge which, when detonated by the fuse, caused thousands of high speed metal fragments to be directed in a ring around the missile body. As the missile entered the terminal guidance phase, a fuse sensed the proximity of the airframe and sent a detonation pulse to the warhead. On the AIM-9L this fuse was improved by adding a target detector with four infra-red emitters and associated detectors. The four small glass windows on the forebody of the AIM-9L were evidence of this improved fuse. Unlike the Sparrow, the Sidewinder was a 'fire and forget' missile. Once it had acquired the target and the trigger was pressed, the crew had no further part to play. It guided to its target entirely autonomously.

In addition to live missiles, which could be distinguished by yellow bands on the missile body, there were drill rounds that were used for training groundcrew and could be carried for photographic events or air shows. These looked exactly like the real thing but blue dots were painted on the fins of the Sparrow. Drill Sidewinders sometimes did not have rear fins, and the word 'drill' was clearly marked in blue boxes on the missile body. This ensured that a live load could never be accidentally put on an aircraft by mistake. Acquisition rounds were also available for training purposes. A fully capable seeker head fitted to a missile body could be carried on the LAU-7 missile rail. Although both front and rear fins were missing on an acquisition round, the seeker head acted in every way like a live Sidewinder, and the cockpit indications when it was carried were identical to a live missile. The AIM-9Gs and original AIM-9Ls were not equipped with infra-red countermeasures so were very vulnerable to infra-red countermeasures or flares. Later a rudimentary system was developed, known as 'Genetic', which was subsequently replaced in the AIM-9Li version with a much more capable flare rejection circuitry. This chess battle ensured that the missile fitted to the Phantom kept pace with the developing capabilities of potential enemies.

The Sidewinder was a hugely successful missile and proved itself in many operations from the Falklands to the Gulf. Unfortunately, I managed to prove that it is not infallible. In addition to controlling the missile practice camps, No. 11 Group, the Operational Headquarters for the Phantom Force, could schedule a no-notice firing by a Quick Reaction Alert aircraft. I was happily watching the latest movie on Battle Flight at Wildenrath when the alert klaxon sounded. Once in the cockpit, breathing heavily, I checked in on the telebrief to copy the scramble message. Normally in Germany this would be an easterly heading towards the Inner German Border, perhaps to shepherd a wayward light aircraft away from East German airspace. In the UK, it might be an easterly vector suggesting a training intercept in the North Sea. If it was northerly, it would be a live QRA mission off the north coast of Scotland where the Soviets would be heading around the North Cape and into the Iceland-Faroes gap. For this particular scramble, the vector was westerly, which could mean only one thing: a Battle Flight QRA missile firing. We carried the essential operational information in a small pocket book called a 'Noddy Guide', hidden in the depths of which were the profiles to be used for a Battle Flight firing.

From Germany it was a long transit from the Dutch border, all the way across the English Channel, across England and Wales to the entry point at Bardsey Island. Throughout the trip, while talking to the air traffic control agencies, my pilot and I were rehearsing the intricacies of the firing profile and trying to suppress the inevitable nerves. Although complex, the procedure was well set out, and we practised regularly in the simulator. Nothing could go wrong. Indeed, nothing did go wrong as we dropped into the routine. As we descended over Wales, armed with a full war load of four Sparrows, four Sidewinders, and a fully loaded gun, we were joined by another Phantom that had been launched from RAF Coningsby to act as the photo chase. The clock ticked down. The profile was a simple look-down stern shot against a Jindivik drone at very low level. We were to fire from a few thousand feet above the target after a late push down towards the target at 'Punch'. The shot was well within normal missile parameters, so it gave no cause for concern. As we ran around the range following the instructions from the controller, things seemed to be running on rails. We received clearance to fire, my pilot called visual, and as the pipper came on, the Sidewinder began to 'growl'. He pulled the trigger and the Sidewinder sped away in a cloud of smoke and we broke out. My pilot reversed the turn as the photo chase tracked the missile's flight, and we watched it guide towards the surface of the sea. The bright orange Jindivik stood out well against the choppy sea. The Sidewinder followed a spiralling path downwards and splashed into the sea behind the target, throwing up small splashes in the water that seemed to be the witness marks from the warhead as it exploded. All seemed fine, as even with a live missile there were procedures to try to avoid killing the drone, and it flew gently on having survived the encounter. After landing for the debrief at RAF Valley, we learned that the missile had failed to guide. For real, a second missile would have been fired to finish the job, but we would never know the reason for the failure as QRA missiles were not equipped with a telemetry pack. It will remain a mystery, albeit an expensive mystery. Sidewinder failures were rare, but it was a shame to be part of the statistics that lowered the success rate.

The Sparrow was replaced by a British-built derivative called the Skyflash which had a much improved capability. Although due to enter service on the Phantom in the late 1970s, it began to emerge on UK-based aircraft in the early 1980s, but did not appear in any numbers in Germany until 1983. Skyflash became the standard weapon for the Phantom, but it had been developed principally to equip the Tornado F3, which was about to enter service at that time. The Operational Conversion Unit did not teach Skyflash tactics for the Phantom until well into the mid-80s, so, as with many other disciplines, the training was delegated to the squadron weapons instructors. In reality, few changes were needed, as the missile merely provided improved performance. Although it shared a very similar missile body, looked similar to the Sparrow, and fitted into the underbelly housings without modification, the Skyflash had a significantly longer range due to the fitting of a much improved motor. It was fitted with a Marconi XJ521 monopulse seeker head that performed well against electronic jamming, so its big advantage was that it was much more capable in the electronic jamming environment that the Phantom was expected to face. It was easily identifiable because of the black strip antennas down the centre body of the missile which supported a new fuse. As with any weapon system update, the radar was modified to support the new missile. Small pennants on the small ancillary intake on the nose indicated which weapons update was fitted to a particular aircraft. One small pennant was an original standard missile control system, two was an interim standard, while three pennants designated a fully modified, Skyflash capable, weapon system.

For training purposes, weapon simulators were fitted so that the crew would see indications in the cockpit to make it appear that real weapons were being carried. A large concrete Sparrow, minus its fins and painted blue, was always carried on one of the front fuselage stations. Contrary to popular belief, this was not a dummy Sparrow but was fitted to add weight at the front of the aircraft to improve the centre of gravity. Normally two dummy Sparrows were fitted unless a strike camera was needed. As the camera also fitted to the front Sparrow launcher, the dummy missile was joined by the camera pod. The Phantom, without that missile, became rather unstable in pitch, particularly with fuel in the aft No. 7 tank, so the front missile was always the last to be fired in anger. In reality the Sparrow simulator was a small electronic plug called a target acquisition unit fitted into one of the other launchers. When fitted, the lights on the missile control panel in the front cockpit lit up as if four missiles were loaded. As simulated missile shots were taken, the lights disappeared. In the case of the Sidewinder, the acquisition unit was mounted on a missile body but was easily identifiable as it was not fitted with fins. This 'acqui(sition) round', as it was known, was linked to the weapon system via an umbilical plug that fitted into the missile rail and acted exactly like the real missile, providing a 'growl' in the headsets. Under normal conditions, after a Sidewinder was fired, the weapon system cycled to the next live missile on an adjacent launcher. After a simulated shot with the acquisition round, the pilot had to cycle through the sequence, returning to the launcher carrying the practice round.

Although some versions of the Phantom, such as the German F4F, were equipped with an integral gun, the RAF version was not. The British Phantom had its heritage in the early US Air Force C/D models and the US Navy J model. At that time, the USAF had decided that the day of the gun was over, so when the decision was reversed there was no option but to design a podded gun to fill the gap. The RAF bought the SUU-23 gun pod, which was carried on the centreline station. Weighing 1,730 lbs, the pod was fitted with a six-barrelled M61 Gatling gun that carried 1,234 rounds of 20-mm ammunition and could fire at up to 6,000 rounds per minute. Different types of bullets could be loaded, ranging from inert training rounds, known as ball ammunition, through high explosive incendiary rounds (HEI), to armour piercing rounds. HEI was normally loaded on a live air defence mission. Stripped of the front aerodynamic fairing, the barrels extended to almost half of the overall length of the pod. Immediately behind sat a complex linked feed mechanism that moved the rounds from the ammunition can into the firing breech where they were electronically fired. At the rear of the pod another aerodynamic housing covered the electronics package that controlled the firing process.

The gun was extremely useful in certain environments. On a QRA mission, the gun would be a great persuader should it be necessary to fire a warning shot to convince an intercepted aircraft to comply with instructions. A missile was indiscriminate and could result in the loss of the intercepted aircraft, escalating the situation unnecessarily. A few rounds of high explosive incendiary bullets were much more subtle and would probably do the trick. The gun also proved useful in providing a limited air-to-ground strafing capability for air defence crews in the Falkland Islands. Until reinforced by dedicated ground attack aircraft, the air defence Phantoms could have offered a rudimentary capability against enemy ground forces using the gun.

The gunsight controls, immediately in front of the pilot, had the hugely snappy title of LCOSS or lead computing optical sighting system. The main controls were on the radar repeater. The sight could be 'caged', in other words fixed to the weapons boresight, or released in a dynamic lead computing mode by selecting 'uncaged'. It projected a limited set of symbols onto the sight glass

The pilot's radar scope with the gunsight controls on the right.

which helped the pilot aim the gun. In 'caged' mode, a fixed cross was locked to the weapon's boresight and a fixed depression could be set using a rotary knob, allowing the sight to be configured for air-to-ground strafe. In this mode the radar could be used to provide a range to the target, and this information was displayed by a moving range ring around the outside of the sighting symbology. Once 'uncaged', a moving dot, or pipper, showed where the bullets would fall once fired. In this air-to-air mode, the pipper was corrected for all the parameters that could affect the bullets, such as lead angles, gravity drop, and velocity jump. Radar range was fed in automatically when the radar was locked to the target.

Whilst in theory this sight could solve any air-to-air firing solution, in practice it had its limitations. To begin with, the sight had a built-in lag caused by the analogue sighting computer needing about one second to complete its calculations. This meant that when attempting to achieve a guns tracking solution on a target, the pilot would have to have a perfectly stable tracking solution for at least one second if the shot was to be valid. Very few targets were sufficiently understanding to fly in a stable predictable path for several seconds just to allow the Phantom pilot to close for his guns kill. The second problem was that at medium to long range, any tiny variation in the Phantom's manoeuvre was amplified by the sight. The cure to this problem was for the pilot to partially deaden the sight by using a switch on the outside of the left throttle. Again this was referred to as caging the sight – just to be confusing! With this 'caged' switch pressed backwards by the pilot's left-hand little finger, the sight was de-sensitised so that it did not overreact to the Phantom's manoeuvres. As the range reduced during a guns attack the calculations became less reactive, and at a range of about around 1,000 feet the pilot would release the switch to uncage the sight. At this point he would have a usable sighting solution. In the real world, this took a great deal of skill and practice.

The way in which RAF crews practised air-to-air gunnery was a throwback to the past, having changed little in the years since the Second World War. Only the tow aircraft had been updated. A Canberra operated by No. 100 Squadron would tow a banner behind the aircraft, albeit at the amazingly slow speed of 180 knots.

The banner was attached to the towline, and heavy weights on the end of the spreader bar made the banner fly upright. The banner was made of a tough woven fabric that felt like a tennis net. It was edged in black to make it more visible at higher speeds, a large black spot in the centre providing an aiming mark. A darker section was painted at the back of the banner to indicate the overall length. Flying alongside, you could see the banner flapping in the airflow. If it was towed at a much higher speed, the banner would literally be shredded in the airflow. The fact that it was towed so slowly caused significant issues for high speed fighters.

There were a number of firing patterns, but the most common for Phantom squadrons was the 'figure of 8'. On a call of 'commence' from the Phantom navigator, the Canberra pilot would start a turn. The navigator would then control a pattern, aiming to roll in behind at about a mile and offset by 10 degrees. He would then give a range commentary to the Phantom pilot, who would close in and eventually track the banner with the pipper. At an appropriate range, the pilot would release the gunsight into 'uncaged' mode and fire a short burst. The tracking picture was a black art, with the pilot initially aiming towards the front of the banner before relaxing slightly to track the aiming mark painted on the banner. This compensated for errors in the Phantom's gunsight caused by the slow speed of the tow aircraft. After the rounds had been fired, a violent breakout in the opposite direction to the turn was initiated. In the front, the pilot moved the controls roughly from one extreme to the other. In the back, the breakout felt violent and often put the head perilously close to banging on the canopy glass. At this point the Canberra straightened up before reversing its turn to fly the second part of the 'figure of 8'. The Phantom navigator would then control a further set up before the firing procedure was repeated for a second pass in the other direction. With the huge differences in speed, the separation

A 100 Sqn Canberra towing a banner which is just visible in the circle. This shows how difficult it was for a Phantom pilot to visually acquire the banner on a 'hot' pass.

An air to air gunnery banner. The black stripe to the right is the towing strop and the banner is stabilized by a heavy spreader bar.

between the high speed Phantom and the low speed banner at the breakout point reduced to well less than 300 yards. At the point of closest pass, the separation between the Phantom and the banner was literally feet, and yet, remarkably, there were no instances of collisions. The whole procedure was extremely rapid and lasted only a minute or two, and the overtake speeds were breath-taking. The absolutely critical safety aspect was that firing pilots should always ensure that they stopped firing if the angle-off fell below 15 degrees. Angle-off was the angle between the Phantom's heading and that of the Canberra. This ensured that the bullets were never aimed directly at the Canberra. Inside 15 degrees and Canberra crews became extremely nervous, as not only the banner but also the Canberra would appear on the Phantom's gunsight film. Many Canberra crews told me that they could hear bullets whistle past when the angle-off became too shallow. Beer changed hands for this infraction.

Marking a banner was always a 'blood sport' and extremely competitive. The Qualified Weapons Instructors ruled the roost on an armament practice camp and their word was gospel. The bullets were tipped with paint, so any that passed through the flag left not just a hole but a coloured mark; typically red, blue, yellow, and green were used. Up to four aircraft fired on each banner, so each jet was allocated a different coloured round. After the sortie the Canberra would jettison the banner over the runway and it would be returned to the squadron for marking. The number of bullet holes was carefully recorded for each pilot. Whilst this sounds simple and appears to have no possible room for error, there was one small technical detail that generally led to arguments and complaints. The ball ammunition used for practice air-to-air gunnery left the factory painted blue. When searching for colours on the flag it was not unusual to find an extra large number of green hits (unfortunately, yellow and blue mix to form green), virtually no yellow, and a few multicoloured holes. Again the squadron QWIs had the final say on what colour a hole actually was. Needless to say, much beer changed hands when an individual required just one more hole to qualify. After marking the flag, the crews would retire to the squadron darkroom for the subsequent debrief which would invariably show why the bullets hit at certain points of the banner – or missed, as was often the case. Scores in the region of 10 to 20 per cent were typical, and 50 per cent plus was a good score. Whilst this sounds poor, the barrel of the Gatling gun was deliberately loose to give a certain amount of bullet dispersion. The logic was that it was better to 'spray them around a little' rather than to be precise but miss the target. To put it in context, as little as three hits from high explosive rounds were needed to down a typical fighter target. A dispersed pattern from a Gatling firing at 6,000 rounds per minute would often be good enough to down an opponent.

One of the features of an armament practice camp was the 'Pigs Board'. Because gunnery was an infrequent phase, yet one of the more dangerous events on the calendar, any deviation from the rules was recorded as a 'pigs'. At the end of the week, the number of 'pigs' awarded was totted up and a contribution made towards a barrel of beer at 'happy hour'. Although it was kept light-hearted, it was a good way to focus attention on the serious nature of operating with live weapons.

Every year each air defence Phantom squadron detached to the Mediterranean for an armament practice camp, shortened to APC. My first APC was at RAF Luqa in Malta in 1977, but that was a delight which proved short-lived: the RAF was asked to leave, for political reasons, by the Prime Minister of the day, Dom Mintoff. The withdrawal ended a long association between the RAF and the Malta, made famous during the Second World War. Three Gloster Gladiators of No. 1435 Flight, named *Faith*, *Hope*, and *Charity*, gamely battled the might of the Luftwaffe during the early years of the Second World War. This was an association I was to rekindle during my time as boss of 1435 Flight in

Finalising the daily flying programme in Operations at RAF Akrotiri.

A 56 Squadron weapons instructor marks the banner with the crew.

The German exchange pilot returns from a gunnery sortie discussing his efforts with a QWI.

A gun armed Phantom taxies past a well riddled banner in Malta. The dark witness marks are the colour flashes made by the bullets.

the Falkland Islands. The APC Squadron operated from its own dispersal on the airfield. I suspect the huts that housed the squadron also dated back to the Second World War, so the whole operation was a slightly surreal experience – a complex mix of high technology and history. At that time, the squadron was tasked with contingency reinforcement. After deploying the aircraft from the UK behind a tanker, immediately on arrival the jets completed an operational turnround and fresh crews launched to set up a combat air patrol in the vicinity of the island. Had the alert been real, the aircraft would have deployed armed, allowing a CAP to be mounted within hours of leaving the UK. As a young Flying Officer at that time, I had yet to understand the significance of 'No Fly Zones' and such concepts would come later, but this was the first demonstration for me of the flexibility and capability of the Phantom as a war machine.

Luqa was a magnificent airfield. Although a new 11,000-foot runway had just been built, we were barred from using it other than in an emergency, as a result of the friction between the two governments. We were briefed that if we ever put a wheel onto it, our own government would pick up a large proportion of the construction costs, so it proved easy to resist that temptation. The Phantoms, and the resident Nimrods and Canberras, operated from the shorter 7,800-foot strip. This was no hardship, as leaving Runway 06, the aircraft crossed Grand Harbour, giving perhaps the most amazing views on departure that I had ever experienced from a Phantom cockpit. During our time on the island, HMS *Ark Royal*, then equipped with Phantoms and Buccaneers, pulled into harbour on a final visit before retiring from service. It was something of a daily chore to rotate into the vertical directly over the moored ship to make sure the Navy were aware of our presence. That said, the sight of the naval fast-jet aircraft arranged on the flight deck – a capability the UK will lack for some years to come – was magnificent.

After the somewhat undignified withdrawal from Malta, it was decided that future APCs would be run from the Sovereign Base Area at RAF Akrotiri in Cyprus. The 56 (F) Squadron detachment in 1978 was only the second APC following a long gap since the troubles in 1974. The locals were extremely pleased to have fast-jet activity again as the station had been very quiet in the intervening years. Strangely enough, the novelty quickly wore off as the station was invaded by raucous Phantom crews every eight weeks, causing temporary disruption to normal life for the residents.

Deployments were normally behind a tanker routeing from the UK, through France, and down the Mediterranean. It was rare to see other aircraft apart from a passing airliner, but occasionally the French would send up a Mirage as we passed through their airspace to make sure we had the correct number of aircraft in the formation. One of the more interesting moments was during a US 6th Fleet exercise: our formation was intercepted by the alert aircraft from a US carrier. As we headed east towards Crete, the radar warning receiver began to bleep rhythmically and we spotted a pair rolling in from the south. A few minutes later, a US F14 pulled alongside in full QRA fit as his No. 2 dropped into 1 mile trail. Not a peep from the radio on the guard frequency, so I guess we were not passing close to the task force. Even so, it was an unusual feeling for the 'boot to be on the other foot', given that we flew the transits unarmed.

A typical APC lasted six to eight weeks, depending on the number of crews that had to be qualified to NATO standards. As the aircraft were flown without external tanks, sorties were short and lasted only 15 to 20 minutes. The first wave launched at 07:00 as soon as the airfield opened, with typically four banners a day and four to six aircraft on each banner. This meant that the whole squadron had to deploy to provide enough aircraft to meet such a demanding flying programme. That said, the Phantom loved the sunshine. Serviceability could be quite poor in the UK with the constant rain and the pressures of keeping the sometimes temperamental weapon system operative. Once in the sun, like the crews, the aircraft seemed to relax, and sortie after sortie could be flown with the jet reporting serviceable every time. In fact, these detachments underlined how significant the high power pulse Doppler radar was in relation to the overall serviceability of the UK Phantom. Rarely used on an APC, suddenly the overall volume of radar faults diminished markedly.

There was little briefing to be done. The gunnery profile was repetitive, so, unlike UK sorties where it took 90 minutes from starting the briefing to getting airborne, crews would arrive 15 minutes before take-off and still make the planned launch time. The weather was invariably bright blue, so a flying suit and T-shirt were the order of the day. This was a refreshing change from the heavy immersion suits needed for North Sea operations. Air-to-air gunnery had to be conducted in good weather. For safety reasons, we had to be certain that no small boats had strayed into the range, as firing was conducted under 'clear range procedures'. The first aircraft at the holding point in the morning was the Canberra. The groundcrew hooked up the shackle to the tug and it would trundle down the runway, with the banner bouncing in its wake, on the dot at 07:00. The control agency would check the area on radar for surface contacts, and the tug pilot would carry out a visual sweep of the range area before declaring it clear. If a boat strayed into the range, a section would be declared off limits for firing. After a short wait at the threshold the first armed Phantom would take off, followed every 15 minutes by the next. The range was literally a few miles off the southern coast of Cyprus, so after a short transit and a hand-off to the radar unit at Mount Troodos – callsign 'Olympus' – the firing exercise began. A standard load for an academic sortie was ninety rounds of ball ammunition, so at the incredible rate of fire of 6,000 rounds per minute it took only a few passes to use the bullets. Pilots had to be judicious in their use of their trigger finger to make sure they completed a number of passes using short bursts. One ill-timed or inaccurate long burst could translate into an embarrassing zero score. Normally, crews flew two or three sorties per day. Occasionally, it was slightly bizarre to land back at Akrotiri at 07:15 having completed your planned flying for the day. Suffice it to say that APC was a good time to build squadron morale – and the brandy sours, which were the signature drink in the bar of the Officers' Mess, were generous and cheap. Even so, the first wave of flying came round quickly and the 8 hours 'bottle to throttle' rule was always in the back of everyone's mind.

The gunnery exercises concluded with a Limited Academic and an Operational Shoot. Unlike the academic profiles that consisted of a number of planned passes, op shoots were 'free game'. On the call of 'commence', the Canberra began the first of two 360-degree turns. The Phantom crew set up firing passes as quickly as possible and could take as many firing passes as they could achieve, expending their allocated ammunition before the tug completed the turns. Instead of the short staccato burp that was the trademark of an academic shoot, an op shoot was a deeply satisfying full burst, the noise of which is difficult to describe but was a long throaty buzz. Naturally, scores were generally lower under the pressure of a time limit, but the occasional pass would produce amazingly good scores when everything came together.

Ironically, Cyprus was one of the areas where the Cold War produced some of the closest contacts between East and West. Limassol was a hotbed of intrigue, and the arrival briefings always warned of the risks to the unwary from hostile intelligence forces. One of my scarier moments occurred during an early morning gunnery exercise off the Cyprus coast. The Soviet Navy had established a mooring to the south of Akrotiri, known as the South Cyprus buoy. Soviet vessels regularly moored for a few days at a time to complete maintenance tasks and probably to listen to our activity on the islands. Our own authorities were keen to know which vessels were moored, so we were often asked to fly a buoy check at the end of a sortie. On one occasion during a detachment with 92 (East India) Squadron my pilot and I were asked to conduct the check on the way out to the banner, presumably because the resident vessel was planning to depart. We launched as the airfield opened at 07:00, and as our Canberra tug made its way into the gunnery area we headed out to the buoy that lay south-east of the airfield. The sun was just rising and the light levels were still low as we set heading at 250 feet above the sea. I fired up the radar and went into pulse mode to paint the buoy which was easily visible, particularly with a vessel moored. A small correction to the heading had us pointing directly towards the buoy. As we closed, the radar warning receiver began to chirp with the regular bleeps of a search radar, and the strobe began to pulse on the screen. My pilot eased the throttles up as we hit 10 miles, as it was almost mandatory to wake the sailors with a fast pass over the ship. At about 8 miles we could see the bulk of the vessel on the buoy when the RWR suddenly shrieked with the alarm tone of a pulsed radar lock on and the strobe and warning lights illuminated. The normal counter to a surface threat was to break hard through 90 degrees, and just as I called the counter I heard a loud expletive from the front cockpit. As I looked towards the Soviet vessel, I suddenly understood. A smoke trail was streaking away from the aft of the ship and aiming directly towards us, arching high into the still dark sky. As the adrenaline kicked in, my pilot racked the Phantom into a hard defensive turn and we steadied up on the beam. The ship had launched a surface-to-air missile! I cannot vouch for my pilot, but my own heart was racing at twice its normal rate as the smoke trail reached its apex. Suddenly, there was a visible pop and the parachute flare began to bob gently back down to Earth. What was supposed to have been a high speed pass over a Soviet vessel turned into a gentle orbit and a rather subdued pass to identify the type of ship. I think it fair to say that, on that occasion, it was 1-0 to the Soviet Navy.

A visit to the Cyprus buoy also showed the lighter side of squadron humour. In Cyprus we flew as a crew, so my pilot and I had relaxed into a comfortable working routine. After one gunnery sortie we asked for a buoy check and were cleared by our ground controller to make a pass. As we approached I could see that there was a Polnocny class landing craft moored alongside, bobbing gently on the Mediterranean swell. I also noticed that the speed was creeping up, and my pilot intended that it should be a spirited flypast to say good morning to the Russian crew. In my experience, all naval personnel enjoyed a flypast to break up the monotony of life aboard. As we swept past the ship at 250 feet and well over 600 knots, the needle on the machmeter was just shy of Mach 1, although it was just subsonic. I noted the hull number on my kneeboard and we set heading back to Akrotiri. As we walked back from the line hut, a concerned-looking Duty Authoriser said simply, 'Boss's office now; hats on.' This was never good. As we dropped off our flying kit and retrieved or headgear, my pilot was going over what we had done during the sortie. The gunnery event had been unremarkable and all the passes had been legal, so no suggestion of a problem there. It had to be the buoy check.

As we stood on the boss's carpet, his face was like thunder. He was good at that. He was probing me, asking how fast we had been going and how low, even though he knew I didn't have a radio altimeter. He explained calmly that the Commander British Forces Cyprus had just received a complaint from the Soviet

Consulate in Limassol and registered a diplomatic incident. I was in no position to question whether the Soviet Consul could do that. Apparently, a Phantom had passed at supersonic speed over a Soviet vessel moored on the Cyprus buoy, breaking windows on the ship and knocking a seaman into the water. As we were the only aircraft in the area at the time, identification was not in doubt. My pilot had absolutely no idea how fast we had been travelling at the pass as he had been concentrating on keeping the aircraft steady at 250 feet above the waves. A high subsonic pass was perfectly legal, but a supersonic pass within thirty miles of the coast, particularly near a ship, would be a transgression. Twenty knots variation in speed could be the difference between a little harmless fun and a diplomatic incident. My pilot was a first tourist; with well over 1,000 hours on the aircraft, I was the sortie authoriser and supposed to be the adult in the crew. The boss turned his attention to me and gave me a roasting for failing to act as a responsible authoriser, saying how disappointed he was in my lack of professionalism, and threatening all manner of retribution. I protested our innocence and repeatedly assured him that we had been subsonic. His face stayed absolutely deadpan and despite my repeated assurances of our innocence, even I was beginning to wonder if we had screwed up.

It was possible to drop a sonic boom below the Mach, but normally that occurred only in a shallow drive or if the aircraft manoeuvred violently at around Mo.98+. We had done neither and had carried out a level pass at about Mo.98. It had been fast but should have been entirely legal, albeit 'high spirited'. Even so, I was doubting myself and beginning to feel very nervous. We were dismissed and, after threats of doom, we saluted smartly and retired hurt. As with all squadron 'spoofs', it wasn't kept going for long; as we made our way back to Operations there was a bank of grinning and cheering aircrew lining the corridor. The reports of damage and injury were pure fiction. My pilot and I were dragged bodily into the courtyard, tied up with webbing, and laid out on a gunnery banner before the cameras were pulled out to capture the 'arrest'. Such were the joys of squadron life. Afterwards, we found out that our controller had called the Duty Authoriser explaining that we were doing a buoy check. He had assumed that the pass would be fast and set up the whole spoof on a whim. We had, of course, remained subsonic and the whole event was a wind-up, but aircrew never allowed facts to spoil a good joke.

Detachments concluded with the return 'trail' to the UK, again assisted by tankers. The four-hour sortie followed a standard route from Cyprus, heading west along the Mediterranean before turning north and coasting-in at Nice in France. Normally, the fighters would refuel up to four times en route, but the highlight of any return trail was the sight of a Phantom plugged into the tanker over the Alps. After that view, somehow the routine of normal squadron flying and the flat English landscape of Suffolk or the murky North German Plain seemed dull in comparison.

A trophy was awarded annually for the best performing squadron at air-to-air gunnery. Known as the 'Seed Trophy', it was donated by Mr Clifford Seed in 1979, with the winner nominated by HQ 11 Group. It was an accolade for No. 56(Fighter) Squadron to be awarded the trophy as the first winners in 1979, just a few years after its formation as a Phantom squadron. The cynics, however, were less impressed, as the presentation involved a formal parade.

CHAPTER 13
Opponents

Operating in UK airspace, the Phantom had few real enemies. The aircraft was procured to fight the long range battle against Soviet bombers in a hostile electronic battlefield well out over the North Sea. From static, defensive Cold War positions, the likely intruders would have been the Tupolev Tu-20 Bear and Tu-16 Badger and, to a lesser extent, the Myasishchev Mya-4 Bison. The medium bombers, such as the Tu-22 Blinder and Ilyushin Il-28 Beagle, would have been stretched to make even coastal targets. Armed with 23-mm radar-laid tail guns, the bombers operated by the Soviet Long Range Air Force undoubtedly had the ability to inflict damage, but it would have been a naïve Phantom crew that strayed within guns range once a shooting war began. With air-to-air missiles it would have been possible to stand off from these bombers and engage using the Sparrow or Sidewinder missiles. What might have prevented that was electronic jamming, but there were effective countermeasures built into the AN/AWG-12 radar that would have allowed the Sparrow to track even under electronic attack.

Other than the aircraft carriers, none of the Soviet fighter aircraft would have had the range to threaten even the outer combat air patrols in the early stages of a conflict. Whether carrier-based aircraft would be a threat was a point of debate. The Soviet Union developed a vertical take-off aircraft during the early 70s with a clear intent to deploy a Carrier Battle Group into the Atlantic Ocean. The original vertical take-off and landing aircraft was the Yakovlev Yak-36, known to NATO as the 'Freehand'. This was in all respects a prototype and did not offer any realistic operational capability, only a few ever being produced. It was the advent of the Yakovlev Yak-38 Forger, deployed aboard the Soviet carrier *Kiev*, that caused the first potential concern to UK-based Phantom crews. The Forger gave only a rudimentary deployable force, which was more politically than operationally significant. Fitted with large and heavy twin lift engines behind the cockpit, it could indeed take off and land vertically but lacked

A Bear 'Delta' showing its tail guns which were directed by the 'Beehind' tail warning radar. UK MOD Crown Copyright (1977).

any real performance. The weight of these engines crippled the aerodynamic performance, and the fact that it was armed with only four AA-8 Aphid infrared guided air-to-air missiles meant that it had little credibility. Reportedly, its effective range was a mere 65 miles, which was worse than the original British Harrier GR1s. Add to that the usual procedural difficulties of operating aircraft from a carrier, and this would have given it a pitifully short time on task in an operational area. Contrast this with the Phantom's extensive fuel reserves, and it would have been a very nervous Forger pilot who entered an engagement at any significant range from its carrier where fuel was life.

There was an even bigger limitation. Soviet doctrine produced engines that lasted only hundreds of hours of flight time before being discarded, unlike western engines that offered many more hours and could then be refurbished. There was much fanfare when the Kiev Battle Group deployed into the Mediterranean in 1976, and RAF aircraft shadowed the fleet as it made its way around the UK coast and through the Strait of Gibraltar. We were keen to see how the much vaunted new capability played out. However, of the few aircraft deployed, and reportedly the number was only six, barely any were still operational during the return voyage. Reports at the time suggested that the lift engines had a service life measured in tens of hours. Operating on a carrier with the obvious problems of resupply would have been difficult. In war, such an unreliable piece of equipment would have been operational suicide. It was safe to say that the threat to the UK during the Cold War from the Soviet Carrier Group could be discounted.

For Phantoms operating in the Falkland Islands after the war, the picture was more complex as the Argentinians were equipped with some capable, albeit ageing, fighters. The US-built A4 Skyhawk was a basic fighter-bomber aircraft but with performance quite similar to the MiG-21. The French-built Mirage III, and the Israeli-built Dagger, were also capable fighters. During the time when the Phantom operated in the South Atlantic, the Argentine Air Force suffered from a lack of capable air-to-air weapons. The Mirage III was fitted with an early version of the French-made Matra R530 semi active missile although later versions were able to carry the more effective Magic infra red missile. The Dagger carried the Israeli Shafrir missile. By then, the UK Phantoms were equipped with Skyflash missiles and AIM-9L Sidewinders, both of which could operate at all aspects. This was a massive advantage for the Phantom crews, most of whom had the opportunity to train against the Mirage III and V versions operated by the French and the Belgians. With a large delta wing configuration, the Mirage could operate at all altitudes, although it was less stable than the Phantom at low level. Being single engine, it suffered from lack of thrust. Entering a combat engagement, Mirage pilots were able to generate a high rate of instantaneous turn, but this came at the cost of a rapid loss of energy. If a Phantom crew chose to stay and turn, the advantage would quickly switch to the Mirage pilot. As against most agile aircraft, the secret was to keep the Mirage or Dagger at arm's length and seek to disengage in order to set up a more advantageous tactical approach. A Phantom crew would have beaten both these Argentinian types by employing a Sparrow missile from beyond visual range. Luckily, geography was a great ally. Sitting about 400 miles from the mainland, the Falkland Islands were at the limit of endurance of both these fighter types. Only the Skyhawks were AAR capable, but the Argentinians had only a few C-130 tankers, so fighters would have been operating with very small fuel reserves and a prolonged combat engagement would have been difficult. Despite having a reheated engine, the Mirage could not afford to use it at such extreme range, which limited the aircraft's performance significantly. Phantom crews, however, enjoyed the full performance of their aircraft and could afford to use high speed to maintain separation from the threats and look for tactical opportunities to launch a Sparrow. Tactics were determined to ensure that this could be achieved.

Over German airspace the story was quite different. Phantom crews faced a large array of potential opponents from aircraft operated by the Group of Soviet Forces Germany in the shape of the 16th Tactical Air Army. Surprisingly, the list of potential opponents was quickly whittled down to a small number of likely opponents. Types such as the Su-9 Fishpot were operated only by the Soviet Air

Defence forces, the PVO Strany, and would have been unlikely to venture outside Russian airspace. The older types could not be totally discounted as they were still manoeuvrable aeroplanes, albeit armed with older, less capable air-to-air missiles. One postulated scenario was that waves of obsolete fighters such as the MiG-15 and MiG-17 would have been launched across the front line in advance of the main Soviet thrust. These could have acted as cannon fodder, drawing fire from both NATO surface-to-air missiles and fighters. Given that our own Phantoms had maybe only three missile reloads before stocks would have had to be replenished, this could have been a valid tactic. There would, however, have been advanced warning should this strategy have been contemplated. Jet aircraft need basing and support, and these older types would have to have been deployed forward. There would have been warnings and indicators that analysts would have seen during heightened tensions.

The principal threats to the Phantom in the Central Region would have been the MiG-21 Fishbed, shown in Plate71, and the MiG-23 Flogger. Both types were operated by the Soviets and their allies in the Warsaw Pact.

Understanding the threat during the Cold War was difficult. The majority of intelligence data was theoretical and produced by analysts from first principles. It was only the fall of the Berlin Wall in 1989 that allowed access to both hardware and former Warsaw Pact pilots, giving a more comprehensive picture. Nowadays, by typing 'MiG-23 Flogger' into a search engine I can watch online videos of former East German Air Force Floggers operating from their airfield at Peenemünde as easily as I can watch a Typhoon at an air display in England. During the height of the Cold War, such footage would have been intelligence gold. Defence analysts from all the NATO partners pored over designs and simulations to give their best guess at the performance and capabilities of our Soviet opponents. Aircrew, being essentially simple beings, turned to an easier reference source: the *Jane's Defence* series of publications. Essential reading in the squadron crewroom, *Jane's* gave a simple unclassified assessment that could be easily accessed and used without risking the wrath of the RAF Police, unlike the official summaries. We all pored over the descriptions of potential foes, forming our own opinions of strengths and weaknesses based on personal experience of other types we had flown against.

The MiG-21 was a formidable point defence fighter about which very little was known, despite the fact that some of the UK's traditional allies operated the aircraft. A few British test pilots and flying instructors had the opportunity to fly the two-seat variant during liaison visits to allies such as India. With the exception of the 'Constant Peg' programme in the Nevada Desert, only recently declassified, it was only really after the fall of 'The Wall' in 1989 that western pilots began to fly this former Soviet Union fighter in earnest. It seems hard to believe that there are now examples in private hands, flying at air displays in the United States.

From a squadron perspective the MiG-21 was respected, although it had distinct weapon system limitations. Like the older British fighters, it had only a simple pulse radar, originally the 'Spin Scan' and later the 'Jaybird'. The early versions fared even worse, equipped only with a simple gun ranging radar and two air-to-air missiles, albeit this increased to four on the later Fishbeds. It was a classic delta wing fighter with characteristics representative of that design. Lightweight, with thrust from its single engine of about 13,000 lbs in afterburner, it had a good thrust-to-weight ratio given that the airframe weighed only 15,000 lbs. It had a decent turn of speed, yet was still controllable at extremely slow speeds. Its huge advantage was that it could pull 7G and turn extremely tightly, and even as the speed bled off in air combat, it had sufficient nose authority, or response to the controls, to be able to keep pointing at an opponent. In combat, this ability is extremely intimidating. Despite the lessons having been hammered home repeatedly, it could sucker Phantom crews into staying in a flat turning fight trying to match its turn performance. This natural reaction of a true-blooded fighter pilot to stay and turn is understandable, but the correct response for a Phantom was to leave the fight as quickly as possible. It was a small aeroplane – even in profile it would be hard to see – but if it turned nose on, it would almost disappear until very close. In air combat, losing sight meant losing the fight. Being so small, a well-flown MiG-21 could get close to its opponent and be inside missile parameters before being seen. Flying against the aggressor F5s, this fact was demonstrated repeatedly to ensure that Phantom crews had taken on the prime lesson. In comparison, the Phantom was a huge, smoking 'barn door'. The offset for Phantom crews was the Phantom's radar, which gave tactical situation awareness that the MiG pilot lacked in the absence of ground control.

Although few had the opportunity to do so, the best way to fight a MiG-21 in a Phantom was to exploit its weaknesses. Close contacts with Soviet forces during the Cold War were rare. Jagdgeschwader 71, The 'Richthofen' Wing from the German fighter base at Wittmundhafen provided the German exchange crew on 56 (F) Squadron and we had close links with the German Squadrons. I remember being enthralled hearing the story of Phantom crews encountering two armed Mig21s during a sortie in the Baltic Sea at the height of the Cold War. The fighters from JG71 were escorting another Phantom from the nearby base at Leck which was conducting a reconnaissance mission over the Baltic Sea. The Quick Reaction Alert from Jagdgeschwader 9 of the East German Air Force at Peenemünde, was scrambled and the two formations met over International waters. After the merge, one of the Phantom crews maneuvered into a guns

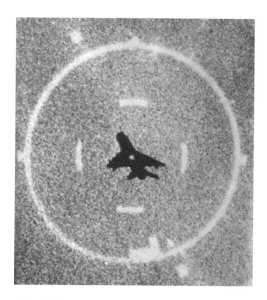

Above left: Gun camera film from the German Phantom. The target is being tracked inside the 25-mm inner ring and the pipper is centred on the Mig 21. © Klaus Berke.

Above right: The Mig 21 descends to low level to evade the Phantom. A ship is clearly visible in the background. © Klaus Berke.

tracking position in the 6 o'clock of one of the Migs and captured the event on their gun camera. This proved that a well flown Phantom was more than a match for a Mig 21 flown by a Warsaw Pact pilot and the pictures became legendary among NATO fighter crews at the time. One of the pilots remembers reading the transcripts from West German intelligence intercepts showing that the MIG pilots passed only aircraft type and tail number to their controllers and made no mention of the combat maneuvering which had followed. Stories told in the crewroom over the years may have embellished the facts suggesting that the Mig pilots, despite being out-maneuvered, had asked for clearance to engage. Substance did not reflect reality and, typical of Cold War rhetoric, before returning to their home base, the Mig pilots reported 'we have driven them off'.

The best fighting ground for the Phantom crew was below 20,000 feet and above 420 knots. In a flat fight the MiG-21 pilot might have to trade height for speed if he was to continue being aggressive. He would struggle to match the vertical manoeuvring of a well-flown Phantom and could never match the acceleration of the larger twin engine fighter. By taking the MiG up into the vertical at the merge, it would rapidly bleed off energy. The trick was then to keep it at arm's length. Extensions that widened the combat circle, keeping the

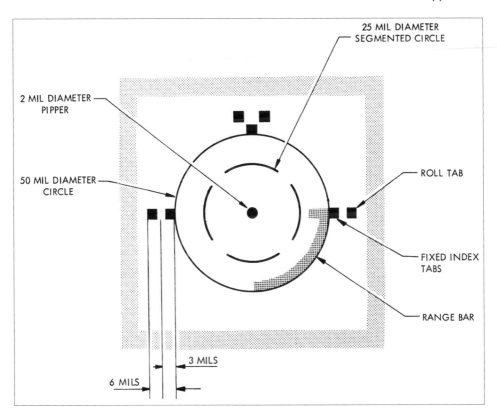

The Phantom gunsight display. With the radar locked the pilot sees target range on the range bar.

The two East German Mig 21s over the Baltic sea 20 miles north-east of Rügen. © Klaus Berke.

MiG outside of its small weapons envelope, would keep the Phantom alive. By slowly widening the circle with extension manoeuvres, a point could be reached at which there was enough separation to execute a turnback manoeuvre for a high speed head-on pass. This allowed the Phantom to leave the lethal circle. Once well clear, a further pitch back to engage with a front sector Sparrow shot might achieve a kill, but needed snappy radar work by the navigator. Stay and manoeuvre, and the MiG-21 would slowly arc the turn, eventually closing for a missile or gun shot. The result would be inevitable. Western technology gave another advantage in that the 'G' limitations of the Soviet AA-2 Atoll infra-red missile carried by the MiG-21 were thought to be much worse than our equivalent Sidewinders. Analysis suggested that the AA-2 was susceptible to infra-red decoys, which meant that even if the Soviet pilot achieved a missile shot against the Phantom it did not guarantee that the engagement was lost; missiles could fail and flares might seduce the Atoll missile away from its target. Regrettably, there was no countermeasure against a bullet, so Phantom pilots were trained to execute a last-ditch guns jink manoeuvre to disrupt a guns tracking solution. In this manoeuvre, as the attacking fighter closed to guns range, random and violent inputs were fed into the controls, producing violent gyrations that could prevent an aggressor pilot from tracking the Phantom smoothly. The key was to make the Phantom fly 'out of plane' by using a rapid roll followed by a snatch pull or push, followed by another random roll, and so on. Inside the Phantom the effect was pure mayhem, but hopefully the bullets would go wide.

The best replication of the MiG-21 for training purposes was the Northrop F5E, and it was no surprise that the American Aggressor squadrons used this type to prepare crews for combat against the MiG-21. The two types were similar in most respects, and although the F5 had slightly better performance in terms of energy management, the MiG could turn tighter. Crucially, the view from the cockpit was similar in both types, meaning the Phantom crew trained against a pilot who had to live with the same strengths and weaknesses.

It was only the Germany-based Phantom crews that might actually have encountered the MiG-21. Its small size meant that it carried very little fuel, so it really was a point defence fighter. It would not have had the range to operate in the NATO rear areas in Germany or to reach UK airspace, and lacked any air-to-air refuelling capability. Even as the Soviets pushed forward into West Germany, it was unlikely that forward basing would have been possible before Phantoms would have been forced to fall back to the UK. Perhaps the only chance of encountering a MiG-21 would have been if the Phantoms were pushed forward onto Army support CAPs close to the forward edge of the battle area. The only other scenario would have been if the Phantoms were tasked to escort bombers into hostile airspace, but this option was rarely practised. Paradoxically, the escort role would have been advantageous to the Phantom crew, as it would have given unfettered use of the forward hemisphere capability of the Sparrow missile. It was much more likely to meet a foe rather than a friend in hostile airspace, and the crew could say almost certainly that a blip on the radar would have been an enemy.

The MiG-23 Flogger was less well understood and, with hindsight, crews gave it more credibility at the time than perhaps it deserved. There were some fascinating insights into its qualities in Steve Davies's book *Red Eagles*. The pilots who flew the aircraft in the USA under the 'Constant Peg' programme reported that the controls were heavy. It had a yawing movement throughout the flight envelope, with a disconcerting tendency for the nose to hunt back and forth but apparently at random. One of the more bizarre features was a pilot 'aid' known as a 'knuckle rapper'. At angles of attack greater than 17 degrees, a plate literally rapped the pilot's knuckles as a reminder to ease off on the control column. That said, with a marked habit of departing from controlled flight at high angles of attack, perhaps the feature was a prudent reminder for a Flogger pilot.

At the squadron level, we assumed that the flying characteristics would be similar to the Tornado, which was just entering service at the time. Feedback from our own test pilots of the advantages that variable geometry wings gave, suggested to us that the Soviets had replicated the capability. This proved to be completely wrong. We knew that the Flogger accelerated quickly and, with the wings swept, it had transonic capability at low level. Experience showed that 900 knots at low level was entirely possible, and the aircraft could outrun an F111, which from my own experience was blisteringly fast at low altitude. My later experience of the Tornado F3 proved that a swept wing was easily capable of speeds of 850 knots at low level, which was the design limit for the F3. The tactical lesson here was that it was unwise to try to outrun a MiG-23.

One major disadvantage proved to be that if external tanks were fitted in order to extend the Flogger's range, the wings were fixed because the Soviets had not perfected movable pylons. The Flogger pilot would be constrained by the wings being fixed in the forward position, because unless the tanks and pylons were jettisoned he could not take advantage of the dash capability, negating the aircraft's major strength. It also had a poorly designed canopy that gave an appallingly bad view from the cockpit. Sitting in a Flogger many years later at the Nellis AFB Threat Training Facility, it was clear to me that the view to the rear was restricted by the spine of the airframe. The fact that a rear-view periscope was fitted to try to improve the rearward visibility was telling. The heavy ironwork around the front canopy and a thick armoured windscreen meant that the view through the front was equally poor, although a Phantom pilot would have had some sympathy, being equally 'visually challenged'.

However, like the MiG-21, the MiG-23 had a very small cross-section when viewed head on. Also like the MiG-21, it would have been difficult to detect an attacking Flogger visually if flown carefully by an attacking pilot who followed a pure pursuit course into an intercept.

With greater access to the aircraft during squadron exchanges came a realisation that we had seriously over-estimated its capability. Unlike the Tornado, where sweeping the wings forward gave much improved turn performance, the MiG-23 reportedly would become a real handful as it was manoeuvred at high angle of attack. One test pilot who had the opportunity to fly the MiG-23 suggested jokingly that the aircraft should be provided free of charge to all our enemies so that they could do themselves mischief before a future conflict. The weapon system proved equally flawed, albeit it was designed in the 60s so reflected its generation. The two-seat trainer version of the aircraft, known as the Flogger 'Charlie', was fitted with an older 'Jaybird' radar and had only limited combat capability. The B model air defence variant was fitted with a 'High Lark' AI radar, which although of the older pulse variety was equipped with moving target indication or MTI. In theory this gave a pseudo look-down shoot-down capability, particularly at medium level. Later in my career, I was able to discuss this system with pilots who had flown the aircraft with one of the old Warsaw Pact air forces. To say that they were dismissive was an understatement. Having said all that, Soviet doctrine was to control the intercept from the ground, asking the pilot to make simple switch selections and fire the weapons. This relied on comprehensive radar coverage from ground installations and a complex data link control system. Under these conditions, the MiG-23 was capable of doing the job it was designed for. It did, however, benefit from an upgrade in air-to-air armament over its predecessors. The arrival of the AA-7 Apex missile gave the aircraft a head-on capability that had to be honoured in an engagement. The Apex was a semi-active radar guided missile and, like the Sparrow, relied for guidance on a continuous wave radar signal provided by the 'High Lark' radar. It carried two of the large missiles on pylons mounted on the wing glove. Unlike the Phantom where the missiles were carried in semi-conformal launchers under the fuselage, the Apex sat prominently on the pylon and must have added significantly to the aerodynamic drag, reducing performance yet further. Performance assessments at the time were vague, so we had to assume that the missile conferred a similar capability to the Sparrow.

However basic in the beyond visual range arena, Phantom crews now had an opponent with similar capability. The AA-8 Aphid was a vast improvement over the AA-2 Atoll, and finally gave a respectable IR capability. It was a much more agile weapon than the Atoll it supplemented, and we assumed that it was to give the Flogger pilot a weapon he could use in close combat. Up to four missiles could be carried on complex underfuselage pylons, again adding to the aerodynamic drag. In reality, Soviet tactics were much more scripted and the AA-8 was intended for another purpose. Again, we were driven by our assumptions that the Soviets intended to engage in air combat manoeuvring, which proved not to be true. I recall vividly that we were briefed on Soviet decoy tactics where one formation of MiG-23s would turn at about the range where a Phantom would be launching a Sparrow. This manoeuvre would have negated the Sparrow shot, as the target would remain outside the missile lethal range. The missile would have burned out before reaching its intended target. The decoy turn would pull the offensive Phantoms into a long tailchase as the MiG-23 formation accelerated away. Meanwhile, a second pair of MiG-23s would manoeuvre behind the Phantoms, hoping to take advantage of an unseen tail shot. It was here that they planned to employ the AA-8 missile. What we could not know was that these tactics exploited the highly controlled nature of Soviet doctrine and that there was still a marked reluctance to be drawn into air combat. There was much speculation that the Soviets were developing an air combat capability, but the reality was that their profiles were little more advanced than the fist basic steps we would take on our operational conversion to the Phantom. At that time it was light years away from the normal cut and thrust on a NATO squadron.

The MiG-23 had one huge advantage over the British Phantom in that it was equipped with an early generation infra-red search and track system. This sensor, thought to be developed from a missile seeker, detected hot spots from the target's engine exhaust. If it could be cued onto a target by the radar, it would track the incoming aircraft passively. For that reason, if a MiG-23 pilot could be directed by a ground controller and track an incoming Phantom passively using IRST (Infra-Red Search and Track) he could turn off his radar, unless it was required for an Apex missile shot. In the absence of a warning on the Phantom's radar warning receiver, the Phantom crew would be unaware of its approach unless they picked it up on their own radar.

We gave much credibility to the MiG's Sirena-3 passive warning receiver and assumed it was a match for our ageing ARI 18228s. In fact, it was a very simple system which gave only rudimentary warning of a threat. It was also extremely inaccurate and really gave little more help than highlighting which quadrant a threat was approaching from. In comparison, our own equipment gave quite an accurate bearing and would have greatly assisted our tactical awareness during an engagement. Many of our tactics were based on the assumption that the Soviet opponent would be aware of our approach through his sensors. In reality he would have almost certainly relied on his ground controller. In the complex environment of the Central Region at low level we were crediting our opponent with more capability then he actually had. A Soviet pilot when asked his opinion

A Mig 23 Flogger Bravo of the Polish Air Force shown at the Newark Air Museum.

of his radar warning receiver replied that it didn't really work. When challenged further, he seemed confused and asked why it was even needed when his ground controller would tell him where the attacking aircraft was. It showed the gulf in tactical thinking between the opposing power blocs. One feature was that the 'High Lark' radar sounded extremely distinctive when intercepted by the Phantom's radar warning receiver. It featured a 'nod down scan' for the MTI that gave a recognisable separate tone amidst the usual electronic warble. I felt sure I would recognise a Flogger 'Bravo' if he illuminated me with his radar, even in the heat of an engagement.

The quality of the Soviet electronic jamming equipment was the area where we felt at a disadvantage. Soviet doctrine stressed the importance of dominating the electronic spectrum. We knew the MiG-23 had an active jammer, and pictures showed the aircraft carrying various pods. In true Soviet style, it proved to be well equipped with chaff and flares, and Soviet propaganda films showed Floggers dispensing flares aggressively over Afghanistan. Ironically, the tactics were designed to defeat Stinger missiles supplied by the Americans to the

Mujahedeen, and we were to face similar risks many years later in the same country. At squadron level during the Cold War, the knowledge of the electronic warfare threat was poorly disseminated. Our analysts suggested that even though the MiG-23 pod was technologically reasonably basic, it could still give our AN/AWG-12 radar a difficult time. Any kills we attempted would probably be achieved in a hostile electronic environment. In the post Cold War area, these systems were marketed openly, so we were able to analyse how we might have fared. Subsequent discussion with Warsaw Pact pilots who had flown with the equipment suggested it was indeed a capable threat. What we could not know was that when the jamming pod burst into life, it made a much more effective job jamming the radar in the Flogger than it might have against a powerful AN/AWG-12. In fact, as the pod responded to an incoming Phantom, the Flogger pilot effectively became blind, as his own radar was affected adversely by the transmissions.

There were also a number of dedicated ground attack aircraft that could not be ignored. The mainstays of the 16th Tactical Air Army were the Flogger 'Deltas' and the Fitter 'Charlies' which equipped many of the attack squadrons. Both were rugged ground attack aircraft that seemed to enjoy good serviceability, albeit armed with simple unguided bombs and older generation direct fire rocket pods. Despite being relatively unsophisticated, they were available in large numbers and could have overwhelmed the West's defences. Like their air defence brethren, they carried self-defence jamming pods, chaff and flare dispensers, and Sirena-3 radar warning receivers. They would undoubtedly have provided a challenging target to intercept and were by no means 'easy meat'. Most had pylons that could carry AA-2 Atoll infra-red guided missiles, so rolling into a tight formation of Soviet bombers would have left Phantom crews open to opportunity shots. More ominous was the fact that the Soviets were developing precision guided munitions. As we sat in our hardened shelters during operational turnrounds, we felt relatively invulnerable from dumb bombs. The Gulf War was to demonstrate how precision guided weapons would change that.

One of the imponderables was that of the attack helicopter. The Mil-24 Hind was a formidable attack helicopter and would have been prolific in the battle area. Phantom crews practised tactics to engage helicopters, but they were not an easy target. The advancing rotor blades caused a phenomenon on the radar known as 'turbine modulations', more commonly seen when looking directly down the intake of an opposing jet fighter. These signals were seen by a pulse Doppler radar as additional targets at different speeds to the actual target and could be interpreted by the radar as electronic jamming. Whether the AN/AWG-12 would have stayed locked to a helicopter or what effect the false signals would have had on the guidance system of the radar guided Sparrow was moot.

Coupled with that was the fact that a helicopter is slow and therefore difficult for a pulse Doppler radar to detect and track. For those reasons, a Sparrow engagement might have been problematic. Many helicopters had small infra-red signatures and were further protected by suppression devices bolted onto the engines that reduced the signature even more. There was some doubt as to whether a Sidewinder could even lock on to the helicopter's emissions.

In Germany, Phantoms were fitted with the SUU-23 gun, and a modification of the air-to-ground strafe technique could be adapted to engage a low flying helicopter. The pilot would effectively carry out a strafe pass against the low, slow flying helicopter as if it was stationary on the ground. One Squadron Commander even advocated a minimum separation supersonic pass to set up a shock wave that would make the helicopter impossible to control. Suffice it to say that a helicopter was not an easy target to engage, but there were tactical alternatives. The basic tactics were practised against a passive opponent, but what if the helicopter was armed with a simple air-to-air missile or a gun? Speed would have been the only factor to separate the Phantom from the Hind. A missile fired from a Phantom was normally fired with overtake against the target; in other words, the Phantom would be travelling faster than its target. At co-speed or slower, the range of the missile collapsed to a mile or less. The Hind pilot would have faced similar problems, so would need to be close to the Phantom for success. For the Phantom crew, avoiding that tight bubble would have been critical. Maybe the close pass or gun shot against a Hind would have proved to be the undoing of an unwary Phantom crew. Luckily, it was never put to the test.

In the latter years of the Phantom's service, the situation deteriorated markedly with the introduction to service of the Soviet air superiority fighters, the MiG-29 Fulcrum and Su-27 Flanker shown in plates 72 and 73. The first line drawings, followed by grainy images, appeared on the squadron in the late 1970s. Originally referred to by their design bureau designations, the Ram-K and Ram-L were clearly intended to match the F15 and F16s against which we had begun to train. The American fighters had started to erode the superiority the Phantom had enjoyed, and if those experiences were extended to our opponents we had much to worry about. We were reassured by our analysts, who stressed that the Soviet Union still did not train its fighter pilots as well as we did in the West. Undoubtedly, they did not enjoy the same continuity or level of flying hours that we did. It would take a change in mindset to move away from the highly scripted, ground controlled operations that had been the feature of Warsaw Pact doctrine.

There was one incident which challenged that assessment, albeit some years later. Reported in the *Daily Mail* on 15 September 1987, a chilling picture, taken by the aircraft captain, showed a fully armed Su-27 Flanker in extremely close formation with a Norwegian P3 Orion over the Barents Sea. Its AA-10 Alamo missiles were clearly visible under the wings and fuselage as the Soviet fighter approached on the left, reportedly closing to within 7 feet of the Norwegian maritime patrol aircraft. According to the crew, 'in a spectacular manoeuvre the Sukhoi rolled sideways and disappeared', but within 15 minutes, the Su-27 returned. After removing his gloves and making hand gestures, the pilot flew his aircraft under the right wing of the Orion. Either through over-confidence, lack of skill, lack of practice, or misjudgement, the fighter flew so close that its tail section struck the Orion's outer right-hand propeller, causing severe damage. Debris from the shattered propeller scythed through the fuselage, leaving a large hole, and the Orion was forced to divert to Vardø in northern Norway, having declared an emergency, landing safely some time later. The incident caused concern. The Orion, although outside Soviet airspace, was reportedly operating well beyond the Norwegian border off the North Cape. The Su-27 being fully armed, was presumably the Soviet QRA aircraft. What was alarming was the pilot's reaction. UK rules give firm guidance on how close an intercepting pilot can fly his aircraft to the aircraft being intercepted. If adhered to, this minimum separation range avoids such incidents. Up to that time, Soviet fighters intercepting western aircraft had stuck strictly to the rules and given a healthy leeway between aircraft. For the first time we saw a Soviet pilot flying a well armed and highly manoeuvrable fighter at extremely close quarters, taking extreme liberties. Assuming the pilot made a mistake, it was a warning bell that reverberated around every crewroom in NATO. The hitherto predictable rules of the Cold War were changing.

With the collapse of the Warsaw Pact in 1989, anything seemed possible and much of the proffered wisdom was to be challenged in so many ways over the following decade. As we began to have contact with the former Soviet Union and, particularly Russia, after the fall of the Berlin Wall, it became apparent that the Su-27 Flanker was a formidable aeroplane. The first real opportunity to inspect the aircraft at close quarters came when it attended the Farnborough air show in 1990. Most significantly, unlike all its predecessors, the Flanker carried huge amounts of fuel and was capable of air-to-air refuelling. It could, for the first time, threaten UK aircraft operating in the North Sea, making the concept of a UK interceptor without an air superiority capability obsolete. It was the death knell of the Cold War mentality, for the Phantom and to a certain extent the Tornado F3, and was to be the catalyst for developing an air superiority fighter in the shape of the Eurofighter Typhoon.

The Su-27 Flanker is a formidable fighter aircraft and represents a massive step forward in operational capability. The basic configuration is similar to the F15,

The OLS27 IRSTS on the nose of an Su27.

with twin vertical fins and a low wing loading. The forward fuselage is broad to accommodate the complex air-to-air radar in the radome. Blended leading edge root extensions and a very thin rear fuselage all show its air superiority credentials. The weapons are carried externally, suggesting that stealth was not a major design driver, as external stores add significantly to the radar signature. Two AA-10 Alamo missiles are mounted on semi-conformal launchers under the central fuselage, with a further two on cheek pylons under the engine intakes. The Flanker is normally seen with a further 2 AA-10s on inboard pylons under the wings, with an additional two underwing pylons carrying AA-11 Archer short range missiles. Wingtip pylons carry the final pair of AA-11s and also the radar jamming equipment. This gives the Flanker an impressive payload of ten missiles, yet it still sports a 30-mm GSh-301 gun with 150 rounds of ammunition. For the first time a Soviet fighter was provided with a comprehensive avionics suite from the outset. The Phazotron N001 Zhuk pulse Doppler radar, known to NATO as 'Slot Back 2', introduced a rudimentary track-while-scan capability, which is displayed on a TV tab display in the cockpit. The radar is integrated with a helmet-mounted sighting system that directs the seeker heads of the air-to-air missiles. The pilot can take commands from an onboard data link system communicating directly with ground controllers. It also sports an onboard jamming system, chaff and flare dispensers, and an updated SPO15 radar

A Mig 29 Fulcrum of the Soviet Air Force at the Farnborough Airshow carrying an AA 11 Archer on an under-wing pylon.

warning receiver. Yet another step change is the impressive OLS-27 infra-red search and track system mounted on the top of the radome which incorporates a laser range finder. Just looking at the sensor, it is apparent that it is much more complex than the earlier Soviet designs. Internet sources suggest that the sensor is fully integrated, with the radar and missiles giving a useful range of 27 miles at medium level, although the laser ranging is limited to about 5 miles. The ability to select the optimum sensor to suit the tactical scenario gives a Flanker pilot a huge advantage over less well equipped opponents. It boasts exceptional performance and can match its western equivalents in 'G' capability. Amazingly, prospective fighter pilots can now fly the aircraft using remarkably accurate computer games on their home computer.

The MiG-29 Fulcrum is a smaller fighter, closer in performance and specification to the F16 but still offering a quantum improvement over the MiG-21 Fishbed and MiG-23 Flogger that it replaced. It also has the distinction of being the first ever Russian-built fighter to serve with NATO when the Luftwaffe inherited a Wing of Fulcrums from the former East German Air Force. In 1988, JG3 acquired twenty-four aircraft forming two squadrons, initially at its base at Preschen and then re-forming as JG73 at Laage in 1993. The Fulcrum was intended to provide air superiority over the battlefield, operating from austere airfields out to about 100 miles range. Like its larger brother, it was fitted with a vastly improved integrated weapon system based around the 'Slot Back 1' radar and a slightly less complex and shorter range IRSTS.

NATO had its first look at the fighter when six Fulcrums deployed from their base at Kubinka in 1986 to the Finnish fighter base at Rissala. At about that time, Finland was looking for a replacement for its ageing MiG-21s, and the Soviet fighter was a strong candidate for the requirement. An impressive solo display in addition to a four-ship flying display showed the true capability, not only to the Finns but to the whole of NATO. It was clear that the Fulcrum was highly manoeuvrable, and the platitudes about lack of quality among Soviet pilots were severely questioned as the team displayed their prowess. It was a spirited display, and the pilot showed the jet's potential using all of the 9G capability and full reheat.

Although I was never lucky enough to fly the aircraft, I was given an opportunity to form a firm impression. As an MOD staff officer later in my career, I attended the bilateral Airman to Airman Talks at the former RAF base at Gatow with my 2-Star Commander. The talks were held within a year of the fall of the Berlin Wall so Gatow in Berlin was a fitting venue. The German Chief of Staff briefed his British counterpart on the complexities of assimilating the former East German Air Force personnel into the Luftwaffe. It would be indiscreet to relay the content of the discussions, but one of the briefings concerned the MiG-29, which was of great interest to the NATO service chiefs at the time. Although the German Chief was naturally hesitant, given the delicate state of the withdrawal of Soviet forces, the details of the MiG briefing, although highly classified at the time, are now openly discussed on the internet. I subsequently read an excellent summary of the aircraft's abilities from the Luftwaffe's *Oberstleutnant* Johann Koeck, who for many years was an F4 pilot and one of the early MiG-29 Squadron Commanders. His open source description mirrors the view I formed. He explained that the main limitation, of which we were all aware, was fuel. With its limited internal fuel capacity and lack of air-to-air refuelling capability, coupled with speed and 'G' limitations on the external tanks, at tactical speeds the combat radius was 100 miles at best. He also identified weaknesses in the avionics fit, with a limited navigation system and a single radio. The radar was unreliable, had poor displays, difficulties discriminating between targets in close formation, and could not be repaired on the squadron. Despite his gloomy assessment of the problems faced by MiG-29 plots, his summary of the strengths would have left many Phantom crews extremely nervous had they been aware of its true abilities or faced the aircraft in anger. His summary is worth quoting:

... But when all that is said and done, the MiG-29 is a superb fighter for close-in combat, even compared with aircraft like the F-15, F-16 and F/A-18. This is due to the aircraft's superb aerodynamics and helmet-mounted sight. Inside ten nautical miles I'm hard to defeat, and with the IRST, helmet sight and 'Archer' I can't be beaten. Period. Even against the latest Block 50 F-16s the MiG-29 is virtually invulnerable in the close-in scenario ... with a 28deg/sec instantaneous turn rate (compared to the Block 50 F-16's 26deg) we can out-turn them. Our stable, manually controlled airplane can out-turn their FBW [fly by wire] aircraft. But the real edge we have is the 'Archer' which can reliably lock on to targets 45 degrees off-boresight.

Chilling indeed. Subsequently, staff at the NATO Tactical Leadership Programme were able to make detailed assessments when the aircraft took part in the NATO course. Not only were the airframes a massive step forward for the Soviet designers but a new series of weapons was introduced at the same time. The AA-10 Alamo was a massive leap in capability over its predecessor the AA 7 Apex. Produced in five major variants, these included radar guided and infra-red guided short range versions, designated AA-10A and AA-10B by NATO. The long range radar and IR versions were designated AA-10C and AA-10D, plus a fearsome anti radar version, the AA-10E, which homed on the radar emissions of a target aircraft. The AA-10 was a huge missile and for the first time matched the range performance of the US Advanced Medium Range Air-to-Air Missile, or AMRAAM, which was its western equivalent. The long range versions significantly out-ranged the Sparrow and Skyflash missiles that equipped the Phantom, leaving the older aircraft out-gunned by an opponent for the first time. The short range AA-10 was evaluated during live fire exercises at the test ranges at Eglin AFB in Florida in 2003. The results proved that the missile was indeed a formidable weapon as NATO feared.

The AA-11 Archer was truly innovative. Designed as a short range combat weapon, it was easily a match for the Sidewinder that armed the Phantom. Its key strength, however, was the addition of thrust vector control, or TVC, to give it amazing agility in the close-in fight. Small paddles were fitted around the exhaust ring of the missile and can be seen in Plate 74. In addition to the normal aerodynamic control provided by the wings on the missile body, the paddles could pop out into the exhaust plume and direct the thrust to slew the missile rapidly in the direction dictated by the guidance system. This not only meant a huge increase in the missile performance envelope but it almost precluded any type of escape manoeuvre by a target aircraft. The missile was just massively more manoeuvrable than its victim in all respects. It was also equipped with complex infra-red countermeasures systems that protected against typical flares, making it a formidable opponent. The Flanker and Fulcrum pilots also had the ability to designate targets using a helmet-mounted sighting system. By merely looking at the target and hitting a designator button, the seeker head would lock on and the weapon could be launched. With TVC, the weapon could literally be designated to the limits of the pilot's vision in the cockpit, giving a massive advantage in an air-to-air combat engagement. For the first time, over the shoulder missile firings were becoming a realistic option. This was a far cry from the early limited stern hemisphere capability of the original RAF Phantom. Chillingly, the Russians were marketing their technology around the world. Phantom crews finally realised that without defence funds to update the aircraft, its capability was waning. Without modern avionics, a helmet-mounted sight, and a longer range missile, the aircraft was losing its edge. The advice went out to the crews, and even modern-day RAF Typhoon pilots should take heed: 'Don't try a knife fight in a phone box with a Flanker.'

CHAPTER 14
Other Events

Some events stand out from the day-to-day activities on a Phantom squadron. The 60th Anniversary Commemoration of the Alcock and Brown transatlantic crossing in 1979 was one of those special occasions when the important milestone in aviation history was commemorated during my time on 56 (F) Squadron. On 14 June 1919, John Alcock and Arthur Whitten Brown successfully flew non-stop across the Atlantic Ocean for the first time. After taking off from Lester's Field in St John's, Newfoundland, and flying through terrible weather, they unceremoniously crash-landed their converted Vickers Vimy bomber in an Irish bog. Their flight lasted 15 hours 57 minutes.

Tony Alcock, the nephew of the pioneering pilot John Alcock, was a Flight Commander on 56 (F) Squadron in the late 70s. He persuaded the Air Force hierarchy that it would be appropriate to mark the feat, albeit this time in something slightly faster, and crafted a plan to cross the Atlantic as a 60th Anniversary Commemoration. An ex-Lightning pilot, Tony was by then flying the Phantom. Luckily, finding an appropriately named navigator was relatively easy, although a compromise had to be made on the spelling. Norman Browne, a Buccaneer navigator who had previously flown the Phantom, willingly volunteered to accompany Tony on the trip. In the months prior to the event, two of the squadron's Phantoms, XV424 and XV486, were beautifully prepared in a commemorative colour scheme. The aircraft were painted in gloss light aircraft grey with red, white, and blue fuselage stripes and a raked Union Flag on the fin. Commemorative inscriptions on the nose and 'Sargent Fletcher' wing tanks linked the Rolls-Royce Eagle engines of the Vimy with the Speys of the Phantom. The event coincided with the thirtieth anniversary of NATO, so the badges of the NATO nations ran down the spine of the aircraft to mark the occasion.

A media and press day was arranged just before the event. The nation's media arrived en masse at RAF Wattisham to capture the event for TV and the newspapers, and the aircraft were rolled out for the photographs. At the

Replica of the Alcock and Brown Vickers Vimy at the RAF Museum Hendon.

appointed hour, Tony taxied the primary aircraft out to the runway and took off. A sortie was flown alongside a tanker to provide pictures to support the news bulletins, before the aircraft recovered to Wattisham. All had appeared to go well, but there was a problem. Although the pictures had been sent to the news desks, back on the ground the aircraft were being prepared for the actual transatlantic journey. Unfortunately, the exquisite hand-crafted RAF crests on the intake ramp had proved less than durable and had begun to peel. It was obvious that drastic surgery was needed in the short time available between the media day and the commemoration. In true fashion, the midnight oil was burned and they were lovingly restored. On the day, no one was aware of the drama, although a speed limit was placed on the aircraft to prevent a recurrence.

The splendor of the commemorative scheme is shown better in the colour plates 75 and 76. The commemoration occurred sixty years to the day. XV424

XV424 and XV486 are prepared for the media sortie.

XV424 Lined up for departure on Runway 23 at RAF Wattisham.

XV424 rolls to meet the Victor tanker.

XV424 refuelling from a Victor tanker. UK MOD Crown Copyright (1978).

XV424 in the RAF Museum.

flew the actual sortie carrying three external fuel tanks but taking some additional assistance from a Victor tanker. Tony and Norman launched from Goose Bay, Newfoundland, and headed east across 'The Pond'. Refuelling in flight from Victor tankers of No. 57 Squadron, they landed in the UK after a 5-hour 40-minute flight. In a nice touch, the crew carried the black cat mascot 'Twinkletoes' that had been carried on the original flight in 1919.

Although the aircraft carried the commemorative paint scheme for only a few weeks, I flew the spare aircraft, XV486, on an overland intercept sortie. We were tasked to intercept a formation of Buccaneers in the Welsh Low Flying Area. After crossing the main airways at high level, we descended into the low flying area and set up a combat air patrol in the south of the area waiting for our opponents. The Buccaneer was a difficult target, as the crews used the radar warning receiver to great effect. One sniff of a lock from a Phantom and they would break onto the beam, making themselves undetectable by the Phantom's pulse Doppler mode. For that reason, Phantom navigators would stay in search mode and carry out a stern attack, sacrificing the head-on Sparrow shot and hoping to talk the pilot into a visual engagement. My wingman and I rolled out behind our respective targets and took simulated Sidewinder shots on the trail Buccaneers before accelerating to run down the front pair. There was surprisingly little reaction from the Buccaneers, who usually evaded hard as

The first iteration with smaller roundels but the original sized fin flash. UK MOD Crown Copyright (1978).

we rolled in. As we accelerated, drawing alongside the back marker, the guard emergency frequency crackled into life: 'Who's a pretty boy then?' At that point, all efforts to press the kill on the front of the formation fell apart.

That year, the jets were the stars of the show, opening the International Air Tattoo at Greenham Common before being returned to their air defence grey colour schemes. Ironically, XV424 now sits in the RAF Museum at Hendon and wears the colour scheme of 56 (F) Squadron. For some years, the commemorative scheme was on display at the RAF Museum at Cosford, albeit on the nose section of a different Phantom, XV591, which was actually an FG1 version.

On 31 July 1992, XV424 was retired from service and earmarked for display at the RAF Museum at Hendon. It was transported by road from RAF Wattisham to London in November of that year and now sits in the Historic Hangars at the RAF Museum. Who knows; perhaps on a subsequent commemoration it may reappear in the 1979 scheme?

In the days before the Air Warfare Centre, the Central Tactics and Trials Organisation (CTTO) did not control its own aircraft. In order to test concepts or to develop capability, the trials officers had to rely on the squadrons to

56 (F) Squadron and 92 Squadron Phantoms in formation during Exercise Bold Pointer.

provide aircraft and crews. It was realised for some years that the grey and green disruptive camouflage that had been the standard colour scheme for RAF fast-jet aircraft for many years was not particularly suitable for air defence duties. While it was good against the fields of northern Europe when seen from an attacking fighter sitting above, it was poor against a sky background. Although it blended well when the aircraft was sitting on the ground, the advent of the hardened shelters meant that the aircraft would be hidden from sight during turnrounds, so this advantage was not particularly useful. The Royal Aircraft Establishment at Farnborough had conducted studies into the best colour scheme for a fighter, and CTTO was tasked to run a trial to evaluate the various options. A 56 (F) Squadron Phantom, XV474, was selected to test a new camouflage scheme. CTTO named the prototype *The Grey Ghost*, although the uncharitable nickname that stuck among squadron crews was *The Grey Goose*. As with all trials, the initial installation did not go smoothly. It was found that the paint selected for the trial was not suitable for the radome, as it would have adversely affected the radar performance. Although the aircraft appeared in its new grey tactical paint scheme, for some weeks XV474 flew around with an extremely prominent black radome, shown in Plate 77, completely negating the aim of the trial. Coupled with the stark, dark-coloured national markings, the tone down seemed destined for failure. The trial was put on hold until a suitable paint could be identified and a new radome painted to match the rest of the aircraft.

The trial was flown using XV474, shown in Plate 78, and detection ranges were assessed against typical backgrounds. The new scheme was set against bright blue sky backgrounds, clouds, rain, and different terrains. The visual detection ranges were compared against those of a disruptive camouflaged aircraft to check for improvements. Although the aircraft stood out against the sea or against typical British countryside, it was decided that the improvement against sky and cloud backgrounds, which was where the Phantom would be seen, was enough to warrant a change. An interim light grey scheme was introduced on a limited trial. This modified scheme was somewhat lighter. Although the infamous toned down pink and light blue markings that became the norm replaced the RAF dark red and blue, the interim aircraft carried full-sized versions of the insignia. In order to benefit fully from the revised colour scheme, the MOD sought dispensation from the international authorities to adopt smaller markings. At the same time, the huge underwing registrations disappeared. If the red tape could be overcome, the scheme had potential.

A prototype was allocated to 92 (East India) Squadron in Germany and flew on the squadron for some months to gain further feedback. Refinements were made, leading to the definitive scheme that entered service, including fully toned down roundels, fin flashes, and darker panels for the upper wing surfaces. There were few pictures ever taken of the interim scheme. Fortuitously, 92 (East India) Squadron arranged a posed picture during a detachment to Cyprus in 1980, shown in Plate 80. The photograph captured a camouflaged Phantom flanked by the prototype *Grey Ghost* and a squadron aircraft in the new air defence grey scheme. The outcome is history – the modified colour scheme was adopted fleet-wide. Over the following years, Phantoms were slowly repainted in air defence grey as they completed their major servicing at RAF St Athan. By the time the aircraft retired in 1992, there were no camouflaged Phantoms still flying. One of the few, perhaps the only remaining airframe, that carries the old disruptive camouflage scheme is XT 891 at RAF Coningsby.

The Soviet effort to restrict access to West Berlin, which led to the Berlin Airlift, was one of the most evocative periods of the Cold War. The airlift had shown how easily links between West Berlin and the West could be adversely affected. During the lead-up to the crisis, Soviet MiGs had intercepted and harried Western aircraft routeing along the Berlin Corridors. Any deviations from the authorised routes would have resulted in the aircraft being forced to land in East Germany.

Understandably, the western powers were paranoid for many years afterwards, so an exercise was arranged annually in which British, French, and American fighter crews gathered to develop plans to protect a transport aircraft from interception. The NATO exercise practised the techniques for Berlin Corridor policing missions using fighters to exercise the privileges of access to RAF Gatow and Berlin Tempelhof airport. The exercise was given the 'Bold' prefix, so when I was nominated to take part in September 1978, I set off for RAF Wildenrath to take part in Exercise 'Bold Pointer'. Although it rotated between three of the four post-war allies, not surprisingly, the fourth allied power, the Soviet Union, did not take part in the exercise. In 1978, the participants were Phantoms from 56 (F) Squadron and 92 (East India) Squadron, Phantoms from the US Air Force from Ramstein, and Mirage IIIs from the French Air Force based at Colmar. As the aim of the exercise was to practise escort procedures for transport aircraft, No. 60 Squadron from RAF Wildenrath provided a Pembroke as the potential victim that would have been at risk from Soviet MiGs. On this occasion, the US 526th Tactical Fighter Squadron was nominated to lead the missions and did so in the usual efficient style that we expected of US fighter aircrew.

Tactics were dictated by the type of aircraft being protected. Jet transport aircraft were relatively easy, as they could match the speed of the fighters allocated to protect them. Fighters could fly alongside in a close escort position or fly in front or behind the airliner. Close escort sent a powerful media message and guaranteed that any attacking fighter would be drawn towards the escort. An attacking aircraft would have to penetrate the protective screen before being able to hit the airliner, particularly using primitive air-to-air missiles. That said, being tied to a relatively slow airliner inhibited tactical freedom, so it was unpopular among the fighter crews. Depending on rules of engagement, being a few miles ahead or behind meant that any move by an attacker could more easily be countered and, with luck, the attacker could be shepherded away from the transport. In extremis, the attacker could be destroyed.

It was much more difficult to protect a slow-moving aircraft such as a Pembroke, which was why it was chosen. If fighters tried to formate, flying 'S' manoeuvres over the top, it made them slow and vulnerable. For that reason, the normal tactic was to fly a racetrack pattern at tactical speeds over the top of the transport, rolling forward as the transport progressed along track. Even then, it was important to protect the flanks of the formation yet remain within the tight boundaries of the Berlin Corridor. Choosing where the various assets at his disposal were deployed was the task of the nominated mission leader. For the exercise, a hypothetical corridor representing the boundaries of the real air routes into Berlin had been set out over German airspace. Each nation was given the tactical lead for a sortie, and various procedures were briefed, tested and

USAF F4Es participating in Exercise Bold Pointer.

evaluated. An aggressor fighter was tasked to attack the transport, and various escalations in alert state and revisions of rules of engagement were practised. At the end of the exercise, the best options were recorded and published in national tactics manuals that acted as a reference if ever the option had to be used in anger. Most importantly, it demonstrated the will of NATO to keep the Berlin Corridors open with unfettered access to West Berlin. Crucially, the exercise was flown at medium level in full view of the Soviet monitoring sites along the Inner German Border, and there could be no misinterpretation of the intent.

Just when we had all settled into a comfortable routine operating with our allies, a bizarre incident at the end of one of the final missions acted as a reminder that NATO collaboration could be complex. We had been briefed to lead the French single-seat Mirage pilots back to Wildenrath after the mission. The Low Level North Recovery was complex, particularly if Wildenrath was operating on the easterly runway, as was the case on that day. The exercise had been run in the medium level airspace over the North German Plain, and once released by the mission leader, the British Phantoms, accompanied by the Mirages, dropped into the low flying area for a standard recovery. The Mirage had much less fuel than the Phantom, so it had been the French pilots who had called 'fuel minimums' first. We knew from the briefing that even though they

A Mirage III ready for an Exercise Bold Pointer sortie.

were carrying external tanks, they were reasonably tight for fuel. All was well as we threaded our way south through the complex airspace, avoiding the military zones around Laarbruch and Brüggen. Turning west to the south of Wildenrath, we passed abeam the airfield before turning hard back to 'initials', avoiding Dutch airspace. The Mirage pilots were quiet but seemed to be holding their briefed position in close trail formation. I watched the radar warning receiver throughout the recovery and the tell-tale blink of the I Band radar carried by the Mirages sat firmly in our 6 o'clock position. Our formation leader had briefed the French pilots that once they were overhead Wildenrath they would be clear to break into the circuit. He would mark the break point by waggling his wings and the Phantoms would press on into Low Flying Area 3 for a further 15 minutes until down to landing fuel, at which time we would recover to base. As we pushed the speed up to 400 knots for the break, the Mirages hung in nicely. As briefed, the leader waggled violently as we passed over the runway threshold and pushed on east, aiming for the gap to the south of the Cologne/Bonn air traffic zone. Worryingly, the I Band strobe behind still blinked relentlessly, and I craned my neck to look into the 6 o'clock. The two Mirages sat tucked in tight, despite the fact we were some miles east of Wildenrath and heading away. The Mirages would now be extremely short of fuel. I called the problem to the leader, who decided that a simple plan was the order of the day. We called Air Traffic Control and turned back towards the airfield to repeat the original procedure. Given the failure of Plan A, the leader elected to break into the circuit and overshot, leaving the Mirages, by now on fumes, to land first. Why they had missed the break is still a mystery, and in the true NATO spirit of compromise, little was said at the debrief in order to save face. The challenges of international operations were underlined yet again.

EPILOGUE
The Demise of the Phantom

The Conventional Armed Forces in Europe Treaty guaranteed the demise of the Phantom. There is no doubt that the aircraft could have soldiered on for some years to come, even though it was rapidly being out-gunned by the modern generation of fighters. The biggest saving to the defence budget is when a fleet of aircraft is retired. Along with the basic running costs for the airframes such as fuel, go the support costs including such diverse aspects as avionics and personnel. With governments keen to realise a windfall after the end of the Cold War, the Phantom was an obvious candidate. Reductions in the number of combat aircraft were agreed between nations, and with the Tornado F3 in service, the older airframes were the prime candidates. The finer details in the treaty identified measures to verify that the aircraft had been withdrawn from use and rendered unflyable. It was this specific clause that would make the withdrawal of the Phantom such a sad sight to those who had been associated with the jet.

Over the year preceding its retirement, there were many celebrations as each individual squadron proudly retired its Phantoms. I was fortunate to deploy to RAF Wildenrath in a Tornado F3 for one last visit shortly before the station closed. 92 (East India) Squadron had arranged a Families Day, but various UK squadrons were able to send aircraft to help celebrate the demise of the aircraft. A commemorative blue paint scheme had been applied to one of the squadron's Phantoms, XV408 *Zulu*, harking back to the days when the squadron aerobatic team, the Blue Diamonds, had displayed at air shows during the Hunter days in the late 50s. Gone was the disruptive camouflage green and grey or the air defence grey of the Cold War years, replaced by a gloss blue finish over the whole airframe. The toned down pink and pale blue roundels had been replaced by the traditional RAF roundels in red, white, and blue. The intake roundel sported the arrow in the squadron colours of red and yellow, and the cobra emblem on the fin was returned to its full height. Finally, the chequer board had returned to the

XT897 in profile comparing the lines of the Phantom with the newer Tornado F3.

top of the fin. Number 92 (East India) Squadron said goodbye with a great deal of style. The aircraft is pictured in Plate 79.

Having flown the Phantom for over 10 years and with just a few hours short of 2,000 hours on the aircraft in my log book, I was to cross paths one final time before the Phantom retired. With the impending transfer of the 56 (Fighter) Squadron numberplate to the Tornado Operational Conversion Unit, our Tornado F3s had already been painted in the colours of 56 (Reserve) Squadron. The Tornado scheme closely resembled the original paint scheme that had graced the Phantom on my first tour on the squadron. I was able to plan a final commemoration sortie, and the respective squadron bosses agreed that a pair of Phantoms would launch from RAF Wattisham and join a pair of F3s over the North Sea to capture the handover in pictures. A third Tornado sortie was launched to act as a camera ship, and I invited the renowned aviation photographer Geoff Lee to take part. I also managed to persuade a sympathetic Boeing E3D Sentry captain to allow us to join up for some final pictures. As was usual, it had to be completed as part of a productive training sortie and we had the chance to fight against the Phantom for one last time. Although the event was published in the aviation press at the time, no pictures have ever been released from within the formation until now. It had been many years since I had experienced close formation with a Phantom, but the thrill of the experience never waned. The aircraft simply had character. The pair of Phantoms, shown at Plates 81 and 86, joined formation resplendent with the red fin that had become

A 56 Squadron Phantom with a 56 Sqn Tornado F3 joining in formation.

The 56 (F) Squadron Phantoms depart.

the trademark of 56 (F) Squadron in its final days. The full-sized Phoenix had gone, although the red and white chequer boards adorned the RWR antenna on the top of the fin and flanked a smaller Phoenix emblem on the nose. Without the constraints of fatigue conservation, the ugly external tanks had been dropped and the aircraft carried only the LAU-7 pylons for the Sidewinders, giving it a much cleaner profile. With the impending retirement, the jets were being operated to the absolute limits of their performance, so it must have been heady times for the remaining crews, unconstrained by normal fatigue management. The sortie gave the chance to compare the lines of the Phantom against the newer Tornado F3 for what would be for me one last time. The F3 could be extremely photogenic in certain poses, but it never matched the brutal functionality of the Phantom. Since the retirement of the Tornado F3, the photographs now have even greater significance.

The formal retirement of the Phantom came in the autumn of 1992. In the months following, the aircraft were towed to a dispersal on the airfield at RAF Wattisham that became known as 'the graveyard'. The aircraft were laid out and marked with large black crosses on the airframes to signify their retirement, and to allow Soviet satellites to verify their decommissioning. Over the coming months, the airframes were slowly dismantled before being transported to local scrap yards to be shredded. The pictures were stark, and I have yet to meet any pilot or navigator who flew the Phantom who did not experience a massive feeling of sorrow and regret at the sad demise of this once powerful war machine.

A former Air Officer Commanding No. 11 Group, a former Phantom pilot and a keen member of the historic aviation community, directed that a number of Phantoms should be stored at Coningsby in the vain hope that they could be kept airworthy for the future. Sadly, complex civilian rules under which 'warbirds' are flown virtually exclude the possibility of keeping modern fast jets in flying condition. It is extremely unlikely, given the tribulations experienced by the 'Vulcan to the Sky' project, that the Spey-powered Phantom will ever grace the air show circuit in this country.

Although there are no British Phantoms still flying, happily many aircraft survived and are on display in museums or as gate guardians at RAF airfields. XV409 escaped the fate of its fellow 1435 Flight airframes that ended their lives in a flooded pit in the Falkland Islands. XV409 sat on show beside the passenger terminal at RAF Mount Pleasant as the first reminder to the incoming personnel that their role during their detachment is to protect the islands from air attack. Sadly, its fate was sealed; the airframe deteriorated as it was battered by the elements. The airframe could not be economically returned to the UK, so it was dismantled. Only the nose survives but is destined to be displayed in a museum as a small reminder of 1435 Flight's contribution to the defence of the islands.

XV409 outside the Air Terminal at RAF Mount Pleasant.

XV497 was acquired by a former commander of 23 Squadron. As an ex-Phantom navigator, he saved the airframe from the scrap yard, and it is displayed outside the 8 Squadron buildings at RAF Waddington and shown in Plate 93. Ironically, the aircraft outlasted 23 (Fighter) Squadron whose standard was retired when the E3D fleet was downsized in 2010. It remains as a fitting reminder of the task of the Sentry Force, which still controls fighters in its primary role.

Only the cockpit of XV490 has survived, although I captured it when it was still flying and shown in plates 16, 56 and 58, but it has been lovingly restored by Mike Davey. Mike is typical of the selfless people who invest their own hard-earned cash to protect the history of this fine fighter. The cockpit is almost fully restored and retains 74 Squadron markings on the nose. Although it spent a good few months at Newark Air Museum, it will find a final home on display at RAF Wattisham, where it flew its final sorties before retirement.

The most famous survivor, XV424 of Alcock and Browne fame, holds pride of place in the centre of the Historic Hangars at the RAF Museum, Hendon, sporting the colours of 56 (F) Squadron, which operated the aircraft in its final years before retirement. It is displayed in an unusual configuration in that it carries external fuel tanks and a gun. Only the RAF Germany squadrons operated in that fit operationally. Even when deploying to Cyprus for armament

The cockpit of XV490 wearing a 74 Squadron badge is owned by Mike Davey at Newark Air Museum.

Mike prepares XV490 for a Museum Open Day.

practice camps, UK-based Phantoms transited in 'Delta' fit or with three external tanks. The guns were shipped separately by air or sea and the fuel tanks removed on arrival.

Although not a true airframe, one of the original Phantom mission simulators survives at the Newark Air Museum. One of two simulators installed at RAF Coningsby in 1969, the simulator was designated DB001 or M1 during its service at Coningsby and lived within the simulator complex until 1988. When the Phantoms moved north from Coningsby to RAF Leuchars, the simulator was moved to RAF Wattisham, which had not had a simulator for many years. It trained Wattisham crews for its final years before being retired in 1992. In its heyday, the simulator was controlled by a huge computer complex that would probably fit into a number of PCs nowadays. The instructors supervised the mission from the attached control room. In its original form it had a rudimentary visual system to make ground attack missions more realistic. A small suspended camera moved across a modelled landscape and projected onto a screen in front of the front cockpit. Deemed unrealistic and largely unnecessary for air defence scenarios, the visuals were removed in the late 70s. From then on, the simulator became largely a procedures and emergencies trainer, although intercept training was part of a normal simulator sortie. Mounted on large hydraulic rams, there was some movement, but in the absence of any simulation representing 'G' it was too obvious to crews that they were sitting in a simulator, as it lacked the immersive experience offered by modern flight simulators. Efforts to add modern graphics were never funded, so crews trained in the dark. The simulator is still operational and is fired up on special occasions by museum staff.

XT891 was delivered for RAF service on 23 August 68 at RAF Coningsby. The last sortie was by a 74 Squadron FGR2 in October 1992 from RAF Wattisham when the squadron disbanded. A commemorative formation including Hawks and Tornados was led by a single Phantom. The true final flight was on 1 November 1992. Two 74 Squadron Phantoms were joined by a single Hawk for a final display. After a number of passes over the airfield, one Phantom rolled down the main runway before returning for a high speed afterburner flypast departing into the vertical. The other aircraft in the formation, XV474, had already left Wattisham bound for Duxford, where it is now displayed. Although the last flypast was the most dramatic, the crew of XV474 received the accolade for being the last operational RAF Phantom in the air. Ironically, the last actual flight was probably by the Phantom FG1, XT597, based at the Aeroplane and Armament Experimental Establishment, Boscombe Down, although this was not a squadron aircraft.

The Cold War windfall that saw the Phantom retired early in 1992 was both a blessing and a curse. The Russian air superiority fighters were not really

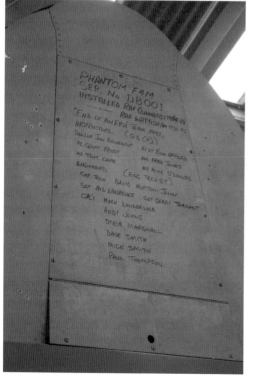

Above: The Phantom Mission Simulator on display at Newark Air Museum.

Left: The commemoration note from the final Simulator staff.

deployed in large numbers before the Phantom was scrapped. For those early post Cold War years, Russia became less of the threat it had been during the height of tensions, and political attention moved to other regions. The new potential opponents operated older aircraft against which the Phantom could still compete. As world events unfolded, whether it was the might of NATO or the lack of political will, most of the new adversaries failed even to launch an effective air defence.

The Phantom's last call to action came as the coalition forces squared up to Saddam Hussein after Iraq's invasion of Kuwait. The Tornado F3 was the new kid on the block, but was ill-prepared for operations in 1990. When the UK was called upon to deploy forces in support of Operation Desert Storm, the Phantom was considered but passed over in favour of the newer aircraft. The Tornado F3 was rapidly modified and deployed to Saudi Arabia, the Phantom being deployed to Cyprus to act as a base defence force for RAF Akrotiri. However, the Iraqi Air Force barely operated outside Iraq, and an attack on Cyprus was never really likely. Its lack of real action during the Gulf War meant that the RAF Phantom in its fighter role never faced worthy opposition in anger.

On retirement, many of the airframes had flown well over 5,000 hours – sterling service for a 'stopgap' purchase. The pilot with the most hours topped the 4,000 mark. Ironically, it was not technical reasons but one of the many defence reviews, *Options for Change*, and the desire for a Cold War windfall, that ultimately sealed its fate.